THE GULF COOPERATION COUNCIL PROJECT

1981-2016

The elusive potential for economic gain through regional integration

“Diplomacy and Strategy”
English Series
Directors: Fouad Nohra and Michael J. Strauss

Diplomacy and Strategy is a collection initiated by the academic directorate of the Centre d’Etudes Diplomatiques et Stratégiques to promote the outstanding scientific work presented by Ph.D. graduates, professors and researchers. The scope of subjects covered is as wide as international relations itself, encompassing disciplines such as political science, economic science, international law and sociology.

Other titles

ZERMOUNI Hakim, *Smart Power in Barack Obama’s Foreign Policy. A Systemic Approach to Diplomacy with the Gulf Cooperation Council*, 2016.
CARTA Gianni, *Berlusconi and the Power of Television: 2008-11*, 2016.
SADIA Antoine, *Democratic Governance and Foreign Aid in Sub-Saharan Africa,* 2013.
Alena F. DOUHAN, *Regional Mechanisms of Collective Security. The New Face of Chapter VIII of the UN Charter?*, 2013.
SOLVIT Samuel, *Dimensions of War. Understanding War as a Complex Adaptive System*, 2012.
DUQUESNE Isabelle, *Nepal, Zone of Peace. A Revised Concept for the Constitution*, 2011.
STRAUSS Michael J., *The Viability of Territorial Leases in Resolving International Sovereignty Disputes,* 2010.

Kambiz Zare

THE GULF COOPERATION COUNCIL PROJECT

1981-2016

The elusive potential for economic gain through regional integration

L'Harmattan

5-7, rue de l'Ecole-Polytechnique, 75005 Paris

http://www.editions-harmattan.fr

ISBN : 978-2-343-16448-9
EAN : 9782343164489

Simply, to Darya, who is endless

Human beings are members of a whole,
in creation of one essence and soul.

If one member is afflicted with pain,
other members uneasy will remain.

If you have no sympathy for human pain,
the name of human you cannot retain.

– Saadi (1184-1283)
Persian Poet

ACKNOWLEDGMENTS

I am so grateful to professors A.M.S. Fatemi, Serge Besanger, Michael Strauss, Hassan Mansoor and Fouad Nohra, who during the past years in many different ways assisted, encouraged and most importantly inspired me in finalizing this work.

TABLE OF CONTENTS

MAP OF THE GULF COOPERATION COUNCIL MEMBER STATES

U.S. Library of Congress

CHAPTER 1

INTRODUCTION

Background

In the 1970s, the Arab elites living in the southern part of the Persian Gulf region, mainly in Bahrain, Qatar, the United Arab Emirates (UAE) and Kuwait, attempted to create a monetary union. At the time, it was simply supposed to be done through coordinating a few aspects of their monetary relations. The idea, as the term monetary union implies, was to ultimately bear fruit with a common currency, a "Gulf Dinar," which would freely circulate in the region. However, it was obvious that the efforts made to realize such a big dream were not to produce any results in the short term.[1]

In the 1980s, the aforementioned countries decided to resume work on the left-behind project, this time in a more thoughtful way and with two more players on board, Saudi Arabia and Oman. In 1981, the six countries signed a charter that established the Gulf Cooperation Council (GCC).[2] Its many objectives included concepts and directives such as coordination, integration and inter-connection among members in all fields, and the formulation of similar regulations in economic and financial affairs, commerce, customs and communications. In connection with the new attempt and the charter, on the 25th of May 1981, in Abu Dhabi, the member countries signed a document called the Unified Economic Agreement, which had the main objective of articulating principles that would pave the way toward their desired economic integration and would ultimately give birth to a common currency.

Article 22 of the Unified Economic Agreement is dedicated to principles related to financial and monetary cooperation. It states:

> Member States shall seek to coordinate their financial, monetary and banking policies and enhance cooperation between monetary

[1] Ahmad Alkholifey and Ali Alreshan, "GCC Monetary Union," *IFC Bulletin no. 32*, Bank for International Settlements.

[2] Charter of the Gulf Cooperation Council: https://www.files.ethz.ch/isn/125347/1426_GCC.pdf.

agencies and central banks, including the endeavor to establish a joint currency in order to further their desired economic integration.[3]

However, as of this writing, in 2016, the Gulf Cooperation Council, as a regional project with its designated executive and administrative bodies, in executing Article 22, has faced and is continuing to encounter difficulties that are not easily surmountable. Many of these hardships are not technical ones. For instance, in 2009, though it was previously agreed that Riyadh in Saudi Arabia would be the GCC central bank's location, the UAE objected to the idea and shared its unwillingness to be part of the GCC monetary union. The main reason, as reported by the news media at the time, was that most of the GCC's building institutions are located on Saudi soil.[4] In addition to that, political differences and economic rivalry are hard to mitigate, and compromises seem to be not within reach.[5]

The technical issues, however, are the most important ones in lengthening the decision-making process concerning the launch of a new currency. For instance, Islamic financial and economic jurisprudence must be considered. The main objective of the Islamic system is the implementation of the economic and financial principles of Islam in the banking and financial fields within Muslim communities. The issue, covered in a later chapter, has multiple facets. For instance, the Islamic system of banking defines a bank as a financial institution whose statutes, rules and procedures expressly state its commitments to the principles of Sharia'ah. Thus, as such, interest collections and payments are prohibited. Islam upholds that money, income and property, in the first place, belong to Allah and that wealth is to be used for the good of the society.[6] Though it is practiced and used in many Muslim countries, at first glance, it is clear that such a system lacks standardization and compatibility with the world banking system and financial institutions.

Moreover, other issues such as the inadequate availability of Sharia'ah-compliant financial instruments, underdeveloped Islamic interbank markets and existing legal frameworks[7] have slowed down the realization of any "economic integration project," which since the beginning must be based on economics and economic integration theories, but not only those. Any regional integration project must be also able to take advantage of other

---

[3] Unified Economic Agreement: http://gulfmigration.org/the-unified-economic-agreement-between-the-countries-of-the-gulf-cooperation-council/?print=pdf.

[4] http://gulfnews.com/business/sectors/banking/uae-to-skip-gcc-monetary-union-agreement-1.469; Robin Wigglesworth, "UAE quits Gulf Monetary Union," *Financial Times*, 2009.

[5] Economist Intelligence Unit, "The GCC in 2020: Outlook for the Gulf and the Global Economy."

[6] Shah Abdul Hannan: http://www.shahfoundationbd.org/.

[7] Ritu Basu, Ananthakrishnan Prasad and Sergio Rodriguez, "Monetary Operations and Islamic Banking in the GCC: Challenges and Options," International Monetary Fund, 2015.

experiences elsewhere in the world, whether these were successful or not. Additional monetary-related issues can be also mentioned. For instance, some of the currencies of the GCC member countries are pegged to US dollar. The GCC was likely to announce the US dollar as the backing for its currency, but the option of being tied to a basket of currencies is still open to discussion and on this point not all of the GCC members agree.[8]

It must be affirmed that although a common currency has yet to see the light, after four decades of various initiatives, dedicating resources and more importantly leaving behind other opportunities, there is still no sign of a Gulf currency in a foreseeable horizon. However, it is worth affirming that as of today, the project has been successful in achieving, for instance, the launch of the GCC customs union.

The Research Problematic

In the past decades, the global economy has experienced the proliferation of regional blocs. In particular, we have been witnessing countries get together with the honorable intent of integrating their economies, either for resolving their internal economic-related problems or because free trade and non-interventionist foreign policies are key requirements for world peace.[9] However, on the one hand, most of these regional bloc agreements have failed to deliver what they were promising in terms of economic growth and prosperity; and on the other hand, neighboring states are still interfering in each other's internal affairs, either directly or indirectly, peacefully or aggressively. We need to bear in mind, however, that being part of a regional bloc, integrating national economies and using the same currency no longer depend on decisions made by ambitious politicians, rulers or groups of qualified technocrats. Today, people, particularly in democracies, can change the route, or the way they want to see their beloved country function, sometimes directly through a simple referendum. Brexit is a vivid case.

In countries where citizens are free to express their thoughts on important issues and where governments and politicians do not have a fear of organizing referendums on decisions and choices relevant to the future, we

---

[8] Issac John, "GCC to stick to Dollar peg," *Khaleej Times*, 2016: http://www.khaleejtimes.com/business/banking-finance/gcc-to-stick-to-dollar-peg; John Pratap, "Qatar, GCC Countries with Dollar peg to face challenges when Fed hikes rate," *Gulf Times*, 2015: http://www.gulf-times.com/story/463341/Qatar-GCC-countries-with-dollar-peg-to-face-challe; "The GCC Monetary Union, Choice of Exchange Rate Regime," International Monetary Fund, 2008; John Whittaker, "The Gulf Currency, Lessons from Euro," Lancaster University, 2010: http://www.lancaster.ac.uk/staff/whittaj1/Gulf%20Currency%20Report%20Final.pdf.

[9] M-W. Palen, "Free-Trade Ideology and Transatlantic Abolitionism: A Historiography," *Journal of the History of Economic Thought*, 37(2), 2015, pp. 291-304.

are witnessing more and more participation of citizens in the decision-making process. In regards to the phenomenon of economic integration or the creation of simple trading blocs, sometimes the citizens' vote is in clear opposition to any further integration or to the continuation of an existing one. The problem could be with the idea itself, or the way it is perceived, discussed, decided and implemented in a particular context. Thus, the reaction and opposition to it could be based on an undelivered promise of economic prosperity and/or durable peaceful relations.

The idea of integrating national economies, though it sounds interesting, unfortunately, by just bringing politicians and policy makers from different backgrounds and neighboring countries to sit around a table in order to share their wills and perspectives by signing different agreements, may not give birth to a functioning "union," whether it is an economic union or a monetary one. In theory, we accept the widely shared rationales behind integrating different economies. In general, it would create wider and far better opportunities for everybody. Governments could not easily interfere in the markets, resources would be allocated efficiently and in the long run economic growth would be attained.[10] However, during the past decades, in many cases, as mentioned, the desired results could not be achieved. These failures have triggered belated studies aimed at offering solutions to undesired consequences of integration attempts and initiatives. Therefore, at the end of the day, in terms of the concept of opportunity cost, the cost of a failure can be even higher than the one calculated before launching it.[11]

Many studies have been concluded in the field of international economics and have covered many problematics pertinent to the area of "economic integration." Precious theories and fresh experiences would be lighting any desired journey toward any form of regional integration. Integration projects, whether they aim to create simple trading blocs or complete unions, if properly done or studied in detail, would avoid the main problem of undesired and costly damages to national economies in terms of time and resources. A well-studied regional integration project would offer the possibility of an eventual best alternative available to a nation. For instance, it may be the case that resources and opportunities available to a nation must be exploited unilaterally rather than through creating regional blocs. Therefore, the opportunity cost of a choice must be calculated on a larger scale for a hypothetical country.[12]

---

[10] https://thoughteconomics.com/regional-and-global-economic-integration/.

[11] European Parliament, "One Belt, One Road (OBOR): China's regional integration initiatives," 2016: http://www.europarl.europa.eu/thinktank/en/document.html?reference=EPRS_BRI(2016)586608; Carlos Lopes, "Inching toward Integration," *Finance and Development*, 53(2), 2016.

[12] Finn Laursen, "Theory and Practice of Regional Integration," Jean Monnet and Robert Schuman Paper Series, 8(3), University of Pittsburgh, 2008; Ministry of Economy, Trade and

The Research Objective

Here I do not discuss the vast field of "regional integration." Foremost, regional integration is considered as a process. It can be simply defined as signing agreements that would enforce cooperation between different states. The term itself is not very clear and many of those signed agreements ambiguously define objectives that are not "SMART" (specific, measurable, achievable, realistic and time-bound). Rather, here I remain concentrated on analyzing the GCC project of integration. Since the first two building blocks of any economic integration is establishing a free trade area and a customs union, and since GCC countries claim the implementation of the two, I will review the existing literature on the subject with the aim of providing an understanding of the main body of relevant theories. Once the main theories are reviewed and the different stages of an economic integration articulated, I will go through each of the GCC members' economic and institutional particularities, considering the role and importance of socio-economic factors for any successful integration. In concomitance with international trade theories and those related to economic integration, I use the analytical framework offered by Walter Mattli, developed in chapter four, to identify a set of conditions that are indispensable for any successful integration project.

Countries integrate their economies if there could be an economic gain from it. The integration would take place and be considered as implemented based on required and functioning institutions to deliver and safeguard the economic gain. Therefore, I will analyze an eventual economic gain concerning Gulf Cooperation Council countries based on their trading activities and the identification of their respective partners. Since the project is defined within a region where Islam is omnipresent, a review of both the conventional financial system and the Islamic one is considered necessary. Finally, the flows of finances within each GCC country and among them, including through foreign direct investment activities and portfolio investments, are analyzed. Based on the aforementioned conditions, the feasibility of a GCC integration project is evaluated.

Limitations

Although an effort has been made to go through papers, reports, textbooks, articles, theses and televised debates concerning the subject matter,

---

Industry, Japan, "Regional Integration," http://www.meti.go.jp/english/index.html; European Central Bank, "Regional Economic Integration in Global Framework," G20 Workshop, 2004; Asian Development Bank, "ADB's Work to Support Regional Cooperation in Asia and the Pacific," https://www.adb.org/themes/regional-cooperation/overview.

the main issue remains the availability and reliability of data that even sometimes are not revealed to statistical organizations. I hope that as GCC countries try to adhere to standardized approaches as well as respect internationally accepted and observed procedures, the quality of data, indispensable for a detailed study of the project, would improve in time. However, for now, I have been forced to conclude this research while being limited by two realities: (1) an inability to travel to conduct field studies, and (2) data reliability and discrepancies due to the nature of statistics bureaus, power structures and policies.

CHAPTER 2

THEORETICAL FRAMEWORKS

Review of Literature on the GCC

In the past decades, various studies have been conducted with the aim of assessing the feasibility of creating a monetary union out of nothing in one of the most tumultuous regions on earth, the Middle East. As is often the case for any scientifically researched issue, the result as of today is not a definitive yes or no. The camp is divided between those that are in favor of the feasibility of such a union and those that reject it.

In 2002, Belkacem Laabas and Imed Limam tested whether the GCC is an optimal currency area. They found that GCC countries do not meet the preconditions for establishing a currency union and discussed the lack of evidence on converging macroeconomic fundamentals. However, they also did a test based on purchasing power parity and figured out that the exchange rates are closely related, and though to a different measure GCC countries are ready for a currency union. They put forward the idea that the GCC would probably meet the monetary union criteria ex-ante rather than ex-post.[13]

William H. Buiter (2008), after discussing both technical economic arguments and political economy considerations, concluded that there is no overwhelming case for a GCC monetary union, and that the lack of economic integration among GCC members is striking since they could not thus far create effective supranational political institutions that would result in political accountability. For Buiter, the creation of an eventual GCC monetary union could be the result of a successful political integration.[14]

Shinji Takagi (2012) reviewed the GCC project since its start and stated that political and bureaucratic capacity dictated the way the GCC evolved as a conceived regional security alliance. Since it could not make clear progress in security cooperation, a framework in which mutual security would be enhanced through economic cooperation had been put in place. He

---

[13] Belkacem Laabas and Imed Limam, "Are GCC Countries Ready for Currency Union?" Arab Planning Institute, 2002.

[14] Willem H. Buiter, "Economic, Political, and Institutional Prerequisites for Monetary Union Among the Members of the Gulf Cooperation Council," *Open Economic Review*, 19(5), 2008.

argued that even though a common market had been launched, national interests and bureaucratic capacity delayed the implementation of necessary measures to allow a true free movement of goods, services, capital and labor.[15]

Takagi made a comparison between the Asian integration process and the one of the GCC. Though the building process was slow and difficult in Asia, the heads of states of the GCC since its inception had unanimously upheld the idea of a common currency. This was more than a decade before the launching of the European common currency, the euro. Takagi identified the lack of regional institutions and unwillingness to give up sovereignty by the region's monarchs as two main hurdles to the GCC's advancement. He concluded that political will and leadership alone are not sufficient conditions and that as long as the GCC remains a "monarchs' club" there will not be a surrender of sovereignty to any regional institution.[16]

The GCC project is an enormous one. It can be analyzed through different fields of study. For instance, Bassem Kamar and Damyana Bakardzhieva (2006), from the econometric results they produced in their research, concluded that the exchange rate behavior determinants are different in four out of the six partner countries, which confirm different macroeconomic policies. Therefore, policy harmonization, which is a required step toward building a successful monetary union, has not been observed.[17] On the other hand, since 2013, the monetary policy of the GCC was supposed to be governed by a single central bank. In this connection, Onur Tas (2012) analyzed the differences in monetary dynamics among these countries since it was essential to an optimum monetary policy. An alternative test of endogeneity was done to analyze the short-run relationship. Granger causality tests of the long-run dynamics of the relationship between money and price levels had been conducted as well, with the aim of making comparisons between related works done previously. The result was that "the short-run relationship was identical and the long-run one was significantly different." The author concludes that the monetary dynamics prove that the GCC countries are suitable for a monetary unification, though the central bank should consider the differences in the dynamics of the long-run relationship between monetary aggregates and price levels.[18]

A quantitative assessment done by Nasser Al-Mawali (2015) based on fixed effects panel estimation suggests that Saudi economic growth is an

---

[15] Shinji Takagi, "Establishing Monetary Union in the Gulf Cooperation Council: What Lessons for Regional Cooperation?" Asian Development Bank Institute, no. 390, 2012.

[16] *Ibid.*

[17] Bassem Kamar and Damyana Bakardzhieva, "The Appropriate Monetary Policy Coordination for the GCC Monetary Union, Proposal for the Twenty-sixth Annual Meeting of The Middle East Economic Association," 2006.

[18] Bedri Kamil Onur Tas, "Money-Price Relationship in GCC Countries," *Journal of Economic Cooperation and Development*, 33(2), 2012.

engine for the region, and drives the economic growth of the GCC. The author suggested that based on his findings the GCC should motivate the acceleration of the process of monetary union, started in 1983 and later stalled at the stage of implementation. Accepting the fact that an eventual economic growth of Saudi Arabia would boost the GCC's economic growth and motivate the six partners to accelerate the integration process, recent studies remind us that beyond economic-related aspects pertinent to each country, other factors such as political instability can be considered a main source of risk.[19]

Recently, during the 37th GCC summit, a declaration of shared positions was offered to the public. The statement is in fact seen as the GCC members' keenness to pursue work toward a solid Gulf economy. This Gulf economy would be created through forming an agglomeration that shifts from cooperation to union.[20] Other countries' welfare and security, such as those of the United Kingdom, would be linked to it. Abdul Rahman believes that the GCC project is not about selling a dream of the region to Arab people, and that the GCC countries are capable of forming a unified economy even better than that of the European Union without necessarily having a political union.[21]

Regional Integration and Theories of International Trade

"Integration" means bringing all parts together, to unify.[22] As mentioned earlier, the term "regional integration" *per se* is very general and vague. In the field of international relations, the word "integration" is heavily used to explain different types of projects and initiatives undertaken by heads of state. Countries sign political, economic, environmental and other types of agreements in order to expand their cooperation through the creation of common rules and institutions. However, later on, in most of the cases, it has taken the form of political economy where economic-related initiatives or trade projects were the most common. World Trade Organization members, as was previously the case for those of the General Agreement on Tariffs and Trade (GATT), are required to notify it of the regional trade agreements in which they participate. During 1948-1994, the GATT received 124 notifications of regional trade agreements. Since the creation of the WTO in

[19] International Monetary Fund, "Economic Prospects and Policy Challenges for the GCC Countries' Annual Meeting of Ministers of Finance and Central Bank Governors," Riyadh, Saudi Arabia, 2016.

[20] Saleh Abdul Rahman Al Maneh, "Joint declaration at GCC summit raises hopes and Expectations," *The National*, 2016: http://www.thenational.ae/opinion/comment/joint-declaration-at-gcc-summit-raises-hopes-and-expectations.

[21] *Ibid.*

[22] *American Heritage Dictionary of the English Language*, 5th ed.

1995,[23] more than 400 notifications covering regional agreements on trade in goods or services have been received.

Therefore, it is fair to say that the idea of regional integration is confirmed at the international level.[24] The main reason for being pro-trade, and ultimately doing it, is the fact that trade is mutually beneficial.[25] Trading is fully explained and analyzed throughout history by a rich set of theories.

International Trade Theories

Theories of international trade are mainly divided into two main categories: classical country-based theories, and theories based on the modern firm. In the first category, foremost is the mercantilism theory of international trade, which reflects the idea of an era in which promoting exports and discouraging imports with the aim of accumulating gold was a leading trade policy. The most common strategy was to create barriers to imports. Though it is one of the oldest trade theories, it is still practiced. Germany, for instance, through protectionist policies as well as by subsidizing domestic industry, favors exports and discourages imports.[26] This confirms that the objective of having a trade surplus is still valid for many countries.

In 1776, questioning mercantilism and its policies led to the absolute and comparative advantage theories.[27] Adam Smith, by putting forward the theory of absolute advantage, objected to the idea of regulating trade and argued the case that trade should follow the forces of the market. Following market forces would lead to specialization, which ultimately generates efficiencies. He reasoned that by increasing efficiency the living standard in partner countries increases. He concluded that a particular nation's wealth needs to be measured through the level of the living standard of its population rather than by how much gold is accumulated.[28]

A few decades later, in 1817, David Ricardo introduced the theory of comparative advantage. Slightly different from the absolute advantage theory, Ricardo focused on the relative productivity of trading partner countries rather than on their absolute productivity. Though interactions in the real world are

---

[23] https://www.wto.org/english/tratop_e/region_e/regfac_e.htm.

[24] Kym Anderson, *Regional Integration and Global Trading System*, Prentice-Hall, 1993; Athanasios Vamvakidis, "Regional Integration and Economic Growth," *The World Bank Economic Review*, 12(2).

[25] European Commission, "Benefits of Trade for Developing Countries," http://trade.ec.europa.eu/doclib/docs/2012/january/tradoc_148991.pdf.

[26] Mason A. Carpenter and Sanjyot P. Dunung, "Challenges and opportunities in International Business," v.1.0.

[27] Adam Smith, *An Inquiry into the Nature and Causes of the Wealth of Nations*, London: W. Strahan and T. Cadell, 1776.

[28] Dominik Salvatore, *Schaum's Outline of International Economics*, McGraw Hill, 1995.

far more complex, Ricardo suggested that countries should specialize in what they do relatively better, even if they may do better and are more efficient in different and multiple other fields. However, nations continued to face difficulties in determining where they would do better and be more efficient – in other words, how to identify where their comparative advantages lay. In the 20th century, Eli Heckscher and Bertil Ohlin's factor proportion theory tried to determine how a particular country would exploit the so-called comparative advantage using the production factors that are available to it, and, more importantly, that are considered as abundant. By determining the costs of production factors as a function of supply and demand, the theory states that countries need to specialize and produce export goods that depend on cheaper production factors.[29] However, all of these theories are based on unrealistic assumptions that do not reflect the reality of international trade. While conducting research, it is healthy and helpful to bear in mind that trade theories are evolving continuously.[30]

After World War II, since the country-based theories were not able to explain some of the phenomena of the time, such as intra-industry trade, new theories tried to explain the trade patterns. The new set of modern theories became known as firm-based or company-based theories. In order to explain and analyze the trade patterns, these theories use additional factors such as technology and loyalty as well as quality. For instance, the "similarity trade" theory tried to explain that consumers in countries that are in the same circumstances of economic development would develop similar preferences.[31] The theory proposed by Steffen Linder states that once the domestic market is saturated, firms would try to export, and to that end, markets that are similar in preferences would be targeted. The result is that most of the trade would take place between countries that have the same income per capita, creating more intra-industry trade.[32]

In connection with intra-industry trade phenomena, another company-based theory of International trade valuable to this work is the one developed by Paul R. Krugman and Kelvin Lancaster that helps to understand how multinational companies strive to gain competitive advantage *vis-à-vis* their global competitors. It further discusses that while trying to compete, they face barriers to entry. One of the most important of these barriers is economies of scale. The rationale here is that by considering economies of scale and imperfect competition, we would be able to understand that very similar

---

[29] Robert E. Baldwin, *The Development and Testing of Heckscher-Ohlin Trade Models: A Review of Ohlin Lectures*, MIT Press, 2008; Bertil Ohlin and Bo Sandelin, *Interregional and International Trade*, Routledge, 1998.

[30] http://www2.econ.iastate.edu/classes/econ355/choi/ho.htm

[31] The theory was elaborated by Swedish economist Steffan Linder.

[32] Adam Klug, *Theories of International Trade*, Routledge, 2006; Giancarlo Gandolfo, *International Trade Theory and Policy*, Springer Science and Business Media, 1998.

countries can engage in trade and be able to assess both economic convergence and economic divergence.[33] Therefore, the combined presence of economies of scale and imperfect competition would affect gains from trade and the patterns and volume of trade. It would also affect income distribution as well as factor mobility. All together, it would ultimately lead to intra-industry trade flows. However, the issues of how diversified the involved economies are remain crucial.[34]

In 1990, Michael Porter's work helped to explain the concept of national competitive advantage. He argued that a country's competitiveness in a particular industry depends on two main factors.[35] These factors are simply the ability of a particular industry to innovate and upgrade itself.[36] He developed his theory by identifying four determinants:[37]

1. Local market resources and capabilities
2. Local market demand conditions
3. Local suppliers and complementary industries
4. The characteristics of local companies

Porter's and other firm-based theories of international trade, along with those of country-based ones, served as essential tools to understand the trends and patterns of trade. They helped countries and policy makers to evaluate their decisions, elucidate them for their counterparts and move forward toward national goals. Though these theories had been contradicted several times while being tested in real-world cases, they are still valid, and, as time passes, they evolve as well and continue to offer an understanding of the basics of international trade.

---

[33] Bharati Basu, "Economics of Scale and Imperfect Competition," *International Economics, Finance and Trade*, Vol.1.
[34] Gene M. Grossman, *Imperfect Competition and International Trade*, MIT Press, 1992; Paul R. Krugman, *Rethinking International Trade*, MIT Press, 1994; Elhanan Helpman, "Monopolistic Competition in Trade Theory," Special Papers in International Finance, Princeton, 1990; Marius Brulhart, "Scale Economies, Intra-Industry Trade and Industry Location in a 'New Trade Theory,'" Trinity Economic Papers, Technical Paper, No 95/4.
[35] Michael E. Porter, *The Competitive Advantage of Nations*, Free Press, 1998.
[36] Michael Porter, "The Role of Location in Competition," *Journal of the Economics of Business*, 1994.
[37] Jeffrey Furman, Michael Porter and Scott Stern, "The Determinant of National Innovative Capacity," *Research Policy*, 31(6), 2002.

Economic Integration

Economic integration is a complex topic in the field of international economics that can be studied either as a process or by being distinguished and introduced as various forms of integration. Defining such a complex idea is not an easy task. "The term economic integration, whatever it might have been in its earlier history, only recently became a slogan for action, or what the French call more respectfully, une idée forte."[38] "Dans la hiérarchie des mots obscurs et sans beauté dont les discussions économiques encombrent notre langue, le terme d'intégration occupe un bon rang."[39] The two aforementioned statements concerning the complexity of the subject are still valid in the twenty-first century, confirming the fact that it may not have a clear-cut meaning. It includes different concepts such as international cooperation and social integration within its realm. Obviously, such approaches make the term "economic integration" harder to understand for both policy makers and common citizens.

Bela Balassa proposed a definition of economic integration that considered the phenomenon as both a process as well as a state of affairs. He argued that if integration is considered as a process, it will include measures that would help to abolish discrimination among economic units operating within different countries. If considered as a state of affairs, based on the assumption that discrimination would have already affected the economic activities between two hypothetical countries, it will represent the absence of any form of discrimination between different national economies.[40] While interpreting this definition, we learn that it is essential to differentiate between cooperation and integration. The differences can be either quantitative or qualitative. Cooperation is aimed at lessening discrimination, whereas integration is aimed at abolishing discrimination.[41]

Therefore, such a definition makes economic integration take several forms, each *per se* representing varying degrees of integration itself.[42] Being a process, the first stage is a free trade area, within which tariffs or any quantitative restrictions are abolished with the right for participating countries to decide on their own tariff policies towards nonmembers. In close connection with this, a second stage is a customs union. In customs unions, the partners, in addition to abolishing tariffs among themselves, would make tariffs uniform toward nonmembers as well. A higher form of integration would be observed in a third stage, creating a common market. A common

[38] M.A. Heilperin, "Economic integration: Commercial and financial postulates," in *European Integration*, ed. C.C. Haines, Baltimore: John Hopkins Press, 1957, p.126.
[39] Françoise Perroux, *L'Europe sans rivages*, Paris: Presses universitaires de France, 1954, p. 419.
[40] Bela Balassa, "Towards the Theory of Economic Integration," *Kyklos*, 1, pp.1-5.
[41] Bela Balassa, *The Theory of Economic Integration*, Routledge, 2011.
[42] *Ibid.*

market includes both free trade areas and customs unions, and represents a form of integration in which any restriction on movement is also abolished.

After that comes a fourth stage, an economic union. In an economic union, the main work to be done is to harmonize different national economic policies. Since in this stage discrimination and restrictions on movement are suppressed, disparities in national policies are the main causes that slow down the removal of discrimination. The fifth and the last form of economic integration, globally desired but on many occasions misunderstood and not often achieved, is a complete economic integration, unifying monetary, fiscal, social and countercyclical policies, and ending up with supra-national authorities governing the above-mentioned policies.[43] If such a project is presented to a nation, the main question that can be posed is what its effects would be. The most important effect of such an endeavor is related to trade. The effects of economic integration on trade are of two types, known as static and dynamic effects.

Static Effects

The static effect deals with the immediate effects of integration through concepts such as trade creation and trade diversion. It gives a snapshot of the situation. For instance, we would learn how efficiently resources are allocated. Before the creation of a customs union, each country tries to look for and capitalize on its own comparative advantages in order to be more efficient and competitive in exporting. Barriers to trade such as tariffs, and the fact that countries have different preferences in regards to trading partners, create inefficiency, and producers that are more efficient will see their share of the market reduced. Exporting companies and industries are also affected when other countries retaliate against barriers to trade. Higher costs due to tariffs or other restrictions sometimes lead companies to reduce quality. In addition to the aforementioned consequences, in some cases countries can get into undesired trade wars, which ultimately would affect their income.[44]

In regards to trade creation, a good thing that flows from the falling of barriers, such as in a free trade area, is that when tariffs no longer exist

---

[43] *Ibid.*

[44] Richard E. Baldwin and Anthony J. Venables, *Handbook of International Economics*, Elsevier, 2014; Alexander Yeats, *Trade and Development Policies: Leading Issues for 1980*, Palgrave Macmillan, 1981.

prices will consequently drop and consumers will increase their consumption.[45] This is how more trade is created.[46]

On the other hand, the presence of tariffs could harm an efficient nonmember's exports to the benefit of an inefficient trading partner, in this case causing trade to be diverted; this phenomenon is called trade diversion. This economic inefficiency happens because a low-cost efficient producer cannot benefit from its competitive advantage in order to keep prices low, because the high-cost producer that is also a member of the customs union has free access to the union's market.[47]

Dynamic Effects

The dynamic effects are mainly long-term considerations of national economies' reactions to the creation of the union. Dynamic effects are also considered as important success indicators while examining the effects of economic integration. In the first place, there is the extension of the market. Once a union is created, efficient producers within it will have access to foreign markets that were previously unattractive for them due to restrictions. These opportunities enable them to take advantage of economies of scale, and ultimately eliminate the non-efficient producers within the union. A second effect is on job markets, as temporary unemployment would follow. The third effect is the creation of more competition and innovation. This can be experienced also in concomitance with the other two effects. As a result, producers will no longer be protected by tariffs or any kind of favors, and consequently efficient producers will remain in the market, offering lower prices that would ultimately lead to greater competition and innovation.[48]

Monetary Union

Since the ambitious GCC project was aimed at launching a common currency, further developing this idea would be helpful. A complete economic

---

[45] Bela Balassa, "Trade Creation and Trade Diversion in the European Common Market: An Appraisal of the Evidence," *The Manchester School*, 42(2), 1974; Christopher Magee, "New Measures of Trade Creation and Trade Diversion," *Journal of International Economics*, 75(2), 2008.

[46] Jacob Viner, *The Customs Union Issue*, Oxford University Press, 1950.

[47] Richard G. Lipsey, "The Theory of Customs Unions: Trade Diversion and Welfare," *Economica*, Wiley, 24(93), 1957; Richard G. Lipsey and Kelvin Lancaster, "The General Theory of Second Best," Review of Economic Studies, 24(1), 1956; Chris Allen, Michael Gasiorek and Alasdair Smith, "Trade Creation and Trade Diversion," *Single Market Review Series*, European Commission, 1996.

[48] Josef C. Brada and Jose A. Mendez, "An Estimate of the Dynamic Effects of Economic Integration," *Review of Economics and Statistics*, 70(1), 1988; Uwe Walz, "Dynamic Effects of Economic Integration," *Open Economies Review*, 8(3), 1997.

integration will include a monetary union as well. Like any project, countries that decide to relinquish the ability to be in charge of their own monetary policy will face costs and benefits that sometimes are hard to predict and quantify. A central bank is considered as part of a country's sovereignty, and monetary policy is a very powerful tool used by authorities to manage economic activities. Through monetary policy and the way money is supplied, the whole system will be affected. Beginning from households' expenditures to governments' budgets, each economic unit and institution involved in economic activity will be in some way touched by changes in monetary policies. Therefore, to be part of a currency union, a detailed study of such a project is indispensable since it would affect nations' economies and residents, in both the short and long run, and sometimes without any remedy to the long-run consequences.[49]

The theory of Robert Mundell, "an optimum currency area," published in 1961, offers the tool necessary in evaluating the feasibility of a hypothetical area; within its borders, countries can maximize economic efficiency by sharing a single currency. The theory, based on geographical area, discusses and analyzes consequences of fixed and flexible exchange rates on macroeconomic indices in regards to exogenous specific shocks in a country. It this way, it paves the way to figuring out the main characteristics that are required for unifying different currencies in order to introduce a new shared one. He suggests that countries which have close economic ties may benefit and achieve far more efficient economic results by sharing the same currency.[50] Analyzing the GCC countries, for instance, their respective economic ties could give a hint as to the feasibility of a monetary union, supposing that all other requirements are fulfilled.

Mundell argues that as long as fixed exchange rates and rigid wage and price levels exist, crises of balance of payments that occur at different intervals will persist and prevent the adjustment mechanism from operating properly. Therefore, he states that a flexible exchange rate would serve as a tool to replace unemployment by depreciation when the external balance is in deficit and would replace inflation through appreciation when the balance is in surplus. In discussing this at the international level, he poses the question of whether all national currencies should be flexible. To answer it, he describes the problem in a general way and defines currencies as a domain

---

[49] B. Moss, *Monetary Union in Crisis: The European Union as a Neo-Liberal Construction*, Springer, 2004; "Employment Consequences of European Economic and Monetary Union," Education and Employment Committee, House of Commons Paper Series, 1999; Ugo Fasano-Filho and Andrea Schaechter, "Monetary Union Among Member Countries of the Gulf Cooperation Council," International Monetary Fund, 2003.

[50] Robert Mundell, "A theory of optimum currency area," American Economic Association, 1961; Robert Mundell, *Flexible Exchange Rate and Employment Policy*, University of Toronto Press, 1961.

within which exchange rates are fixed, and then tries to determine what the appropriate domain of a currency area is.[51]

Mundell shows the difference between interregional adjustments and international adjustments. He creates a model of two entities, A and B, initially with full employment and with the balance of payments in equilibrium, and analyzes the effects of a shift in demand for goods in A to goods in B, assuming money wages and prices cannot be reduced in the short run without causing unemployment and the authorities act to prevent inflation. He rejects the idea that the optimum currency area would be the world and affirms that the optimum currency area is a region. The idea under scrutiny is the effect of economic shocks – if shocks strike the real economy, a flexible exchange rate would be a solution.[52]

Mundell considers A and B as countries and observes that a shift of demand from country A to country B affects unemployment in A and a rise of inflation in B. If the prices can change to a certain degree in country B, then the change in trade terms will alleviate the burden of adjustment in country A. However, if B prevents inflation, A would entirely bear the adjustment burdens, such as unemployment. He then considers the situation in which the entities are regions, each with a closed economy functioning by a shared currency, with a full-employment policy. Now in order to fix the unemployment in A, the supply of money due to monetary policy will be augmented. In discussing the currency area and common currency, he concludes that in a currency area with different national currencies the pace of employment in the deficit country depends on the willingness of the one in surplus to inflate.[53]

These are very important considerations. Countries that implement such projects, as mentioned earlier, will deal with not only the short-term consequences, but also sometimes long-term ones that are not remediable. In a real-world analysis, these kinds of shifts would affect the daily lives of large numbers of people.[54]

---

[51] Robert Mundell, "The International Monetary Dilemma," Interamerican Institute of Capital Market, 1979; Anja Zenker, *Currency Speculation in Fixed Exchange Rate Regimes: Theory and Empirical Evidences*, Springer Business and Science Media, 2014; Edward D. Mansfield and Helen V. Milne, *The Political Economy of Regionalism*, Columbia University Press, 1997.

[52] Robert A. Mundell, "A Theory of Optimum Currency Area," *American Economic Review*, 51(4), 1961; Mario I. Bléjer and David M. Cheney, "Optimum Currency Areas: New Analytical and Policy Developments," International Monetary Fund, 1997; Luca Antonio Ricci, "A Model of an Optimum Currency Area," International Monetary Fund, 1997.

[53] Ricci, *ibid.*; Mundell, *Flexible Exchange Rate and Employment Policy*; *Money, Capital Mobility and Trade, Essays in Honor of Robert A. Mundell*, MIT Press, 2001; Peter Bofinger, "Is Europe an Optimum Currency Area?," Center for Economic Policy Research, 1994.

[54] Anna Zamora-Kapoor and Xavier Coller, "The Effects of the Crisis: Why Southern Europe?", PMC: https://www.ncbi.nlm.nih.gov/pmc/.

It is worth mentioning that in a currency region with a common currency, the pace of inflation depends on central authority interventions to allow unemployment in the deficit region, through a decrease in nominal wages/prices, a shift in the supply curve or a change in fiscal policies.

In a nutshell, the optimum currency area theory provides an understanding of how to react to shocks. If shocks are symmetric, either monetary union or a fixed exchange rate is considered as an appropriate response, and if shocks are asymmetric, labor mobility or wage flexibility must be the main response.[55]

Mundell's Criteria

Following the result of the research done by Mundell, countries located in a particular region that are struck by asymmetric shocks would be better off if they share a common currency – in other words, they would have more strategies to implement in order to alleviate the consequences of shocks and ultimately to maximize economic efficiency. However, countries that are part of a currency union must correspond to a set of standards. These are necessary steps which must be respected. Otherwise, struck by asymmetric shocks, the countries would be better off if they react and adjust separately.[56]

Countries must meet four criteria if they wish to join a monetary union:

1. Labor mobility across the region
2. Capital mobility as well as price and wage flexibility
3. A risk-sharing mechanism
4. A similar business cycle

The European case is the one that can be studied through these four criteria. In regards to labor mobility, a lack of cultural barriers such as different languages is an essential point. Being able to intervene and redistribute money in regions that are hit by shocks is a critical issue, and in theory the European Monetary Union does not have such a mechanism. Not confirming to the above-mentioned criteria would undermine the desired objective of economic efficiency not only in those regions that are hit by shocks but also in each single member; the 2010 crisis in Greece is a vivid

---

[55] European Parliament, "Optimum Currency Area," http://www.europarl.europa.eu/workingpapers/econ/104/chap1_en.htm

[56] Johannes Ebert, *Intra Industry Trade and Shock Asymmetry in a Monetary Union: A Study of Trade Evolution in Eurozone*, GRIN Verlag, 2013; Martin H. Wolfson and Gerald A. Epstein, *The Handbook of the Political Economy of Financial Crises*, Oxford University Press, 2013; Alexandra Swoboda and Robert Mundell, "Theoretical Foundation for the European Monetary Union," International Monetary Fund, 1999.

case open to further study.[57] However, we should bear in mind that in regards to Mundell's model and criteria, for participating countries all the prerequisites are considered and assumed as given and perfectly met *a priori*. A real case exists, and is still there: the European Monetary Union. Though the Eurozone was not an optimal currency area, the concept that an optimal currency area can be self-fulfilling was proven false. A study conducted by Richard Baldwin demonstrates that the boost to trade from the single currency is much smaller than what was estimated in the past[58] and in its best estimate would be 9%.[59]

Convergence Criteria

The European Union is an open and real case for study and scrutiny. Since its conception, it has continuously been the subject of additional literature on economic integration. This is why any study elsewhere can benefit from European experiences. In addition to the main body of criteria that may be fulfilled before discussing any monetary union, the treaty of Maastricht that came into force in 1993 offers a set of macroeconomic indicators that are meant to measure the readiness of countries that wanted to join the European Monetary Union. In fact, since countries have different policies in regards to their economies or monetary aspects of them, a mechanism is needed to harmonize these policies. In Europe, a set of five criteria, assessed and monitored by independent institutions such as the European Central Bank and the European Commission, would evaluate the readiness and eligibility of countries to join in terms of identified macroeconomic indicators.[60] The table below shows the five criteria that members had to meet before entering the monetary union and adopting the euro.[61]

---

[57] Roman Horvath And Lubos Komarek, "Optimum Currency Area Theory: An Approach for Thinking about Monetary Integration," Warwick Economic Research Papers, no. 647; Emilio Colombo and Luca Stanca, *Financial Market Imperfections and Corporate Decisions: Lessons from the Transition Process in Hungary*, Springer Science & Business Media, 2005; Bléjer and Cheney, "Optimum Currency Areas."

[58] João Santos Silva and Silvana Tenreyro, "Currency Unions in Prospect and Retrospect," *Annual Review of Economics*, 2, 2010, pp. 51-74.

[59] Richard Baldwin, "In or Out: Does It Matter? An Evidence-Based Analysis of the Euro's Trade Effects," London: Centre for Economic Policy Research, 2006.

[60] Paul J.J. Welfens, *European Monetary Integration: EMS Developments and International Post-Maastricht Perspectives*, Springer Science & Business Media, 2012; Rene Smits, *The European Central Bank, Institutional Aspects*, Kluwer Law International, 1997; Panos C. Afxentiou, "Convergence, the Maastricht Criteria, and Their Benefits," *Brown Journal of World Affairs*, 7(1).

[61] European Commission.

Maastricht Convergence Criteria					
Indicators	HICP inflation	Governments budget deficit	Governments debt to GDP ratio	Exchange rate Stability	Long term interest rates
What is measured?	Price Stability	Soundness of Public finances	Sustainability of public finances	Stability of exchange rate	Durability of convergence
How it is measured?	CPI rate	Government deficit as % of GDP	Government debt as % of GDP	Deviation from central rate	Long term rates
Convergence Criteria	Not more than 1.5%point above the rate of three best performing members	Must not exceed 3% at the end of the preceding fiscal year	Not higher than 60%	Part of ERMII min 2 years and with exclusion of tensions	Less than 2 percentage points above the rate of three best performing members

Through the convergence criteria, inflation was monitored, public finances both in terms of soundness and sustainability were measured, and the exchange rate mechanism (ERM) evaluated deviations from the central rate. Long-term interest rates assessed the durability of the convergence achieved by fulfilling the other criteria. Therefore, countries that are similar in terms of economic performance and also benefit from strong economic ties are more likely to succeed if they decide to create a monetary union.[62]

[62] Anna Lipinska, "The Maastricht Convergence Criteria and Optimal Monetary Policy for the EMU Accession Countries," Working Paper Series, European Central Bank, 2008; Marcin Szczepański, "Adopting the euro convergence criteria and state of play," European Parliamentary Research Service, 2015; Treaty on European Union, Council of the European Communities, Commission of the European Communities: https://europa.eu/european-union/sites/europaeu/files/docs/body/treaty_on_european_union_en.pdf.

CHAPTER 3

GCC INTEGRATION

The Gulf Cooperation Council

The implementation of a regional bloc affects many aspects of those countries that join, and mainly their economies. Today, concepts such as sovereignty and being independent in terms of economic policies are at the heart of the debate in any country, discussed by citizens, political establishments as well as intellectual communities. This is why, in order to give up totally or partly the aforementioned principles and aspects of independence, the gain from joining a regional bloc must really be valuable in terms of economic prosperity. In terms of political independence, also, there must be provided and built acceptable and realistic frameworks of governance. The economy can be considered as the most important factor in bringing prosperity to a nation. This is why any regional integration project must be analyzed and assessed through different branches of economics. Many countries have embarked, and in the future more will embark, on such projects and adventures without any idea of their potential gain and loss in the long run. Projects that are considered as failed as they could not deliver promises, or that are simply invalidated at some point either during the integration process itself or after several years, are not rare.[63]

In 1981, six countries located within the Arabian Peninsula region – the United Arab Emirates, the Kingdom of Saudi Arabia, the State of Kuwait, the State of Bahrain, the State of Qatar and the Sultanate of Oman – which together cover a total area of 2,672,700 square kilometers, with a total population of 50,359,763 (national statistics 2010-2015),[64] finally came to an agreement. The agreement formed a new sub-regional bloc within the Middle East called the Gulf Cooperation Council (GCC). Its charter presents the idea of the project as well as the objectives to be fulfilled. The charter begins with the members' awareness of the ties of special relations, common

---

[63] Bill Lee, "The European Union: A Failed Experiment," *Harvard Business Review*, 2013; "Regional Integration and Food Security in Developing Countries, Regional Integration in Africa," FAO: http://www.fao.org/docrep/004/y4793e/y4793e0a.htm.

[64] http://gulfmigration.eu/gcc-total-population-and-percentage-of-nationals-and-non-nationals-in-gcc-countries-national-statistics-2010-2015-with-numbers/.

characteristics and a similar system founded on the creed of Islam, which bind them. It continues with the desire of effecting coordination, cooperation and integration in all fields. Furthermore, the goal of strengthening cooperation and reinforcement of the links between these countries was introduced, which ultimately would channel their efforts to reinforce and serve Arab and Islamic causes.[65]

The six countries agreed on twenty-two articles in the charter. Article 4 goes to the GCC's objectives as follows:

> To effect coordination, integration, and interconnection between member states in all fields in order to achieve unity between them.
> To deepen and strengthen relations, links and areas of cooperation now prevailing between their peoples in various fields.
> To formulate similar regulations in various fields, including the following:
>
> Economic and financial affairs
> Commerce, customs, and communications
> Education and culture
>
> To stimulate scientific and technological progress in industry, mining, agriculture, water, and animal resources; to establish scientific research, to establish joint ventures and encourage cooperation by the private sector for the good of their peoples.

The constitution of the GCC is also a precise manifestation of a higher desire, which is to make happen the unity of Arab states.[66] These objectives touch almost all aspects of the daily life of citizens and ultimately the nations as a whole. This is why the gain from joining a regional integration project must be enormous and could not be achieved unilaterally. Next, we briefly go through each of the GCC members' specificities in terms of the resources available and the legal and political structures, as well as a few macroeconomic factors.

Resource Endowment

The term "resource" can embrace different meanings and definitions based on the subject matter. In economics, by resources, we mean all those factors that can be explored and exploited through well-defined processes that would ultimately result in final products available for consumption. The amount of resources available to a nation and the way these resources are

---

[65] Charter of the Gulf Cooperation Council; Derek Hopwood, *The Arabian Peninsula: Society and Politics*, Routledge, 2015.

[66] Charter of the Gulf Cooperation Council, *ibid.*

exploited will be a determining factor in how a nation will ultimately develop its economy, make progress and bring prosperity to its citizens. Well-known resources are usually understood as human labor, land and capital. The question of including other capacities such as entrepreneurial talent into the resource endowment of a country is still fresh and debated.[67]

Hand-in-hand with freely God-given resources as mentioned above, and with the aim of achieving economic development, goes the concept of "institution." The term is defined as "a custom, practice, relationship or behavioral pattern of importance in the life of a community or society." Concerning the societal life, and in connection with its importance, an institution is also defined as an established organization or foundation, especially one dedicated to education, public services or culture.[68] As such, institutions and the way they accompany nations to exploit resources available to them are not in the second category of importance. Daron Acemoglu and James Robinson, through two theories of the "drivers of democratic and dictatorial regimes," and "how democratic regimes promote economic growth while dictatorial regimes prevent it," explain the determining role of institutions in the success or failure of a nation. These theories are supported by evidence from the rise of medieval Venice until the period of colonization. Pluralistic and "inclusive" political and economic institutions create a system of incentives that will let people dream and invest in their own future, and ultimately, if everybody flourishes, the nation will prosper as a whole. In such a country, on the one hand, inclusive political institutions would distribute and limit political power through democratic elections and constitutions. On the other hand, inclusive economic institutions would offer a variety of rights such as property rights, a free market, competition and contract enforcement. These institutions will nourish and build upon each other.[69]

There is also the argument that the institutions of nations are extractive – they are put in place to protect the interests of the elite and their wealth, and ultimately would cause the failure of the nation as a whole. These kinds of institutions would nourish and help the repressive and authoritarian elites to make themselves and their entourage even wealthier. Therefore, as

---

[67] Moses Abramovitz, *The Allocation of Economic Resources*, Stanford University Press, 1959; R.M. Auty, *Resource Abundance and Economic Development*, Oxford University Press, 2001; "The Economic Significance of Natural Resources: Key points for reformers in Eastern Europe, Caucasus and Central Asia," OECD, 2011; World Bank, *Natural Resources, Neither Curse, Nor Destiny*, Stanford Press University Press, 2007.

[68] *American Heritage Dictionary*.

[69] Daron Acemoglu and James Robinson, *Why Nations Fail*, Crown Business, 2012; R. Kent Weaver and Bert A. Rockman, *Do Institutions Matter? Government Capabilities in the United States and Abroad*, Brookings Institution Press, 2010; Hendrik Wagenaar, *Government Institutions: Effects, Changes and Normative Foundations*, Springer Science & Business Media, 2012.

history teaches, we may learn that to get the economics right you first need to get politics right.[70]

Developing on resource endowment, and in connection with the institutional aspects, Kenneth L. Sokoloff and Stanley L. Engerman discussed questions such as how and why places that had been once favored due to abundant lands and natural resources, and that had been immigrants' destinations, fell economically. What are the differentials in paths of development, and where do they come from? The inclusive answer was that the divergence in paths is due to the achievement of sustained economic growth. They confirm that if resources are distributed equitably, this will lead to a freely competitive and open economy, and the opportunistic economy will bring prosperity. However, in addition, the path of institutional development may affect economic growth, too. If institutions are designed in a way to give advantage to the elite over a majority of the population that has limited access to economic opportunities, the cost for the society and the nation as a whole would be that disadvantaged groups could not realize their full economic potential. Therefore, if a small group within a nation benefits, and it is differentiated enormously from the rest of the population in terms of wealth, human resources and political influence, that group would strive to limit competition and the rest of the population's access to the resources available.[71]

As we can see, both the work of Sokoloff and Engerman and that of Acemoglu meet at the end by reaching the same conclusion.

GCC Members' Resource Endowments and Institutions

- Kingdom of Saudi Arabia

Saudi Arabia, founded by Al Saud, has existed as a state since 1932. As an absolute monarchy, the King of Saudi Arabia acts as head of state while leading the government's functions. He is the sole decision-maker for the country and his decisions are made through consultations with a body of religious and influential members of the royal entourage. The two institutions of "religion" and the "state" are considered as the main legislative bodies. These are also considered as executive bodies that would ultimately cover whole issues concerning the nation. The state handles internationally related issues such as foreign policy and international economics – in other words, all

[70] *Ibid.*

[71] Kenneth L. Sokoloff and Stanley L. Engerman, "Institutions, Factor Endowments, and Paths of Development in the New World," *Journal of Economic Perspectives*, 14(3), 2000, pp. 217–232; Stanley L. Engerman and Kenneth L. Sokoloff, *Economic Development in the Americas Since 1500: Endowments and Institutions*, Cambridge University Press, 2012; Daren Acemoglu, Simon Johnson and James A. Robinson, "Institutions as a fundamental cause of long run growth," in *Handbook of Economic Growth*, Elsevier, 2005.

the issues that are related to Saudi Arabia's sovereignty. However, internal affairs including education, justice, etc., are conducted by religious establishments.[72] On the legal system, Islamic religious law, Sharia'ah, is considered as the foundation of the country and at the same time its two main sources, specifically Qur'an and the Sunnah of the Prophet Muhammad, are considered as Saudi Arabia's constitution. Although the constitution does not exist in a legally binding written format, it ultimately governs all administrative regulations of the state.[73]

With a population of 31,540,763 inhabiting an area of 2,149,690 square kilometers, Saudi Arabia is the most populous country of the GCC. Although it has diverse natural resources such as gold, iron, copper, etc., throughout the country, the main natural resource that is exploited is oil.[74] The Kingdom of Saudi Arabia, with its proven reserves of 268 billion barrels, has the second largest reserves of such God-given riches in the world.[75] This is why its top industries are formed around the exploitation of this natural resource. The dominant ones are petrochemicals, construction materials and ammonia. These industries, and the service sector that formed in parallel to them, constitute the major part of the country's GDP, which in 2015 was $646 billion.[76] The graph below shows the composition of GDP by sectors.[77]

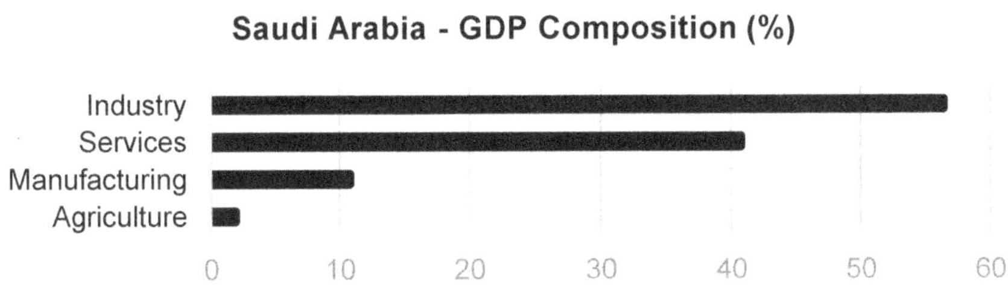

The issue of human resources in Saudi Arabia is also a point that needs to be taken into consideration. With a labor force participation that averages around 51.48%, almost 11 million people were employed in the

[72] http://carnegieendowment.org/2010/10/27/saudi-fatwa-restrictions-and-state-clerical-relationship/6b81.
[73] Abdullah F. Ansary, "A Brief Overview of the Saudi Arabian Legal System," Hauser Global Law School, 2008.
[74] Peter North and Harvey Tripp, *Culture Shock! Saudi Arabia: A Survival Guide to Customs and Etiquette*, Cavendish Square Publishing 2007.
[75] U.S Department of Energy: http://www.eia.gov/cfapps/ipdbproject/iedindex3.cfm?tid=5&pid=57&aid=6&cid=SA,&syid=2010&eyid=2014&unit=BB.
[76] http://data.worldbank.org/country/saudi-arabia.
[77] Global Edge, Michigan State University, http://globaledge.msu.edu/countries/saudi-arabia/economy.

Kingdom in 2015. However, with the introduction of the "Saudization"[78] program introduced in 2011, whose aim is to replace foreign workers with Saudi nationals, the unemployment rate remained unchanged throughout 2016 at 5.6%.[79] To conclude, with a growth rate of 3.6% in 2014 and an inflation rate of 2.7%, the Kingdom of Saudi Arabia has been moving very slowly toward regulatory efficiency and market openness.[80] The potential gain from the free flow of goods and services and trade in general is undermined by a lack of transparency and a heavy bureaucratic system. Foreign direct investment in Saudi Arabia, as will be seen later, amounted to $8 billion, confirming that many sectors of the Kingdom either are not open to foreigners or have limits on their engagement.[81]

- Qatar

The tiny nation of Qatar, once under the control of Bahraini Sheikhs, after surviving submission to Ottoman rule and being a British protectorate, gained its independence in 1971. Ruled by the al-Tahani family, the state of Qatar today is considered as a constitutional monarchy.[82] It is still recognized as such by some authors and commentators after a constitutional referendum in 2003, as the new power structure is not yet institutionalized and the Emir remains the sole executive power.[83]

There are no similarities between the ruler's realm of power and the state as a modern term in Qatar. The ruler is head of state and the power will pass on within the Al-Tahani family. Some authors consider Qatar to be like a corporation, with the Emir acting as a CEO with "unlimited" power that is unparalleled by that of any CEO of a big multinational corporation.[84] The Emir of Qatar is not legally bound by any constitution, for instance. He is the only one who can put immediate limitations on his own power, or break self-imposed restrictions and limitations.[85]

---

[70] James Wynbrandt, *A Brief History of Saudi Arabia*, InfoBase Publishing, 2014.
[79] http://www.tradingeconomics.com/saudi-arabia/unemployment-rate.
[80] http://www.heritage.org/index/country/saudiarabia.
[81] 2014 data unless otherwise noted; K.P.M Basheer, "Saudi Arabia Malayalis jittery as Nitaqat deadline ends today," *The Hindu*, 2013: http://www.thehindu.com/news/national/kerala/saudi-malayalis-jittery-as-nitaqat-deadline-ends-today/article4551294.ece; Anthony H. Cordesman and Nawaf E. Obaid, *National Security in Saudi Arabia: Threats, Responses, and Challenges*, Greenwood Publishing Group, 2005.
[82] http://www.state.gov/documents/organization/160077.pdf.
[83] Jennifer Lambert, "Political Reform in Qatar: Participation, Legitimacy and Security," *Middle East Policy Council Journal Essays*, 18(1), 2011.
[84] Allen J. Fromherz, *Qatar: A Modern History*, Georgetown University Press; 2012.
[85] Katy Schiel, *Monarchy: A primary Source Analysis*, Rosen Publishing Group, 2005; Richard F. Nyrop, *Area Handbook for the Persian Gulf States*, WildSide Press, 2014; Andrew

As for the legal system, as affirmed by the first article of the constitution, Sharia'ah is the main source of legislation.[86] The legal system ultimately covers most of the issues pertinent to the society. In many cases, women are not allowed to give testimony, or when their testimonies are considered they are worth half of men's.[87] As is the case with executive authorities, the Emir has unlimited power over the legal system. He appoints all judges and picks all the justices for the Supreme Court.[88]

Qatar occupies 11,610 square kilometers on a peninsula that borders the Persian Gulf. The majority of its small population of 2,235,355 people reside mainly in Doha, the capital.[89] The main resources available for exploitation, which have brought prosperity to its inhabitants, are hydrocarbons. Consequently, the main industries are formed around this sector. The result is that Qatar in 2013 was the world's fourth largest producer of natural gas,[90] being home to the largest gas-to-liquids facility, and since 2006 it has been the world's leading exporter of liquefied natural gas. Petrochemicals, oil refining as well as fertilizer production are also considered the main industrial building blocks of Qatar's economy. Available data suggest that oil and gas have a share of 50% in the GDP and probably account for 70% of the government's revenue.[91] In Qatar, in addition to the aforementioned industries, and in concomitance with government's plan to diversify the economy, tourism and Islamic/Sharia'ah-based financial markets are also considered as opportunities for investment. The graph below shows the composition of GDP by sectors.[92]

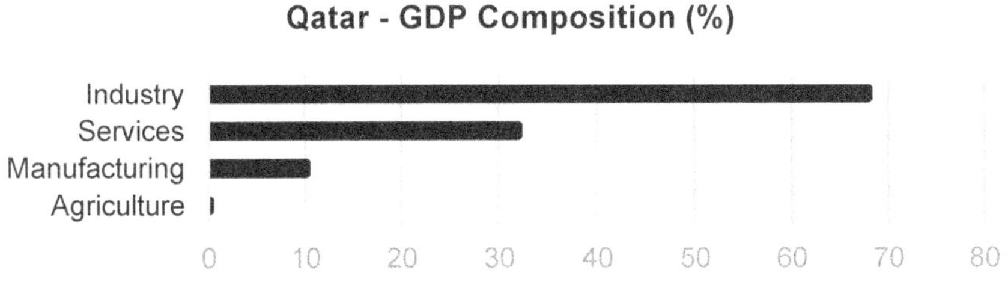

Hammond, "Qatar Leadership Transition, Like Father, Like Son," European Council on Foreign Relations, 2014.

[86] http://www.wipo.int/edocs/lexdocs/laws/en/qa/qa009en.pdf.

[87] http://www.unicef.org/gender/files/Qatar-Gender-Eqaulity-Profile-2011.pdf.

[88] Gabriela Knaul, "Report of Special Rapporteur on the Independence of Judges and Lawyers," Human Rights Council, United Nations, 2015.

[89] http://databank.worldbank.org/data/reports.aspx?source=2&country=QAT.

[90] http://www.eia.gov/beta/international/analysis_includes/countries_long/Qatar/qatar.pdf.

[91] http://www.gulfbase.com/GCC/Index/6.

[92] Global Edge, Michigan State University: http://globaledge.msu.edu/countries/qatar/economy.

A country with a small population size that has access to enormous hydrocarbon resources as the sole factor to be exploited in order to bring prosperity and economic growth evidently will have a different job market structure. Qatar is among these countries, having a labor constraint economy with ample natural resources. This is why Qatar has had to go abroad to satisfy the needs of its booming economy in terms of human resources. While Qatari nationals represented only 12% of the total population based on the 2014 census,[93] the calculation did not consider those nationals residing abroad as well as those with residence permits. Other studies show that foreign workers are 86% of the population and make up 94% of the labor force.[94] Qatar is the country with the highest ratio of migrants to citizens. In connection with the job market structure and the way Qatar's economy and political system function, the average unemployment rate during 2001-2015 was 2.17%.[95] To conclude, with a growth rate of 6.3% and an inflation rate of 3.0%,[96] Qatari nationals are experiencing a high living standard.

- Kuwait

Kuwait, along with Bahrain, the UAE and Qatar, was engaged in the GCC project since the 1970s. It became an independent country in 1961 and two years later it held its first parliamentary election. Though Kuwait's constitution includes the principle of a democratic system of governance, the Emir has the final word and appoints the prime minister. Members of parliament can question and even remove a minister of the cabinet, but they will not be able to remove the Emir's appointed prime minister, who also comes from the ruling family.

The legal system of Kuwait and its constitution encompass principles which are found in many democratic and developed countries' constitutions. However, women do not yet have the right to vote and political parties are not allowed. Sharia'ah remains the main source of legislation, and although the constitution mentions the separation between executive, legislative and judicial authorities, the Emir of Kuwait, a member of the Mubarak Al-Sabah family, is the head of all three authorities with the last word on all matters.[97]

---

[93] http://www.bq-magazine.com/economy/2013/12/population-qatar.

[94] https://www.hrw.org/news/2012/06/12/qatar-migrant-construction-workers-face-abuse; Gabriella C. Gonzalez, Lynn A. Karoly, Louay Constant, Hanine Salem and Charles A. Goldman, "Facing Human Capital Challenges of the 21st Century: Education and Labor Market Initiatives in Lebanon, Oman, Qatar, and the United Arab Emirates: Executive Summary," Rand Corporation, 2009.

[95] Human Rights Watch, "Qatar: New Reforms will not protect migrant Workers," 2015.

[96] http://data.worldbank.org/indicator/NY.GDP.PCAP.CD?locations=QA.

[97] http://www.nyulawglobal.org/globalex/Kuwait.html#thekuwaitlegalsystem; Meshal Al-Sabah, *Gender and Politics in Kuwait: Woman and Political Participation in the Gulf*, I.B.

Kuwait occupies 17,820 square kilometers, and borders Iraq and Saudi Arabia. It is home to a population of 3,892,115 people (2015).[98] Kuwaitis have access to resources from the sea, such as sea foods, although water is sparse internally.[99] The main resources that are exploited systematically in order to bring revenues to the economy remain oil and gas. Beside having classic industries related to hydrocarbons such as petrochemicals and others, Kuwait is home to one of the largest wealth management industries within the GGC countries.[100]

With a GDP of $274.899 billion, the graph below shows its composition by different sectors.[101]

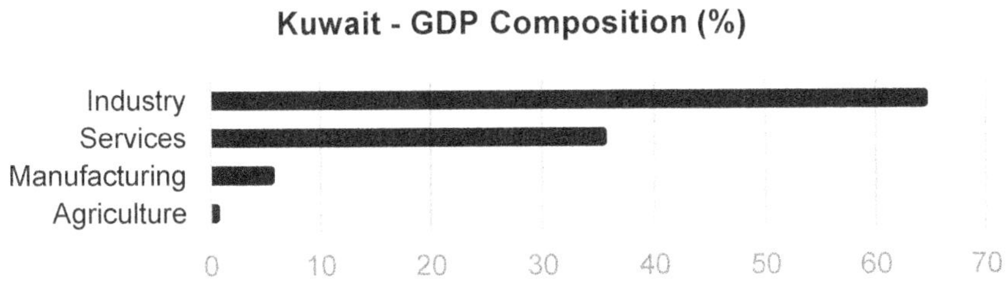

The labor market in Kuwait more and less shares the same characteristics of those in other GCC countries. The public sector, with all its benefits, remains the main employer, and policies such as short-term economic development have been prioritized over long-term policies such as investing in educated and more skilled workers.[102] As the majority of Kuwaiti nationals are employed in the public sector and are better-trained and more skilled but paid less than foreign workers employed in the private sector, we are to conclude that the labor market is not based on meritocracy. As Martin Baldwin-Edwards notes, on the one hand, the overlaying of the national/migrant distinction created a much-segmented market, and on the other hand, the gender segregation reinforced native-immigrant disparities.[103]

Tauris, 2013; Jill Crystal, *Kuwait: The Transformation of an Oil State*, Routledge, 2016; Michel Herb, *All in the Family, Absolutism, Revolution and Democracy in Middle Eastern Monarchies*, SUNY Press, 1997.

[98] World Bank.

[99] http://kuwaitembassy.ca/pages/GeneralInfo/Natural-Resources.htm.

[100] International Monetary Fund, "Kuwait: Selected Issues Paper," 2014; "Fast Growth, Divergent Path: The EY GCC Wealth and Asset Management Report," 2015: http://www.ey.com/Publication/vwLUAssets/EY-gcc-wealth-asset-management-report-2015/$FILE/EY-gcc-wealth-asset-management-report-2015.pdf.

[101] Patrick W. Nee, *Key Facts on Kuwait*, The Internationalist, 2014; Yusuf A. Sayigh, *The Economies of the Arab World*, Routledge, 2014; Global Edge, Michigan State University.

[102] Andrea Salvini, "The Kuwaiti labor market and foreign workers," International Labour Organization.

[103] http://eprints.lse.ac.uk/55239/.

Although the functionalities of the Kefala system[104] for foreign workers have been limited since 2011 and the government has made efforts to introduce and reinforce the Kuwaitization of the market, the number of non-nationals out of the total population during the first trimester of 2015 was 69.2%.[105]

To conclude, the Kuwaiti job market registered a labor force participation of 74.5% during 2015 and averaged an unemployment rate of 1.40% between 1983 and 2013.[106] With Kuwait's growth rate of 1.3% in 2014 and an inflation rate of 2.9%, it is worth mentioning that its institutional deficiencies affect the overall performance of its economy.[107]

- Bahrain

The history of Bahrain is also a very rich one. Like most of the Gulf Cooperation Council countries, Bahrain bore the presence and abided by the rules dictated by regional and international powers such as Assyrians, Persians, etc. It tolerated this until 1971, when it gained its independence from Great Britain. Bahrain is a constitutional monarchy and the amended constitution of 2002 recognizes the existence of a bicameral parliament; however, its Emir, acting as a king, appoints and dismisses prime ministers, judges and other officials. He remains the sole executive power with the final word on all state-related issues and beyond. The legal system affirms that Sharia'ah will remain the main source of legislation.[108]

Being a strategic archipelago located in the Persian Gulf, just 24 kilometers off the east coast of Saudi Arabia, Bahrain occupies a surface area of 770 square kilometers. Bahrain's 33 islands are home to 1,377,237 people.[109] During 2014, 52% of the total population were not Bahraini nationals. The tiny state does not have the same amount of hydrocarbon resources that other GCC countries offer to their inhabitants, and this is why Bahrain has been a leader in the region in terms of diversification of its economy.

---

[104] migrant-rights.org.
[105] Gulf Research Center.
[106] Trading Economics.
[107] http://www.heritage.org/index/pdf/2016/countries/kuwait.pdf;
[107] Economist Intelligence Unit, "Kuwait," http://country.eiu.com/kuwait.
[108] http://www.wipo.int/wipolex/en/text.jsp?file_id=189442; Khalil Mechantaf, "The Constitutional Law and the Legal System of the Kingdom of Bahrain," Hauser Global Law School Program, 2010; Anna Fuchs, *Bahrain: The Exception in the Gulf*, GRIN Verlag, 2013.
[109] http://databank.worldbank.org/data/reports.aspx?source=2&country=BHR.

In 2014, Bahrain's GDP was valued at about $61.9 billion. Its composition, shown in the chart below, highlights the country's economic diversification.[110]

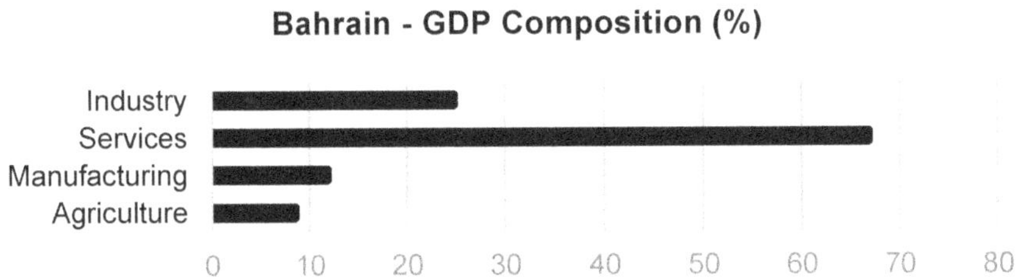

The Bahraini economy offered 635,095 jobs in the second quarter of 2016, with the unemployment rate at 4.1% in 2015.[111] Having an inflation rate of 2.5% and a growth rate of 4.7%, Bahrain also continues to be a leading country in the region for economic freedom.[112]

- United Arab Emirates

The United Arab Emirates gained its independence in December 1971. The UAE is a federation of seven emirates: Abu Dhabi, Ajman, Dubai, Fujairah, Ras al-Khaimah, Sharjah and Quwain. The rulers of these emirates agreed upon a constitution that created a kind of federative system of governance. In accordance with Articles 120 and 121 of the UAE's constitution, parts of the power structure and its related areas of intervention are put under the purview of the federal authorities, and what are left out go to each emirate. The ones under federal control include "foreign affairs, security and defense, nationality and immigration, air traffic and licensing of aircrafts, education, public health, currency, postal, telephone and other communication services."[113] Article 122 clarifies the local powers as follows: "The individual Emirates shall have jurisdiction in all matters not assigned to the exclusive jurisdiction of the federation, in accordance with the

---

[110] *Bahrain Business Law Handbook*, International Business Publications, 2007; Philip Dew, *Doing Business with Bahrain*, Kogan Page, 2002; http://globaledge.msu.edu/countries/bahrain/economy.
[111] https://knoema.com/atlas/Bahrain/Unemployment-rate.
[112] http://www.heritage.org/index/country/bahrain; *The Report: Bahrain 2013*, Oxford Business Group, 2013; Andrew Gardner, *City of Strangers: Gulf Migration and the Indian Community in Bahrain*, Cornell University Press, 2010.
[113] UAEInteract: http://www.uaeinteract.com/government/political_system.asp.

provision of the preceding two Articles."[114] There is no democratically elected authority within the federation.[115] In the United Arab Emirates, the president and prime minister are the main executive actors and all legislative issues are decided through an organization called the Federal Supreme Council, whose members are the hereditary rulers of each emirate. Therefore, it is fair to say that ruling families and other influential ones are the main actors.[116]

The UAE shares borders with Oman, the Kingdom of Saudi Arabia and Qatar. The seven emirates together occupy a surface area of 83,600 square kilometers. Its population in 2015 reached 9,156,963 people and included the highest rate of non-nationals resident within the GCC – 88.5%.[117] The population of the UAE, like its neighbors, has access to hydrocarbon resources such as oil and gas, although these are not equally distributed and Abu Dhabi is the wealthiest emirate within the federation. The UAE considered as a whole is in possession of the world's seventh largest reserves of oil. It is fast moving toward a diversified economy by heavily investing in service sectors such as banking, finance, tourism and entertainment. Registering a GDP of $614.9 billion in 2014, the second highest of any GCC member, the graph below clearly captures the diversification initiatives and the share of each sector in the economy.[118]

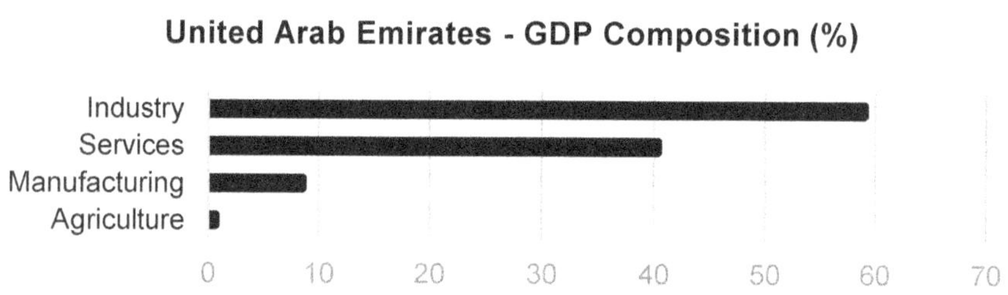

The United Arab Emirates has a total labor force of 6,302,492 and experienced an unemployment rate of 3.6% in 2014. With a growth rate of 3.6% and an inflation rate of 2.3%, it was able to improve itself in many areas of economic freedom. Open-market policies, a business-friendly environment

[114] World Intellectual Property Organization: http://www.wipo.int/edocs/lexdocs/laws/ar/ae/ae017ar.pdf; UN High Commissioner for Refugees: http://www.refworld.org/pdfid/48eca8132.pdf.

[115] U.S Department of State: http://www.state.gov/documents/organization/160079.pdf.

[116] Kristian Ulrichsen, *The United Arab Emirates: Power, Politics and Policy-making*, Taylor & Francis, 2016; Rosemarie Said Zahlan, *The Origins of the United Arab Emirates: A Political and Social History of the Trucial States*, Routledge, 2016.

[117] GLMM, Gulf Labor Markets and Migration.

[118] Global Edge, Michigan State University: http://globaledge.msu.edu/countries/united-arab-emirates/economy; Christopher M. Davidson, *Abu Dhabi: Oil and Beyond*, Hurst Publishers, 2011.

and political stability have helped the federation to increase its position in the Heritage Foundation's index of economic freedom.[119]

- Oman

Bordering the Gulf of Oman, the Arabian Sea and Persian Gulf, Oman has for a long time benefited from its geographic position. Being itself a superpower of the region in the 17th century, though there had been interference from other powers, Oman was always an independent country. It is an absolute monarchy, and as such the Sultan of Oman is the sole ruler and consequently his office is hereditary. The legal system, as in the rest of the GCC members, is based on Sharia'ah and other teachings of the Islamic Prophet.[120] In connection with its judicial system and legislative authorities, the Sultan has the sole power to amend laws and has the final decision on such matters.[121] Occupying a surface area of 309,500 square kilometers, Oman had a population of 4,490,541 in 2015. It is a country rich in minerals and metals such as gypsum, copper, asbestos, oil and gas as well as limestone, just to mention a few. Oman's main industries are formed around the resources that have been available. Oil and gas production, oil refineries and natural gas production are the most important ones, and their huge contribution to the economy are easily noted. The composition of Oman's GDP by sectors affirms that industry makes the greatest contribution to the economy, followed by services. The GDP in 2014 (purchasing power parity) was $163.641 billion.[122]

Oman - GDP Composition (%)

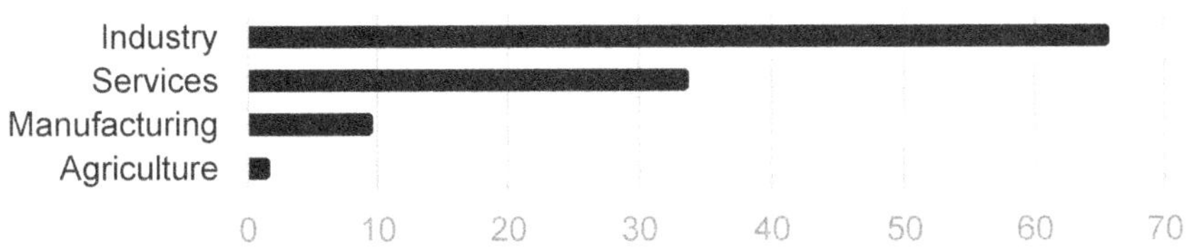

The Omani job market had a total labor force of 2,215,647 people, and experienced an unemployment rate of 7.2% in 2014, which was less than

[119] http://www.heritage.org/index/country/unitedarabemirates.
[120] http://www.omansultanate.com/politics.htm.
[121] U.S Department of State: http://www.state.gov/documents/organization/160076.pdf; Marc Valeri, *Oman: Politics and Society in the Qaboos State*, Hurst Publishers, 2009; Jacqueline S. Ismael, Tareq Y. Ismael and Glenn Perry, *Government and Politics of the Contemporary Middle East: Continuity and Change*, Routledge, 2015.
[122] Global Edge, Michigan State University.

the average rate registered between 1991 and 2014.[123] Oman's economy, with a growth rate of 2.9% and an inflation rate of 1% in 2014, had to deal with state interventions in the private sector which affected the economic dynamism of the country. However, in advancing toward economic freedom, Oman did much better if compared with her giant neighbor Saudi Arabia, though it still has a lot to do in that regard.[124]

GCC: Socio-economic Development and Indicators

The term "indicator" in most dictionaries is simply defined as "one that indicates or points out." However, the term in different fields of study can present very profound meanings or have sophisticated interpretations. Economic indicators have a long history in statistical works and their combination with social indicators created the term "socio-economic" and consequently socio-economic indicators. Therefore a socio-economic indicator "should be a measure pointing to or indicating a variable which is different from the one of which it is a direct measure."[125] Using socio-economic indicators with the aim of measuring levels of living in a community was proposed by a United Nations committee in a report on "international definition and measurement of standards and levels of living." [126] Differentiating between levels of living and standards of living, the committee used macro and micro indicators to evaluate actual living conditions and helped policy makers with tools necessary to evaluate social progress at the national level.

Involving social factors as well as economic ones, socio-economic indicators cannot be reduced to aspects such as employment, wealth, consumer price, and wages, working conditions or household incomes. They incorporate a wider range of human-related aspects of life such as health, health services, leisure time, welfare, cultural life and others. Today these indicators are categorized in four groups: health, economic, social, and ICT (information and communication technologies) indicators. Researchers continue to use statistics and methods such as I-distance[127] to synthetize socio-economic development indicators, and policy makers use these results to formulate decisions. Therefore, leaders and policy makers cannot ignore socio-economic development while projecting any future vision.

---

[123] Trading Economics: http://www.tradingeconomics.com/oman/unemployment-rate.

[124] The Heritage Foundation: http://www.heritage.org/index/country/oman; Steffen Wippel, *Regionalizing Oman: Political, Economic and Social Dynamics*, Springer, 2013.

[125] United Nations Economic Commission for Africa.

[126] http://unesdoc.unesco.org/images/0001/000131/013186eo.pdf.

[127] "A multivariate approach in measuring socio-economic development of MENA," *Modelling Economy*, 38, 2014.

Today, the Human Development Index (HDI) is considered as one of the most appropriate tools to evaluate the progress of a country. Besides an achieved and a hypothetical economic growth rate, people and their capabilities must determine whether a country can be considered as a developed one or not. HDI is a normalized geometric mean of three key dimensions of human development: quality of life, health conditions and knowledge. The graph below shows how HDI is constructed.[128]

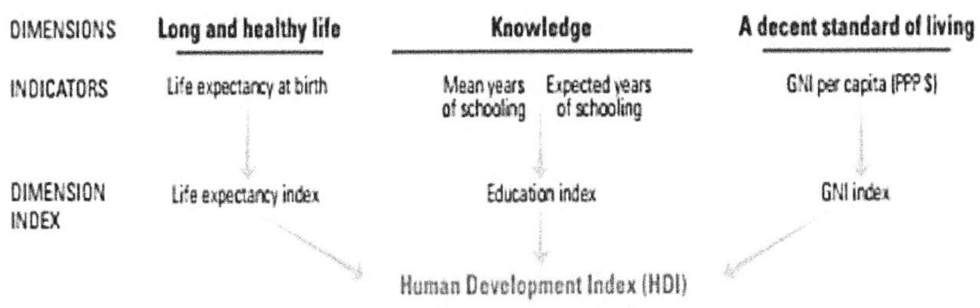

Concerning the GCC countries, the combination of very small populations and the existence of huge oil and gas revenues brought positive changes in their human and social indicators. The distribution of wealth among nationals in various forms, such as subsidizing a wide range of goods and services and/or assuring jobs within the public sector, has occurred within all of these countries. Here we do not enter into a discussion of the sustainability of these achievements since the distribution of wealth *per se* would not guarantee that, and it is not considered a long-term solution.[129] However, based on today's statistics, if some members have done better than others, the overall average for the six countries has shown a steady betterment over the years, essentially starting in the 1980s.

Organization, Structure and Institutions of the GCC

- Political and Economic Approaches

We refer to term "institution" as a founded organization, and/or set of established laws and practices. Regional integration cannot bring unity and implement agreements without appropriate institutions that are essential to its proper functioning. Going through some of the theoretical approaches to integration will clarify the importance of institutions. Institutions play a

[128] http://hdr.undp.org/en/content/human-development-index-hdi.

[129] Kristian Coates Ulrichsen, *Insecure Gulf: The end of Certainty and the Transition to the Post-Oil Era*, Oxford University Press, 2015; Jean-Francois Seznec and Mimi Kirk, *Industrialization in the Gulf, A Socio-Economic Revolution*, Routledge, 2010.

primordial role in forming a successfully integrated region. In political science, functionalism theory elaborates the idea of how to bring nations together, and how to encourage them to work actively together. The functional method considers the fact that sovereignty cannot be transferred through a formula, but through a function, with authorities created that later will replace the old ones. That can also be called the idea of peace by pieces.[130] Integration is considered as a process in which authorities and powers are transferred to a newly created center that possesses or demands jurisdiction over the preexisting centers of power. This involves shifting expectations, changing values and raising to the supranational level the national interest groups and political parties in order to respond to sectoral integration.[131] The Commission of the European Union is an example of an institution that has the power of initiative. It is centrally located and many decisions once made at the national level are now made there.[132]

In an economic approach, theories such as customs unions clearly present a road map on how the integration process must be organized and implemented in order to achieve a particular form and degree of integration, although theoretical approaches would not necessarily cover all aspects of the phenomenon. In the case of customs unions, once they are launched there would be consequences that need to be addressed. After common tariffs are decided and implemented for member countries, losses from tariff revenues are not easily disregarded. This is why properly thought-out and rigorously established institutions need to be set up *a priori* in order to deal with such issues. In the European Union, for example, part of the revenues go to finance common projects or to help countries in difficulty. Therefore, whether tariff revenue goes to each member as income accumulated over time or whether it is considered as the Union's resources, in addition to and in the presence of a presumed mutual trust, a set of mechanisms as well as functioning institutions are required to manage it.[133] Not only do a set of precious theories like those previously mentioned exist to help countries that would like to start a new

---

[130] David Mitrany, *A Working Peace System*, Quadrangle Books, 1966.

[131] Ernst. B. Haas, *The Unity of Europe: Political, Social and Economic Forces*, University of Notre Dame Press; revised ed., 2004, p. 12.

[132] John Peterson and Michael Shackleton, *The Institutions of the European Union*, Oxford University Press, 2012; Andreas Stabb, *The European Union Explained: Institutions, Actors and Global Impact*, Indiana University Press, 2008; Martin Dedman, *The Origins and Development of the European Union 1945-2008: A History of European Integration*, Taylor & Francis, 2010; Leon N. Lindberg, *The Political Dynamics of European Economic Integration*, Stanford University Press, 1963.

[133] Soamiely Andriamananjara, "Customs Unions," World Bank: https://siteresources.worldbank.org/INTRANETTRADE/Resources/C5.pdf; Viner, *The Customs Union Issue*; Brigid Laffan, Rory O'Donnell and Michael Smith, *Europe's Experimental Union: Rethinking Integration*, Routledge, 2013.

regional project, but there is also the hard-earned experience of other nations that went through the same ideas and works.

- The GCC's Organizational Structure

The Gulf Cooperation Council officially declared its creation in 1981, primarily with the aim of achieving external security. Today, being considered as a regional integration project, it is still a work in process. In the GCC, the main actors, players and in general decision makers are mainly states and rulers themselves rather than grassroots groups or institutions below or above the nation-state that must actively and independently harmonize policies and interests that ultimately would coalesce to form a unity. The GCC's supranational organizational structure can be analyzed mainly through three institutions as introduced in its charter and by its Article 6.[134] These are the GCC Secretariat, the Ministerial Council and the Supreme Council.

Briefly, the GCC Secretariat, considered as an independent body, is mainly there to address executive/administrative issues. It assists the other two bodies in organizing their meetings as well as in producing research and background materials.[135] The Ministerial Council is in charge of proposing policies and formulating recommendations. The foreign ministers of the six countries, and a few specialized committees, together will assist ultimately the Supreme Council in making decisions.[136] With foreign ministers of the Ministerial Council meeting quarterly and the Supreme Council's meetings scheduled twice a year, the road to Arab unity, so far, has been long. Compared with the EU and its seven institutions that are put in place to promote and defend its values, objectives as well as interests of its citizens with the final aim of ensuring the coherence, effectiveness and continuity of the EU's policies and actions, the institutional framework of the GCC does not correspond to the defined task.[137] Therefore, it must be affirmed, given the circumstances in regards to its institutional aspects, in addition to its historical background, that the GCC idea and its development was purely a hasty

[134] https://www.files.ethz.ch/isn/125347/1426_GCC.pdf.

[135] World Bank, "Economic Integration in the GCC," 2010.

[136] Rouhollah K. Ramazani and Joseph K. Kechichian, *The Gulf Cooperation Council: Record and Analysis*, University of Virginia Press, 1988; "The Thirtieth Gulf Summit: Accomplishments and Aspirations," Media Committee of the Supreme Preparatory Committee of the Thirtieth Session of the Summit Conference of Gulf Cooperation Council, 2009.

[137] http://eur-lex.europa.eu/summary/glossary/eu_institutions.html; "Detailed Explanations about the Institutions of the European Union," Centre d' information sur les institutions Européennes: http://en.strasbourg-europe.eu/detailed-explanations-about-the-institutions-of-the-european-union,3214,en.html.

reaction to changing circumstances in 1981 rather than a well-calculated move.[138]

- The GCC's Current State of Affairs

This did not stop the multifaceted project from proceeding. It must also be affirmed that the GCC countries, in trying to put the building blocks of their regional integration project in place, had to face serious and insurmountable theoretical and structural issues but nonetheless succeeded in achieving a few aspects of integration. In 1983 a free trade zone had been created, and in 2001 an agreement[139] paved the way for the creation of a customs union. The six countries of the GCC signed the customs union agreement in 2003, and in 2008 a common market was launched and a 5% customs tariff was put in place. As a result, in theory, barriers to trade had to diminish, and restrictions on production factors/resources, including human resources as well as capital, had to ease. Since this research analyzes the economic gain of the GCC's integration through trade flows, it is worthy of mention that the increase in trade among GCC members was achieved through the customs union and common market rather than through real complementarities of production and trade. As shown through the table below, the increase in trade represents only 7.1% of the aggregate foreign trade realized by the six countries.[140]

GCC Intra-Regional Trade (Millions of Dollars, 2013)						
	Qatar	KSA	UAE	Oman	Kuwait	Bahrain
Qatar		2454.39	8381.36	1570.68	1481.28	456.4
KSA	2454.39		8141.18	4623.43	2629.5	5050.85
UAE	8381.36	8141.18		15689.37	1692.18	12.67.4
Oman	1570.68	4623.43	15689.37		777.67	385.55
Kuwait	1481.28	2629.5	1692.18	777.67		279.16
Bahrain	456.4	5050.85	1267.04	385.55	279.16	
Total	$14,344.11	$20,444.96	$26,789.77	$21,476.02	$5,378.51	$6,982.60
Total(all)	$95,415.97					

[138] Bezen Balamir-Coskun and Birgül Demirtaş-Coşkun, *Neighborhood Challenge: European Union and Its Neighbors*, Universal-Publishers, 2009.

[139] 2001 ratified Agreement, Muscat, Sultanate of Oman.

[140] Khalid Shams Abdulqader, "GCC Economic Cooperation and Integration: Achievements and Hurdles," Qatar University, Aljazeera Center for Studies, 2015.

Despite the presence of cumbersome and time-consuming customs procedures at entry points,[141] in 2013 the GDP of the GCC ranked 12th in the world in terms of size, and in terms of trade it occupied the fifth position. Total trade amounted to $1.42 trillion.[142]

Economic Size (Millions of Dollars, 2013)		
1	United Sates of America	$16,800,000
2	China	$9,240,270
3	Japan	$4,901,530
4	Germany	$3,634,820
5	France	$2,734,950
6	United Kingdom	$2,522,260
7	Brazil	$2,245,670
8	Russia	$2,096,780
9	Italy	$2,071,310
10	India	$1,876,800
11	Canada	$1,825,100
12	GCC	$1,628,000
13	Australia	$1,560,600
14	Spain	$1,358,260

Being a multifaceted project, hastily decided and launched, the other item on the wish list was a monetary union. With the aim of creating a common currency and a monetary union going back to 2001, the six countries decided to peg their currencies to dollar, and this had occurred by 2002. However, the fact that important theoretical and procedural aspects of a monetary union were not observed and respected, the fluctuations of the dollar, unfavorable economic circumstances and disagreement about the central bank's location forced three of the six countries – Kuwait, Oman and the UAE – to leave the project. Although in 2010 the launch of a common currency was postponed to 2015, a monetary union still has not seen the light as of today. To conclude on the current state of affairs in the GCC, we should briefly go through a few important basic structures that are necessary for any country that would like to develop and bring prosperity to its people: financial markets, the transport system as well as the role of the private sector.

Regarding financial markets, an integrated financial market does not exist and all the efforts to harmonize policies or affirm rules and regulations

---

[141] *Ibid.*

[142] Stratfor, "The Gulf Cooperation Council: Finding safety in numbers," 2016: https://www.stratfor.com/analysis/gulf-cooperation-council-finding-safety-numbers; Bernard Hoekman, "Intra-Regional Trade: Potential Catalyst for Growth in the Middle East," Middle East Institute, 2016.

to be respected by all members have not yet produced any outcomes. The existence of Islamic finance and banking, which cannot be integrated easily with classical banking and conventional financial systems, is one of the major issues. As we discuss later, the GCC countries had difficulties in issuing Sharia'ah-compliant instruments to manage liquidity, and central banks could not enjoy the required flexibility in terms of monetary operations. Another issue that can be mentioned concerns currency.[143] As the GCC members' currencies are pegged to the US dollar, this affects the monetary policies of GCC countries in search of a certain balance between growth and price stability.

The private sector also contributes poorly to the integration process. Hampered by the presence of the public sector, the private sector is mainly limited to a few importing companies that cannot even develop themselves either for the lack of required capital or the absence of entrepreneurial incentives. It must be affirmed that the GCC governments are the main actors in development, modernization of corporate governance and national managerial elites. The GCC rulers' economic policies, with the lobbying of big businesses, constantly reinforce the convenient status quo and weaken the presence of small and medium-size businesses launched and developed by citizens.[144] In such a business environment, where citizens are not participating in entrepreneurial initiatives and are not even familiar with it, foreigners are also not immune. Restrictions on foreign ownership and/or control over businesses within GCC members, in addition to the aforementioned local issues, make it difficult for the private sector to play its vital role in the integration process.[145]

As an integrated region must have an integrated financial system to handle investments, transactions and other financially related activities of its integrated economies, it cannot handle the daily-life aspects of the economy without a well-developed and fully integrated transport network. Although the air transport and aviation industry within each GCC member has experienced a certain degree of development, roads and railways are poorly developed and managed. The transport system of the GCC is far from an integrated one.[146]

---

[143] Ritu Basu, Ananthakrishnan Prasad and Sergio Rodriguez, "Monetary Operations and Islamic Banking in the GCC: Challenges and Options," International Monetary Fund, 2015.

[144] Steffen Hertog, "The private sector and the reform in GCC," LSE, 2013.

[145] Al Tamimi & Co.; Mohamed A. Ramady, *Political, Economic and Financial Country Risk: Analysis of the Gulf Cooperation Council*, Springer Science and Business Media, 2013.

[146] Tim Niblock, *Social and Economic Development in the Arab Gulf*, Routledge, 2015; Rouhollah K. Ramazani and Joseph K. Kechichian, *The Gulf Cooperation Council: Record and Analysis*, University of Virginia Press, 1988; Stratfor, "The Gulf Cooperation Council: Finding safety in numbers."

CHAPTER 4

ANALYTICAL FRAMEWORK AND REQUIRED CONDITIONS

In this chapter, I examine almost four decades of efforts and hopes for realizing a dream, an Arab Union. It does not matter that the initial motive behind the idea was the "security issue" for the six countries of the GCC; it was clear that the economy would play an important role, of course hand-in-hand with politics. Whether a political union is sought through commerce and trade or an economic union is envisaged through political perspectives, today a set of robust theories as well as unions and regional blocs that have already been created are there to help us evaluate and assess the feasibility of any new project, or reassess any old project or initiative. By reviewing theories and research already done, I present two factors that are vital to any project of integration, and apply them to evaluate the GCC's feasibility. Precisely, it is through applying the demand factor requirement that a potential economic gain from joining a regional bloc can be assessed through the trade flow, later on enriched by another crucial flow, the financial flow. In between, a presentation of the conventional financial and banking system and the Islamic one is given. The chapter concludes with an assessment of the supply factor and institutional aspects of the GCC's regional integration project.

Supply and Demand Factors

Supply and demand factors include conditions or measures such as the potential for economic gain and the existence of committed institutions that would ultimately clarify the feasibility of regional integration. Therefore, a successfully implemented regional integration project requires a combination of market and institutional forces. The latter is called supply factors and the former demand factors.[147] The potential for economic gain from market exchanges must be large in amount, in terms of the opportunity

[147] Walter Mattli, *The Logic of Regional Integration: Europe and Beyond*, Cambridge University Press, 1999.

cost, considered in the contest of an institutional *status quo*. In fact, within a regional bloc, a lack of complementarity in members' economies and a market size that does not offer economies of scale would quickly end the integration process.[148] In connection with economic gain and in the hypothesis that those conditions are met, market players, in addition to other stakeholders and decision makers, need to have access to a regional institutional arrangement. The market players themselves are an indispensable force to demand and create the aforementioned arrangement. Consequently, once institutional aspects of the project are arranged, these institutions would allow the market players and the nation as a whole to reap the economic benefit. However, in order to build that institutional arrangement, a set of conditions must be met in order to have political leaders on board who are determined to move toward that direction. It is worth mentioning that an institution in the context of a regional integration project can be defined as a "set of formal and informal rules, regulations, and compliance procedures designed to constrain and shape human interaction and structure the incentives of actors involved in an exchange relationship in order to maximize the wealth or unity of these actors."[149]

GCC Demand Factors

A determining feature in the GCC's overall economy is a dependency on hydrocarbon resources. In 2013, a huge share of its GDP at current prices came from the oil and gas industry – 46.2% from mining and quarrying (petroleum, gas and mining) and 45.9% from crude petroleum and natural gas. By comparison, the share of agriculture and fishing was a very humble 1.1%.[150]

The GCC members are well-established in the energy sector and are major players in the global energy market in terms of production. The GCC countries are estimated to hold around 40% of global oil resources. Although countries such as Bahrain and Oman are not as rich as other members in hydrocarbon resources, the GCC as a bloc remains the principal producer and

---

[148] *Ibid.*

[149] Beth Yarbrough and Robert Yarbrough, *Cooperation and Governance in International Trade: The Strategic Organizational Approach*, Princeton University Press, 1992; Douglass North, *Structure and Change in Economic History*, New York: Norton, 1981.

[150] Adeel Malik, "The Gulf Economies' Coming Meltdown? How to Prevent It," *Foreign Affairs*, 2015; Kristian Ulrichsen, *The Gulf States in International Political Economy*, Springer, 2016; Atif Kubursi, *Oil, Industrialization and Development in the Arab Gulf States*, Routledge, 2015; GCC-Stat, http://gccstat.org/en/; Gulf Cooperation Council; The World Bank.

exporter of oil and gas. In connection with this, more than 70% of export revenues and government revenues are achieved this way.[151]

Being aware of this reality and of the prospect that the GCC might not benefit from the possession of hydrocarbon reserves in the long term due to the fact that they may run out within the generation to come, great amounts of investment are directed toward exploration and the development of new fields.[152] This is another reason why diversifying the economy is a key challenge for the GCC. It is more pressing for members such as Bahrain and Oman than it is for the Kingdom of Saudi Arabia or Kuwait.[153]

Therefore, it is logical that each of GCC member, in addition to trying to diversify its economy, remains concentrated on the energy sector, which is where its comparative advantage through specialization lies.[154]

GCC: The Complementarity Issue

Complementarity is considered as the needs and/or interests of one country that can be matched with a capacity to supply and serve another country. Complementarity in production and trade is considered as a measure to evaluate the potential for economic gain through a regional scheme of integration. If each of the GCC members specializes in the same sector or industry as the other members, consequently they will produce and export the same goods or services to the same target markets as the others do. There would be overlapping trade flows that would eliminate the economic gain for a hypothetical member. These overlapping trade flows in the first place will reduce the potential for intra-regional trade, and secondly there will be discrimination *vis-à-vis* smaller countries while seeking external markets. As M.J. Trebilcock and Robert Howse assert, "many actual or potential trading blocs offer very small prospects for intra-regional trade expansion, even setting aside their effects on external trade. This is true for many actual or potential trading blocs in Africa, Latin America, the South Pacific and Caribbean, where similarity of natural endowments often sharply limits the potential for mutual gains from trade."[155]

---

[151] Crescent Petroleum: http://www.crescentpetroleum.com/html/oil_gas_overview.html; Stasa Salacalin, "Oil and Gas Reserves, How long Will They Last," BQ, 2015: http://www.bq-magazine.com/energy/2015/02/oil-and-gas-reserves-in-the-gcc; Emilie Rutledge, *Monetary Union in the Gulf*, Routledge, 2015.

[152] European Central Bank, Occasional Paper Series, no. 92, 2008.

[153] International Monetary Fund, "Economic Diversification in Oil Exporting Arab Countries," 2016.

[154] James Gwartney, Richard Stroup, Russell Sobel and David Macpherson, *Economics: Private and Public Choice*, Cengage Learning 2008.

[155] M.J. Trebilcock and Robert Howse, *The Regulation of International Trade*, Routledge, 2013.

- Complementarity in Production

Similarities in terms of economic sectors, main industries and goods and services produced among the GCC members are remarkable. In spite of the efforts they have made to diversify their economies toward non-hydrocarbon industries, however, the main sectors of all the GCC members remain the extraction of raw materials and use of natural resources, after which comes manufacturing. The main products that are ultimately the vital source of revenues for GCC members are minerals, metals, and chemical and plastic products.[156]

As mentioned earlier, the gain from regional integration must be enormous in order to offset what participants in a regional bloc would give up in terms of their sovereignty in the economic sphere. Based on theories, the potential for economic growth for each member can be achieved in three ways. First is that a larger integrated market would help firms and other business units, which are the main market players, to achieve economies of scale. In fact, the extensive intra-industry trade among developed economies would confirm the importance of economies of scale. Since a firm's efficiency is also affected by its size, an increase in scale of production would decrease the average cost and ultimately increase the profitability.

Secondly, larger markets facilitate specialization that is based on each member's comparative advantage. This happens because the marginal opportunity cost of producing a particular good varies in different countries. In third place comes trade creation, which brings economic prosperity and growth.[157]

As mentioned earlier in regards to economies of scale, the main market for GCC members' products is the global energy market, in particular in developing countries rather than in the Persian Gulf region itself. Thus, for the GCC members, which are all mineral and chemical producers, going in search of economies of scale and expanding within themselves cannot be a solution. The gain from expansion ultimately depends on the effects of the initiative on productive efficiency, and for productive efficiency and cutting costs today other solutions are sought – and are available.[158] For instance, turning a successful upstream project into a process that can be replicated offers to oil and gas industries strategic advantages that would include cutting costs. Therefore, for instance, the Saudi oil company merging with the one of Kuwait cannot be a solution. It should be considered that these are mainly

[156] Alan Fisher, Colin Clark and Jean Fourastié, *Three Sector Theory*, Project Gutenberg Self-Publishing Press.

[157] "Trade Creation and Trade Diversion," European Communities, 1997; William Alexander Kerr and James D. Gaisford, *Handbook on International Trade Policy*, 2007; Viner, *The Customs Union Issue*.

[158] Economist Intelligence Unit, "Economies of scale: How the oil and gas industry cuts costs through replication," 2011.

state-owned companies, and "state" in this context means the ruling family and its interests behind that. Idem for a scenario in which, for example, Kuwait would accept Saudis entering its own internal energy market to achieve economies of scale; this is also not foreseeable and is very far from being realistic. Therefore, the concept of economies of scale as a motive that would encourage the main industries and ultimately a ruling family to forgo its autonomy and source of revenues for another ruling family cannot be retained. The second point, specialization and the concept of comparative advantage, also cannot be retained since each country already knows where its comparative advantages lies, and already specializes in that field. For instance, the challenge in that regard, as several studies suggest, is the downstream sector for processing and purifying crude oil and natural gas into other products such as rubber, packaging and plastics. This is logical, and it is why GCC members heavily invested in the past and intelligently continue to invest in the natural resources sector, so they can get the most out of it.[159]

The third motive that can be seen as a potential gain from regional integration is trade creation. GCC countries have already created a customs union and thus the concept of trade creation can be discussed. The idea is that by removing barriers to trade such as tariffs, consumers in a member country would increase their demand for goods, and by doing so, more trade would occur. This simple phenomenon is called trade creation, and it is observed in many other integration projects as well as simple trade agreements. In the case of the GCC countries, most of the products they produce are not consumer goods. Because consumer goods and services are produced elsewhere, outside of the GCC region, the idea of considering trade creation as a motive that can guarantee the success of regional integration is not well founded. The table here summarizes the different sectors and industries pertinent to each of the GCC members.[160]

---

[159] OECD, "Assessing investment policies of member countries of the Gulf Cooperation Council," 2011.

[160] Jacob Viner, *The Customs Union Issue*; Bela Balassa, "Trade Creation and Trade Diversion in the European Common Market, *The Economic Journal*, 77(305), 1967; Anne O. Krueger, "Trade Creation and Trade Diversion under NAFTA," National Bureau of Economic Research, Working Paper no. 7429, 1999.

	KSA	Bahrain	UAE	Qatar	Kuwait	Oman
Main Sectors	Primary, secondary	Primary, secondary	Primary, secondary	Primary, secondary	Primary, secondary	Primary, secondary
Main industries	Minerals, chemicals, plastics	Minerals, metals	Minerals, metals, chemicals, plastics	Minerals, chemicals, plastics	Minerals, chemicals, plastics	Minerals, metals, chemicals
Main products that ultimately would be exported	Crude oil, refined oil, petroleum gas, ethylene, propylene, acyclic alcohols	Refined oil, iron, gold, petroleum gas, aluminum	Crude oil, refined oil, petroleum gas, iron, gold, diamonds, aluminum	Crude oil, refined oil, petroleum gas, ethylene, propylene, fertilizer	Crude oil, refined oil, petroleum gas, ethylene, propylene, acyclic alcohols	Crude oil, refined oil, petroleum gas, acyclic alcohols, fertilizer, iron nail, aluminum

- Complementarity in Trade and Trade Flows

In general, being able to trade depends ultimately on the products that a nation can offer to other nations and the market. A nation must produce goods and services that other nations need. Concerning regional integration, for a sovereign state to relinquish important aspects of its sovereignty and to transfer them to supranational institutions, economic gains in terms of trade must be greater than what can be achieved unilaterally. In other words, the essential demand condition for successful integration under a regional model is that a nation must be better off in terms of economic gain from trade within the region than from unilateral efforts in the world market.[161]

The potential for economic gain through integration and expansion would always exist in theory, mainly because of economics of scale, the concept of comparative advantage and through specialization, as well as through trade creation effects; however, it is important to see whether these are achievable more readily unilaterally or multilaterally. The key analysis would be assessing the complementarity of member states in production and trade flows and whether it happens. The aforementioned conditions existed for the Europeans and helped them through the integration process. Politically motivated through economic incentives, they sought deeper economic integration. This was not the case for many Asian, South American and African initiatives, which had petered out. As mentioned earlier, the GCC countries are producers of almost the same categories of products, and

[161] Mattli, *The Logic of Regional Integration.*

therefore observing and analyzing the GCC's patterns of trade can show where the potential economic gain lies for these countries and how it has materialized so far. To that end, we go through each Gulf Cooperation Council member's external trade. One of the most important aspects of analyzing trade flows is data reliability, but discrepancies happen for different reasons such as poor reporting from a country, differences in algorithms, the way data are calculated or even fraud, so two sources are selected for the purpose of analyzing trade patterns of the GCC countries. These are the World Trade Organization (WTO) and the Observatory of Economic Complexity (OEC).[162]

> *Kingdom of Saudi Arabia: Trade Patterns and Trading Partners*

The Kingdom of Saudi Arabia is the biggest country of the GCC in terms of surface and population. In 2014, Saudi Arabia was ranked the 15th largest exporting country in the world, with total exports of $306 billion. The main exported items were crude and refined petroleum, petroleum gas, ethylene, propylene and acyclic alcohol, and the main destinations were China, Japan, the USA, South Korea and India. In the same year, imports amounted to $146 billion and the main items were cars, refined petroleum, trucks, planes, helicopters, spacecraft and packaged medicine. The main origins of the imports were China, the USA, India, Germany and South Korea. It should be noted that none of the main trading partners of the KSA was a GCC country, although all of the GCC countries are refined oil producers. The Kingdom of Saudi Arabia imported $10.7 billion of refined oil, of which 67% ($7.21 billion) was from India, while the share of neighboring country Oman was only 0.66% ($70.5 million).[163] The KSA's overall trade balance in 2014 was a positive $159 billion.[164]

Slightly different from the OCE's data, that of the WTO confirmed the situation. The difference is that the WTO data showed the United Arab

---

[162] Economists Advisory Group, "Economies of Scale," The Single Market Review Series, Subseries V, 1996; Theodore Hitiris, *European Union Economics*, Pearson Education, 2003; Stephen Davies and Bruce Lyons, *Industrial Organization in the European Union: Structure, Strategy and the Competitive Mechanism*, Clarendon Press, 1996.

[163] United Kingdom, Department for International Trade, "Doing Business in Saudi Arabia," 2016; World Trade Organization, "Trade Policy Review: Saudi Arabia," 2016; European Commission, "Trade in Goods with Saudi Arabia," http://trade.ec.europa.eu/doclib/docs/2006/september/tradoc_113442.pdf; Kingdom of Saudi Arabia and WTO; "Where does Saudi Arabia import refined petroleum?" The Observatory of Economic Complexity: http://atlas.media.mit.edu/en/visualize/tree_map/hs92/import/sau/show/2710/2014/.

[164] "What is Trade Balance for Saudi Arabia? (1995-2014)," The Observatory of Economic Complexity: http://atlas.media.mit.edu/en/visualize/line/hs92/show/sau/all/all/1995.2014/.

Emirates as being among the main five destinations for Saudi exports, with a share of 3.3% for merchandise trade.[165]

> *Kingdom of Bahrain: Trade Patterns and Trading Partners*

At the other extreme is the Kingdom of Bahrain, which is tiny in terms of surface as well as population. In 2014 it was the 81st largest export economy in the world, exporting $33.9 billion of goods and services. Bahrain's top exports were refined petroleum, aluminum, iron ore and aluminum wire. The main destinations were Saudi Arabia, the UAE, the USA, Mozambique and South Korea. In the same year, Bahrain imported $19.7 billion of goods and services; its main partners were Saudi Arabia, China, the UAE, Japan and the United States.[166]

Bahrain imports categories of goods such as transportation equipment and machinery that are not necessarily produced in Bahrain; they are just simply re-exported to other GCC members. It is notable that in 2014, Bahrain was the only county of the GCC to have two other GCC members among its main trading partners. The trade balance in 2014 was negative.[167]

Bahrain is a pioneer among the GCC members in diversifying its economy – one of the main challenges ahead for all of them. Though the breakdown of its exported items is still dominated by fuels and mining products, it was able to put among its export basket more non-hydrocarbon items such as agricultural and manufactured products. Slightly different data from the World Trade Organization confirm the same pattern of trade for the Kingdom of Bahrain. Saudi Arabia and the UAE, both in the GCC club, remain among the main trading partners of Bahrain.[168]

---

[165] World Trade Organization and Saudi Arabia: http://stat.wto.org/CountryProfiles/SA_e.htm.

[166] Alexander Simoes, "What does Saudi Arabia export to Bahrain?" Observatory of Economic Complexity: http://atlas.media.mit.edu/en/visualize/tree_map/hs92/export/sau/bhr/show/2014/; Alexander Simoes, "What does Saudi Arabia import from Bahrain?" Observatory of Economic Complexity: http://atlas.media.mit.edu/en/visualize/tree_map/hs92/import/sau/bhr/show/2014/; Alexander Simoes, "What does UAE export to Bahrain?" Observatory of Economic Complexity: http://atlas.media.mit.edu/en/visualize/tree_map/hs92/export/are/bhr/show/2014/; Alexander Simoes, "What does UAE import from Bahrain?" The Observatory of Economic Complexity, 2014: http://atlas.media.mit.edu/en/visualize/tree_map/hs92/import/are/bhr/show/2014/.

[167] Alexander Simoes, "What is the trade balance for Bahrain?" The Observatory of Economic Complexity, 2014: http://atlas.media.mit.edu/en/visualize/line/hs92/show/bhr/all/all/1995.2014/

[168] World Trade Organization and Bahrain.

> *United Arab Emirates: Trade Patterns and Trading Partners*

The United Arab Emirates was the 26th largest export economy in the world in 2014. The main items among its $186 billion of exports were crude and refined petroleum, petroleum gas, gold and diamonds. The main export partners of the UAE were Japan, India, South Korea, China and Singapore. In the same year, the UAE imported $213 billion of goods and services, with the main sources being China, India, the USA, Germany and the UK. As was the case for the Kingdom of Saudi Arabia, the UAE does not have any GCC members among its main partners. Almost $52 billion of UAE exports were destined for two Asian countries, Japan and China; these exports were valued respectively at $37.5 billion and $14.3 billion.[169]

Although Japan is not among the main sources of the United Arab Emirates' imports, analyzing the data for China's and Japan's exports to the UAE affirms that there are types of products that other GCC members produce, although none is the sole exporter of them to the UAE.[170] These include metals, plastics, rubber and chemical products. This indicates that the UAE prefers to have a diversified pool of partners around the world. Slightly different data from the World Trade Organization confirm the UAE's trade situation.[171]

> *Oman: Trade Patterns and Trading Partners*

Being the largest GCC country in terms of surface after Saudi Arabia, Oman, by exporting $49.9 billion of goods and services, placed itself as the 57th largest export economy in 2014. Like Bahrain, with limited hydrocarbon resources, Oman can be considered as a pioneer in diversifying its economy as well. However, the top exported items in 2014 remained hydrocarbon-based products, specifically crude and refined petroleum, petroleum gas, cyclic hydrocarbons and nitrogen fertilizer. Oman also heavily traded with Asia; its main export destinations in 2014 were China, South Korea, Japan

---

[169] Alexander Simoes, "What does United Arab Emirates Export to China?" The Observatory of Economic Complexity, 2014: http://atlas.media.mit.edu/en/visualize/tree_map/hs92/export/are/chn/show/2014/; Alexander Simoes, "What does United Arab Emirates Export to Japan?" The Observatory of Economic Complexity, 2014: http://atlas.media.mit.edu/en/visualize/tree_map/hs92/export/are/jpn/show/2014/.

[170] Alexander Simoes, "What does United Arab Emirates import from China?" The Observatory of Economic Complexity, 2014: http://atlas.media.mit.edu/en/visualize/tree_map/hs92/import/are/chn/show/2014/; Alexander Simoes, "What does United Arab Emirates import from Japan?" The Observatory of Economic Complexity, 2014: http://atlas.media.mit.edu/en/visualize/tree_map/hs92/import/are/jpn/show/2014/.

[171] World Trade Organization.

and other Asian countries. Among destinations for Oman's exports was the United Arab Emirates, although the amount of $2.02 billion was small compared with the total value of exported items ($49.9 billion). Almost 67% of Oman's total exports to the UAE were hydrocarbon-based products such as minerals, metals, plastics, rubber and other chemical products.[172]

Since 2009, Oman's imports have been increasing at an annualized rate of 10.8%. Imports totaled $31.1 billion of goods and services in 2014, with the main origins being the UAE, Japan, China, the USA and India.[173]

Data from the World Trade Organization, again slightly different from that of the Observatory of Economic Complexity, confirms the same trade patterns, with manufactured and agricultural products among the main import items and fuels and other mining products consisting of 83% of exported items.[174] Oman has experienced a positive trade balance every year since 1995.[175]

> *Qatar: Trade Patterns and Trading Partners*

Qatar, famous for its highest GDP per capita among the GCC members, confirmed itself as the world's 35th largest export country in 2014 ($125 billion). Its main export products include petroleum gas, crude and refined petroleum, ethylene polymers and nitrogen fertilizer. Its main export partners were Japan, South Korea, India, Singapore and China. The same year, Qatar imported $32.8 billion of goods and services; among its main sources were China ($2.98 billion). Its export destinations included one GCC member, the United Arab Emirates, although the amount of exports, $2.42 billion, did not place it among Qatar's main export partners.[176] Data from the World Trade Organization confirms the same trade pattern for Qatar as the OEC reports.[177]

---

[172] Alexander Simoes, "What does Oman export to United Arab Emirates?" The Observatory of Economic Complexity, 2014: http://atlas.media.mit.edu/en/visualize/tree_map/hs92/export/omn/are/show/2014/.

[173] Alexander Simoes, "What does Oman import from United Arab Emirates?" http://atlas.media.mit.edu/en/visualize/tree_map/hs92/import/omn/are/show/2014/, Alexander Simoes, "Oman Import per Category," Observatory of Economic Complexity, 2014: http://atlas.media.mit.edu/en/visualize/tree_map/hs92/import/omn/all/show/2014/; Alexander Simoes, "Oman Export per Category," Observatory of Economic Complexity, 2014: http://atlas.media.mit.edu/en/profile/country/omn/#Exports.

[174] World Trade Organization and Oman.

[175] Alexander Simoes, "What is the Trade Balance for Oman? (1995-2014)," The Observatory of Economic Complexity, 2014: http://atlas.media.mit.edu/en/visualize/line/hs92/show/omn/all/all/1995.2014/.

[176] Alexander Simoes, "What does Qatar Export?" The Observatory of Economic Complexity, 2014: http://atlas.media.mit.edu/en/visualize/tree_map/hs92/export/qat/all/show/2014/; Alexander Simoes, "What does Qatar import?" The Observatory of Economic Complexity, 2014: http://atlas.media.mit.edu/en/visualize/tree_map/hs92/import/qat/all/show/2014/.

[177] Qatar and WTO.

Qatar registered a positive balance of trade in 2014, reflecting a widening gap between exports and imports in recent years.[178]

> *Kuwait: Trade Pattern and Trading Partners*

After the Kingdom of Saudi Arabia, United Arab Emirates and Qatar, Kuwait is the fourth largest exporting economy among the GCC members; it is also the 40th largest exporting country in the world. Kuwait exported $87.4 billion in 2014, and its main exporting partners were South Korea, India, Japan, the USA and China. The main exported items were crude and refined petroleum, petroleum gas, acyclic hydrocarbons and acyclic alcohol.[179] In the same year, Kuwait imported $34.6 billion of goods and services, mainly from China, the USA, the UAE, Japan and South Korea.[180] Data from the World Trade Organization confirms the same trade patterns, specificities and overall trend.[181] Like other energy-exporting countries of the GCC, Kuwait registered a positive trade balance in 2014.[182]

The European Union: Trade Patterns and Trading Partners

Before getting into intra-GCC trade statistics, a look at the European integration project in terms of trade and commerce would be of help in analyzing, in particular, the growth of the GCC's single market and the progress made toward integrating the economies.[183]

Data for the period from 2002 to 2013 shows that although the value of exports of goods varies widely among countries in the EU region (for instance, in 2013 Germany exported 623 billion euros of goods to its EU partners while Cyprus exported less than 1 billion euros), the value of exports increased between 2002 and 2013. Spectacularly, even some EU members like

---

[178] Alexander Simoes, "What is the Trade Balance for Qatar?" The Observatory of Economic Complexity, 2014: http://atlas.media.mit.edu/en/visualize/line/hs92/show/qat/all/all/1995.2014/.

[179] Alexander Simoes, "What does Kuwait export?" The Observatory of Economic Complexity, 2014: http://atlas.media.mit.edu/en/visualize/tree_map/hs92/export/kwt/all/show/2014/.

[180] Alexander Simoes, "What does Kuwait import?" The Observatory of Economic Complexity, 2014: http://atlas.media.mit.edu/en/visualize/tree_map/hs92/import/kwt/all/show/2014/.

[181] World Trade Organization and Kuwait.

[182] Alexander Simoes, "What it the Trade Balance for Kuwait?" The Observatory of Economic Complexity, 2014: http://atlas.media.mit.edu/en/visualize/line/hs92/show/kwt/all/all/1995.2014/.

[183] European Union, "Import and Export," http://europa.eu/european-union/business/import-export_en#trading-in-and-with-the-eu; Michael Pfaffermayr and Peter H. Egger, "The Pure Effects of European Integration on Intra-EU Core and Periphery Trade," *The World Economy*, 36(6), 2013.

Slovakia experienced an almost four-fold increase in the value of exports.[184] In addition to having the majority of members experience an increasing trend, the value of exports had recovered to its levels of before the 2008-09 financial crisis. Most EU members have two or three partners within the region that account for more than 50% of their intra-EU exports.[185]

Evolution of Intra EU-28 Exports of Goods, 2002-13, in millions of euros (Source: Eurostat)

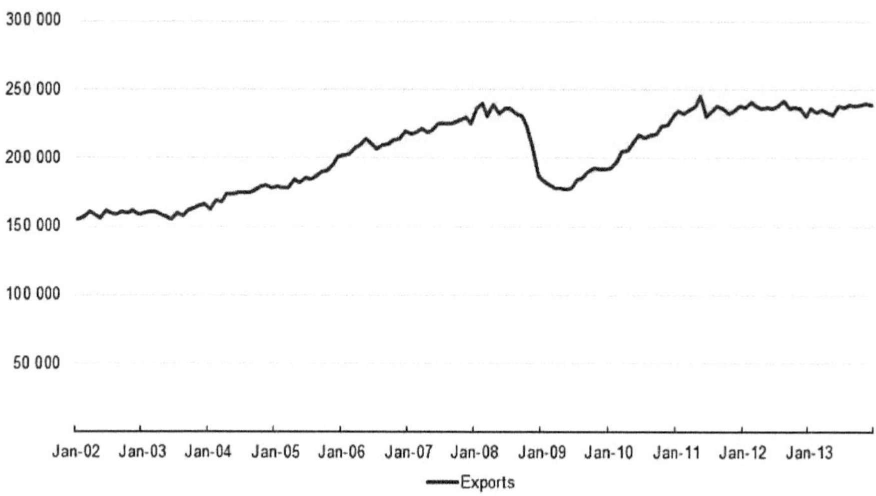

Traditionally, EU members have traded goods within the region rather than with outsiders. This can be observed and confirmed. Foremost among reasons, the geographical proximity helps these countries to reduce and minimize costs associated with trading, such as physical shipping costs, time-related costs and costs related to unfamiliarity. Secondly, EU members have diversified economies. In 2013, more than 77% of intra EU trade was in manufactured products – machines and vehicles accounted for 34%, chemical products 16% and other manufactured goods 27%. EU members are also producers of primary goods such as foods and drinks, and intra-EU trade is strong here as well.

Member states' overall exports by product, shown in the next table, confirm that both larger and smaller economies in the EU have a share of exported manufactured goods that is greater than the EU's average.[186]

---

184 EUROSTAT.

185 Harald Badinger and Volker Nitsch, *Routledge Handbook of the Economics of European Integration*, Routledge, 2015.

186 EUROSTAT.

EU-28 Exports by Products
(Source: Eurostat)

	2002				2013			
	Primary goods	Manutactured goods	N.e.s.	Total	Primary goods	Manutactured goods	N.e.s.	Total
EU-28	15%	83%	1%	100%	22%	77%	1%	100%
Belgium	17%	83%	0%	100%	26%	72%	2%	100%
Bulgaria	21%	77%	2%	100%	29%	71%	0%	100%
Czech Republic	9%	91%	0%	100%	12%	88%	0%	100%
Denmark	32%	66%	2%	100%	37%	61%	2%	100%
Germany	9%	89%	3%	100%	13%	85%	1%	100%
Estonia	21%	79%	0%	100%	27%	71%	2%	100%
Ireland	10%	86%	3%	100%	19%	80%	1%	100%
Greece	34%	64%	2%	100%	46%	52%	2%	100%
Spain	20%	80%	0%	100%	27%	72%	1%	100%
France	16%	84%	0%	100%	21%	77%	1%	100%
Croatia	20%	79%	0%	100%	31%	68%	1%	100%
Italy	10%	89%	1%	100%	14%	85%	1%	100%
Cyprus	42%	58%	0%	100%	30%	65%	5%	100%
Latvia	39%	61%	0%	100%	41%	59%	1%	100%
Lithuania	38%	61%	0%	100%	52%	48%	0%	100%
Luxembourg	9%	91%	0%	100%	13%	87%	0%	100%
Hungary	9%	89%	1%	100%	16%	84%	0%	100%
Malta	2%	98%	0%	100%	19%	81%	0%	100%
Netherlands	31%	67%	2%	100%	35%	64%	0%	100%
Austria	11%	88%	0%	100%	14%	85%	1%	100%
Poland	14%	86%	0%	100%	20%	79%	0%	100%
Portugal	12%	88%	0%	100%	22%	77%	1%	100%
Romania	12%	88%	0%	100%	14%	86%	0%	100%
Slovenia	5%	95%	0%	100%	17%	83%	0%	100%
Slovakia	13%	86%	1%	100%	14%	85%	0%	100%
Finland	13%	86%	1%	100%	29%	71%	0%	100%
Sweden	15%	84%	0%	100%	25%	74%	0%	100%
United Kingdom	16%	84%	0%	100%	31%	69%	0%	100%

To conclude, by elaborating on data from the OEC, we analyze and compare the trade patterns of one of the smallest EU countries, Cyprus, with one of the largest economies within the EU, Italy.

Although the republic of Cyprus, occupying the southern part of the island of Cyprus, exported only $3.64 billion worth of goods in 2014, it can be considered as an example of a diversified economy. Its main exported items were packaged medicine, refined petroleum, passenger and cargo ships, cheese and broadcasting equipment, but the range of its exported products goes well beyond the aforementioned items.[187] Among the main destinations for its exports are Israel and South Korea, but Cyprus also trades heavily with its EU partners.[188]

The same applies to Italy, too. In 2014, Italy exported $509 billion of goods, the main items being packaged medicine, refined petroleum, vehicle parts, cars and valves.[189] Italy's main export partners are Germany, France,

[187] Alexander Simoes, "What does Cyprus export?" The Observatory of Economic Complexity, 2014: http://atlas.media.mit.edu/en/visualize/tree_map/hs92/export/cyp/all/show/2014/.

[188] Alexander Simoes, "Where does Cyprus export?" The Observatory of Economic Complexity, 2014: http://atlas.media.mit.edu/en/visualize/tree_map/hs92/export/cyp/show/all/2014/.

[189] Alexander Simoes, "What does Italy export?" The Observatory of Economic Complexity, 2014: http://atlas.media.mit.edu/en/visualize/tree_map/hs92/export/ita/all/show/2014/.

the United States, United Kingdom and Switzerland. As was the case for Cyprus, Italy also trades heavily with its EU partners. Of its total exports in 2014, $315 billion went to European countries.[190]

As we can see, complementarity in production and trade helped European countries in integrating their economies. This also confirms that these countries joined the regional bloc because they saw more potential in terms of economic gain within the region than outside of it, otherwise they would not have given up some aspects of their economic and political independence.[191]

Intra-GCC Trade: Trade Patterns and Trading Partners

As we have tried to show, for now the GCC members' economies do not meet the essential criteria of complementarity in production and subsequently in trade. Of course, there is no doubt that creating a free trade area anyway would increase trade among the signatories, and this was indeed the case for the GCC countries. In 2010, intra-GCC trade hit a peak, rising from $19.8 billion to $65.4 billion; however, it remained a very tiny fraction of the total amount of their trade at the time. Data for 2013 also confirms that although intra-GCC trade had increased and was almost 7 times greater than the levels registered before the creation of the GCC's customs union, it was only 7.1% of the members' total trade. By contrast, intra-EU trade in the same year was around 62% of the total value of traded goods.[192]

GCC Intra-Regional Trade (Millions of Dollars, 2013)						
	Qatar	KSA	UAE	Oman	Kuwait	Bahrain
Qatar		2454.39	8381.36	1570.68	1481.28	456.4
KSA	2454.39		8141.18	4623.43	2629.5	5050.85
UAE	8381.36	8141.18		15689.37	1692.18	12.67.4
Oman	1570.68	4623.43	15689.37		777.67	385.55
Kuwait	1481.28	2629.5	1692.18	777.67		279.16
Bahrain	456.4	5050.85	1267.04	385.55	279.16	
Total	$14,344.11	$20,444.96	$26,789.77	$21,476.02	$5,378.51	$6,982.60
Total(all)	$95,415.97					

[190] Alexander Simoes, "Where does Italy export?" The Observatory of Economic Complexity, 2014: http://atlas.media.mit.edu/en/visualize/tree_map/hs92/export/ita/show/all/2014/.
[191] Peter A. Hall, *Varieties of Capitalism: The Institutional Foundations of Comparative Advantage*, Oxford University Press, 2001.
[192] World Bank, "Economic Integration in the GCC;" Abdulqader, "GCC Economic Cooperation and Integration;" Ahmed Saddam Abdul Sahib and Fatimah Kari, "Analysis of Intensity of Intra-regional Trade in GCC countries, 1998-2008," *International Journal of Trade, Economics and Finance*, 3(3), 2011.

The short-run increase in intra-GCC trade due to falling tariffs and imposing barriers to imports from non-members does not guarantee long-term sustainable intra-GCC trade for the regional partners. In the absence of complementarity in trade and production, they will lose the opportunity for economic gains within the group. Bilateral free trade agreements with non-GCC countries can be more advantageous for each of the GCC members unilaterally, instead of trading as a bloc. The rationale is as follows: they produce and export the same products and clearly are in competition with each other in addition to experiencing the presence of a constant conflict of interests. This is what Asian countries such as India, Singapore and South Korea did – they used bilateral free trade agreements to have lower prices relative to external competitors. [193] For instance, Turkey is a huge petrochemical market and South Korea has a free trade agreement with Turkey, so South Koreans are in a better position to export to Turkey compared with the exporters within the GCC that are not able to offer their own price to Turkey's petrochemical market.[194] The other rationale for trading unilaterally for countries that lack complementarity in production and trade is that negotiating as a bloc is more difficult and time-consuming. For instance, negotiations on a free trade agreement between the European Union and the Gulf Cooperation Council, a project reportedly under discussion since 1990, had been taken off the table due to political issues in 2008.[195]

To summarize, concerning the demand factors, the economic gain from integration, due to a lack of even minimum complementarity concerning many aspects of the GCC economies, is irrelevant in terms of volume.[196] In fact, being in competition for the same markets, including in tourism and banking, where they are trying to diversify their economies, and the tiny amount of intra-GCC trade suggest that they might do better unilaterally.

Next, we discuss the banking and financial system – the conventional one, which we designate as such in order to differentiate it from the one offered to the Muslim community by Islam. The banking and financial system and the institutions, theories and philosophy behind them are essential for any country that would like to develop and bring prosperity to its people. It is necessary to analyze it since economic theories of integration and trade are formed in that context and shaped, affecting many aspects of the system and its institutions. Regional integration may or may not work in different contexts through different institutions.

---

[193] Courtney Trenwith, "The case for free trade in GCC," *Arabian Business*, 2015: http://www.arabianbusiness.com/the-case-for-free-trade-in-gcc-604126.html.

[194] *Ibid.*

[195] *Ibid.*; European Commission, "EU-GCC Cooperation Agreement," http://trade.ec.europa.eu/doclib/docs/2008/september/tradoc_140300.pdf; Aarti Nagraj, "Stalled EU-GCC Free Trade Agreement Should be Passed – UK's Mandelson," *Gulf News*, 2015: http://gulfbusiness.com/stalled-eu-gcc-free-trade-agreement-passed-uks-mandelson.

[196] World Bank, "Economic Integration in the GCC."

CHAPTER 5

THE CONVENTIONAL FINANCIAL SYSTEM AND ITS INSTITUTIONS

Financial Markets

Having healthy financial markets and institutions are of primordial necessity for any developed economy or any country that tries to develop its economy. All the actors within a country from households to the government, and from firms to investors, are affected by the way the financial system as a whole operates. The only way to move resources of an economy from savers to borrowers, in other words for these actors to invest their excess resources and/or borrow funds for their needs and projects, is through financial markets and institutions. In an economy, the long-term financing required for expansion purposes or the short-term financing needed to alleviate temporary shortages is handled through this mechanism.[197] The importance of a financial system is not only because it assists the aforementioned actors with financing. It is also there to offer alternative opportunities for those interested in investing, which may be individuals, businesses or governments.

Today, in most developed economies, supply and demand of financial resources take place on two main markets. The bond market is a place where businesses and other entities go in order to ask for money and obtain financing from the public. By issuing certificates of indebtedness that are called "bonds," companies or governments seeking financing communicate their obligations in terms of how and when they would repay their loans. With bonds, there are details regarding the interest rate that would be paid periodically as well as the date of maturity. For instance, if an oil company has projects to develop in some part of the world and needs money to finance it, it would go to bond markets where it can borrow directly from the public and from sources that have an excess of funds. Therefore, the buyer of the bonds gives money to the company in exchange for receiving interest payments plus the total amount of the bond at the end of its maturity,[198] whether it is a short-term bond with a maturity of a few months or a long-term bond with a maturity in 30 years. In developed economies, millions of bonds

---

[197] Jeff Madura, *Financial Markets and Institutions*, West Publishing.
[198] N. Gregory Mankiw and Mark P. Taylor, *Economics*, Thomson.

are issued and traded, whether by national governments in need of money to develop infrastructures or corporations seeking financing to develop new products or activities.

The other important market that helps investors and borrowers meet is the stock market. Stock represents the ownership of a company. A company that seeks money in order to finance its projects can sell stock to raise the money. The sale of stock is also called equity finance. In a practical sense, the owner of a company's stock would participate in sharing the company's profit. Once shares of stock are issued and sold to the public, owners can trade these shares on a stock exchange and the prices are based on supply and demand.

In connection with this, stock indices that are an average of a group of shares are created and made available to the public. These indices help investors, analysts, speculators, competitors and other interested groups to observe and monitor prices generally. They also help shape perceptions on the future of firms' profitability. Although many stock exchanges and indices exist around the world, the most well-known are the Dow Jones Industrial Average, based on 30 major American companies; the London Stock Exchange index; the DAX 30 and DAX 100 of Frankfurt; and the Nikkei index in Tokyo that is calculated based on 225 companies.[199]

In developed countries where organized exchange markets exist, the matter of transferring financial resources from surplus units to deficit units is perfectly managed. Therefore, having a well-organized and transparent system of transferring resources within the economy is considered as an essential requirement that needs to be met in order to bring prosperity and growth. The same importance must be given to a financial system at a regional level. There is no doubt that, for instance, the Eurosystem benefited enormously from already efficient functional financial markets within each of the European Union members. In fact, the EU and its mission statement precisely communicate the importance and the necessity of promoting financial integration that would go first through each member's financial system. It is considered as a key aspect for completing any level of regional integration.[200]

Financial Intermediaries

The financial market is an institution itself where interactions between surplus units and deficit units take place directly and continuously.

---

[199] Rick W. Hafer and Scott E. Hein, *The Stock Market*, Greenwood Publishing Group, 2007; Bloomberg Markets, "Americas," Bloomberg, 2016: https://www.bloomberg.com/markets/stocks.

[200] https://www.ecb.europa.eu/ecb/orga/escb/html/mission_eurosys.en.html; Eurosystem, "Financial Integration in Europe," European Central Bank, 2014: https://www.ecb.europa.eu/pub/pdf/other/financialintegrationineurope201404en.pdf.

However, there are also other institutions called financial intermediaries that are there to serve the needs of the aforementioned units. These institutions stand between borrowers and investors and act on behalf of both. The two main institutions from which any developed country can benefit are banks and investment funds. Banks have access to savings of surplus units and, through that, they transfer resources to deficit units. Differences between the interest paid to surplus units and that received from deficit units cover the banks' costs and allow their owners to be provided with some profit. Banks and a banking system are essential, because in addition to what banks do as intermediaries, they also offer a medium of exchange. Banks and the way they operate are very important also because the accumulated wealth and savings of people are all deposited within their realm of responsibility.[201]

The other important intermediary institution that plays a crucial role within advanced economies is the investment fund. These institutions offer their shares to the public and later invest the amount of money received to buy stocks, bonds or both, creating different types of portfolios with the main objectives of seeing their values increase. If that occurs, shareholders will benefit, but in case of a decrease in a portfolio's value they would participate in the loss. Investment funds are targeted by people with small amounts of money, allowing them to diversify and multiply their investments in a way that is otherwise not doable, in addition to becoming owners of firms and businesses. Since these funds are managed by professionals, ordinary people are willing to trust in experts' capabilities rather than doing it by themselves. These institutions are also play a crucial role in circulating money within the economy.[202]

There are many other institutions operating within the banking and financial system such as pension funds, insurance companies, etc., and all of them ultimately serve the purpose of directing resources from surplus units to deficit ones. By guaranteeing the allocation of financial resources, the functionalities of a healthy economy would be guaranteed as well. The management of financial resources in a civilized manner, where contracts are enforced and respected, freedom of choice is guaranteed and alternatives are equally created, would ultimately lead to the best possible allocation of the resources. Such a system is able to accept its shortcomings, improve itself, learn from its experiences and implement the required regulations and reforms necessary to its healthy functioning.[203]

---

[201] Madura, *Financial Markets and Institutions*; Mankiw and Taylor, *Economics*.

[202] Mark St Giles, Ekaterina Alexeeva and Sally Buxton, *Managing Collective Investment Funds*, John Wiley & Sons, 2005; Timothy Spangler, *The Law of Private Investment Funds*, Oxford University Press, 2012.

[203] Asian Development Bank, *Financial System Stability, Regulation, and Financial Inclusion*, Springer, 2015; Angel Gurria, "Regulatory Reform in the Financial System," OECD: http://www.oecd.org/berlin/presse/45262457.pdf.

National Income Accounts and Financial Systems

Whatever happens in financial systems is important and central to what happens next to the economy as a whole. Whatever is experienced within the economy also affects the financial system. As discussed above, financial markets are in the hands of intermediaries that manage and control the flow of savings and investments. Owners of these savings and investments, both surplus and deficit units, are the main actors of a nation. These are citizens engaged in daily life, and the way their incomes, expenditures, savings and investments are managed determine the performance of the country, calculated through GDP as one of the most important measures for the standard of living within it. As shown below through the GDP equation, we see how important macroeconomic variables measure what happens within the financial markets.[204]

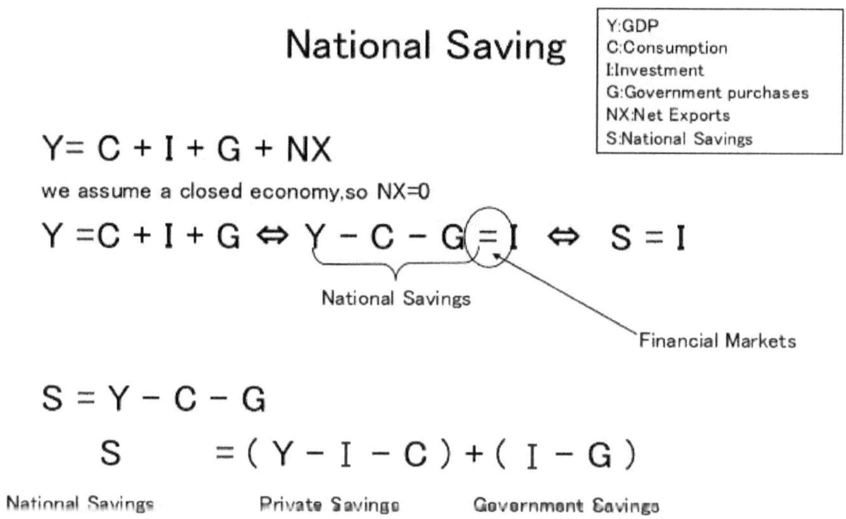

Here, GDP denoted as "Y" incorporates important components of an economy – consumption, investments, government expenditures/purchases and net exports. This means that any change in one of the items located in the right part of the equation would be reflected on the left side and vice versa. With the objective of observing what happens within financial markets, we

---

[204]Lars Osberg and Andrew Sharp, "Comparisons in trends of GDP and the Economic Well-being: The impact of social capital," OECD: https://www.oecd.org/innovation/research/1824740.pdf; Geert Bekaert and Campbell R. Harvey, "Capital Market: An Engine for Economic Growth," Duke University: https://faculty.fuqua.duke.edu/~charvey/Research/Published_Papers/P58_An_engine_for.pdf.

assume that our hypothetical economy is a closed one and thus there is no trade and consequently our net exports, "NX," equals zero. Therefore, within our economy each unit produced and sold would be consumed, invested or purchased by the national authorities. In connection with financial markets, as shown through the above formulas, subtracting consumption and government expenditures from both sides, what would remain from the national income after consumption and authorities' expenditures is "I," or investment: Y-C-G=I. The left side of our equation, "S," represents national savings.[205]

Although we can expand the discussion on savings and divide it into two categories of private and public savings, because of the presence of taxes we remain concentrated on how the equation S=I is related to financial markets. Savings=Investments confirms that in an economy considered as a whole, savings ought to be equal to investments. As simple as that seems, however, behind all the huge amounts of interactions that take place within a country in terms of expenditure, consumption, investments, borrowing, etc., there is a functional financial system and a network of financial intermediaries that place themselves in the middle of the equation S=I. This system directs the flow of national savings toward the nation's investment opportunities. In other words, financial markets and intermediaries coordinate the economy as a whole. The circular flow model to which financial flow is added represents the reality of a functional economy.[206]

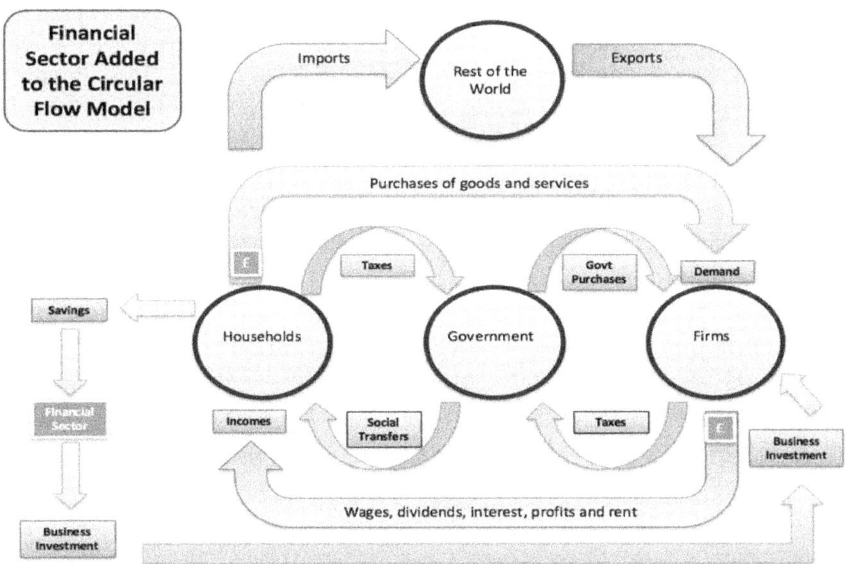

[205] Madura, *Financial Markets and Institutions*; Mankiw and Taylor, *Economics*.
[206] Geoff Rieley, "Understanding the Circular Flow of Income and Spending," Tutor2u Publisher: http://www.tutor2u.net/economics/reference/circular-flow-of-income-and-spending; Paul Samuelson, *Economics*, McGraw-Hill, 2010.

Therefore, a clear and vital relation exists between a financial system's institutions and the overall performance of a country, which ultimately affects the standard of living of its people. The latter sometimes is sought through regional integration and eventual economic gains/benefits that can be reaped.

The Financial Market Model

Analyzing the financial market model is important because in addition to giving us insights into how it is structured, it also enables us to see how various policies affect savings and investments within the system. The idea of building an economic model is to simplify the real-world phenomenon, and to explain it. Here, based on model that N. Gregory Mankiw created[207] for the "market for loanable funds," we assume that this market is the only market that exists in the economy. It is also to be assumed that there is only one interest rate used to calculate both return on savings as well as the cost of borrowing. People go to this market for either borrowing or lending, and as the term itself suggests, loanable funds refers to that part of people's income that they decide to save and borrow rather than consume.[208]

The loanable fund market is governed by the law of supply and demand. Suppliers of loans are those units in surplus and demanders of loans are those that are in deficit. Supply can take two forms: directly, for instance, when a surplus unit buys a bond issued by a firm; or indirectly, as when a household in surplus deposits its savings in a bank. In fact, savings constitute the main source of loanable funds. On the other side, demand for loanable funds comes from units that would like to borrow, for instance in order to make investments. As previously assumed, the interest rate is the same for both borrowers and lenders. It is the amount that borrowers pay for what they borrow and that savers receive for what they lend. With the rule of supply and demand applied, a higher interest rate would make loanable funds less attractive and consequently demand falls. Similarly, a high interest rate makes saving more attractive and consequently the quantity of supplied loanable funds would rise. The following graph shows the interest rate that balances the market forces. In the example, it is 5%, with the amount of loanable funds both supplied and demanded equaling $1,200.[209]

[207] Mankiw and Taylor, *Economics.*

[208] *Ibid.*

[209] *Ibid.*

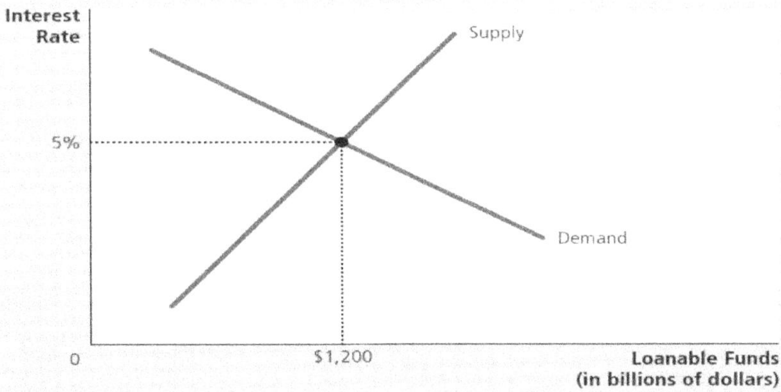

The 5% interest rate and the quantity registered are not eternal. The adjustment process occurs rapidly. Again, the rule of markets and the law of supply and demand intervene. Therefore, if the interest rate were lower than 5%, the quantity of loanable funds supplied would have been less than the quantity demanded. Consequently, the shortage of loanable funds would have been considered as an invitation for lenders to raise the interest rate. Similarly, in the presence of an interest rate above 5%, there would be less demand for loanable funds and at the same time the willingness to supply loanable funds increases. In any case, either due to shortages or excesses of loanable funds, the interest rate would respectively increase or decrease in order to reach the equilibrium point where the quantity of supply and demand are equal.

This model is important because it follows the law of supply and demand and mimics real markets. As Adam Smith put it, there is always an invisible hand, which ultimately would coordinate the behaviors of those participating within a market, adjusting the price as well as quantity. All these adjustments and changes affect the way people live. One of the ten principles of economics states that a nation's living standard and prosperity ultimately depend on how capable that nation is in producing goods and services. Considering the fact that savings in the long run would determine the productivity of a country, if the saving rate increases, the GDP growth rate should increase as well, and as years pass the quality of life within the country will be augmented. However, market mechanisms can be affected by external and internal incentives, too, and consequently responses to the incentives would occur.[210]

Based on the model we have introduced, we assess three different policies and the way markets are affected by them. Governments' revenues are mainly collected through taxing income, including interest and dividends.

---

[210] *Ibid.*

It is clear that taxing interest income would reduce the amount of savings. Ideas and solutions to face this policy are many, such as replacing the tax on interest income with one on consumption, like the value added tax (VAT) in Europe. Here the rationale is that income not consumed is considered as being part of savings. Another solution, to avoid discouraging people from saving, is to expand eligibility for special saving accounts. The graph below captures the response to the policy.[211]

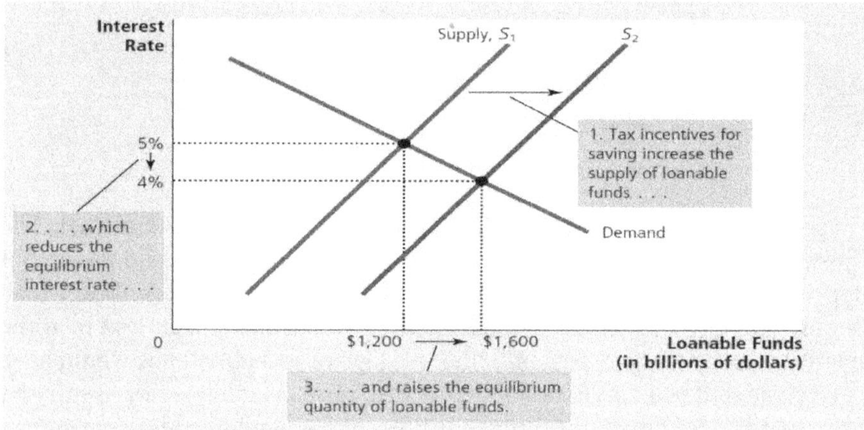

It is clear that these kind of policies/incentives, though, do not affect the demand curve directly since for the borrowers this change is indifferent. They would increase the supply of loanable funds and consequently shift the supply curve to the right. As explained through the graph, the shift to the right increases the quantity supplied and at the same time reduces the equilibrium rate. Therefore, the result is less taxes, more savings and ultimately more and cheaper loanable funds available to borrowers for further investments.[212]

The second policy can be in form of a tax reform, with the objective of making investment easier and more advantageous. For instance, sometimes governments institute investment tax credits. In this way, firms that would like to expand their business, for instance through building new factories or developing new products, would be eligible for some sort of tax advantages. With more demand for loanable funds, the interest rate would be higher too. A higher interest rate for savings would create incentives for surplus units to

[211] *Ibid.*

[212] Henry Aaron and Michael Boskin, *The Economics of Taxation*, Brookings Institute Press, 2011; James Alm, Jorge Martinez-Vazquez and Mark Rider, *The Challenges of Tax Reform in a Global Economy*, Springer, 2005.

save. This reform therefore encourages both investment and causes greater savings.[213]

The third policy that we go through here in order to see how incentives alter behaviors of market players is related to governments' budget deficits and surpluses. An open and continuous debate, mainly in democracies, is about how governments spend money from taxpayers, and if it is spent wisely or not. This happens because a system of checks and balances is put in place and politicians are held responsible while at the helm of their country. The status of a government budget can be either in surplus or in deficit. A budget deficit means the government spends more than it collects. This is usually financed through bond markets. The opposite is a surplus budget, which is rare, however if it exists it would serve to repay previously accumulated debts of the government. Assuming that for different reasons the government runs a budget deficit, we can analyze this through the market for loanable funds introduced earlier.

The ways that budget deficits can affect the market are slightly different. As we recall, national savings (Y-C-G=I) is composed of private and public savings. Therefore, a change in public savings will negatively affect the supply of national savings. However, the demand for loanable funds at any given rate remains intact. This leads to an increase in the interest rate. The difference here is that a higher interest rate discourages families and businesses from investing. Thus, a government's budget deficit harms investments, and since investments are important to the growth rate in the long run the opportunity for economic growth is diminished.[214]

To conclude, financial markets follow the law of supply and demand. Interest rates and prices are adjusted automatically. Incentives and shocks affect the way the markets function. In parallel, they would also change the behavior of market players. Through financial markets, resources of the economy are allocated where they would be most efficient and productive. The way financial markets and institutions function, or the way governments act while in charge of a nation, will have long-term consequences on national economies. As demonstrated, national savings pave the way for more investments as well as develop more opportunities. These cannot be realized without a mechanism that is well-developed and institutionalized. All these affirm the importance of price and the law of supply and demand.

---

[213] Mankiw and Taylor, *Economics*.

[214] *Ibid.*; Alm, Martinez-Vazquez and Rider, *The Challenges of Tax Reform in a Global Economy*.

Financial Market Efficiency

So far, I have briefly introduced the idea of financial markets and institutions; however, related definitions and concepts, as well as financial tools and the way markets are organized, can go far beyond what I have discussed. To elaborate a little more on these items, mainly those that are concerned with the present work, and before getting into financial markets' efficiency, we need to go through few definitions such as "securities."

Securities are simply financial tools that represent an ownership right. They can be, for instance, in the form of a bond or a stock. Securities may be "paper certificates" known as definitive securities, or electronic records known as "book-entry" securities that are evidence of ownership of equity (stock) or debt obligations (bonds).[215] New securities are issued in primary markets, and existing securities are traded in secondary markets.[216] The difference between the two markets is that primary markets provide funds to the initial issuers and secondary markets do not. Therefore, if a government decides to finance its debt by selling new bonds, it would go to the primary market. Similarly, a firm that would like to finance its new projects by offering new shares would go through the primary market as well.

Financial markets in general are divided into two different categories. Money markets deal with managing short-term funds, precisely those with maturities of less than one year. As such, securities traded within these markets are called money market securities. The other category is called the capital markets, dedicated to the flow of long-term funds, and securities traded within these markets are called capital market securities. An aspect of money markets that differentiate them from capital markets is liquidity. Securities that have a maturity less than one year can be liquidated easily and without a loss of value.[217]

Liquidity is important. It means that either a security enjoys a very low bid/ask spread and is highly resilient or that a surplus unit, such as an investor, can make funding available.[218] The two dimensions of liquidity known as funding liquidity and market liquidity must be taken into consideration while analyzing any market. The latter refers to credit availability, and how easily a deficit unit can borrow. The former refers to the ease with which market players can conduct their activities, for instance, to what degree they can make large amounts of purchases and sales without

[215] http://www.nasdaq.com/investing/glossary/s/securities.
[216] Madura, *Financial Markets and Institutions*.
[217] *Ibid.*; Alm, Martinez-Vazquez and Rider, *The Challenges of Tax Reform in a Global Economy*.
[218] Lasse Pedersen, "Liquidity Risk and the Current Crisis," CEPR Policy Center, 2008, http://voxeu.org/article/understanding-liquidity-risk-and-its-role-crisis.

affecting the price level.[219] Here we do not enter into the risks associated with liquidity – liquidity risk and credit risk – which are also very important and in recent years have affected daily life of lots of people. It suffices to affirm that liquidity issues affect many aspects of an economy, and through a financial system, for instance, it can affect mainly shares of small and medium-sized companies that are traded publicly and have market capitalizations of between $300 million and $10 billion. The vast chunk of the traded volume goes to the big firms, which is another cause for shares of smaller firms to have less liquidity.

The daily trading volume for the stock of an average large company can reach millions of shares. Compared with daily trading of Bank of America Corp., which can reach up to 87 million shares, or those of Apple Inc., which can reach the threshold of 54 million shares, building or quitting positions in small and "midcap" (medium levels of capitalization) stocks are hard to achieve.[220] During 2015, an average of about 6.5 billion shares were traded on U.S. stock exchanges.[221] That can be considered as huge liquidity available to the economy; however, there are factors that need to be taken into consideration since this can create lots of volatility as well. For instance, a growing part of the volume traded happens in the first and the last half-hours of the trading sessions, due partly to the increasing use of index funds at the closing. New technologies, such as the way computer models score, are also to blame since they sniff out the best trading minutes. These can create a real problem for the way overall investments are conducted, and for the economy as a whole. This is why attention needs to be dedicated to the issue of liquidity.[222]

Independent institutions and entities work continuously toward, and are essential for, the stability of the system. In connection with this, it is why the Securities and Exchange Commission (SEC) in the United States had to intervene through launching a pilot program in 2016 to resolve the issue of liquidity. It is worth discussing how the program works.

The SEC Pilot Program and Tick Size

In financial markets, a "tick" represents the price fluctuation of a security.[223] It is the minimum price change of a different set of bid and offer

---

[219] Timothy F. Geithner, "Liquidity and Financial Markets," Federal Reserve Bank of New York, Feb.2007, https://www.newyorkfed.org/newsevents/speeches/2007/gei070228.
[220] *Ibid.*
[221] Market Watch.
[222] Allen Berger and Christa Bouwman, *Bank Liquidity Creation and Financial Crises*, Academic Press, 2015; Greg N. Gregoriou, *Stock Market Volatility*, CRC Press, 2009; Madura, *Financial Markets and Institutions*.
[223] http://www.nasdaq.com/investing/glossary/t/tick.

prices related to a particular security, and the minimum price difference that must exist for regulating incoming bids and offers.[224] Therefore, a "tick size" is the smallest increment permitted that can occur in the price of a financial instrument.[225] Tick sizes can be fixed or variable.

Launched through a new National Market System Plan, the Tick Size Pilot Program would widen the minimum quoting and trading increment for small and midcap stocks. These are stocks of companies that have either less than $3 billion in market capitalization, or an average of less than one million shares traded per day. Some of these so-called "pilot securities" will see the tick size widen from $0.01 to $0.05; some quoting needs to occur in $0.05 increments and others perhaps will see both quoting and trading in $0.05 increments. The main objective is to advance the research on the effects of these adjustments and the regulation of liquidity on the publicly traded stock of small and medium-sized businesses.[226]

To summarize, the liquidity issue matters within the economy and cannot be neglected. Many of the financial crises that have been experienced were marked by a variety of liquidity-related problems. BNP Paribas had to suspend liquidity of some of its money market funds. Runs on Lehman Brothers forced it to quite the business.[227] This is why in a developed economy that enjoys robust financial markets and institutions, transparency reigns, and regulatory authorities and financial supervisors actively intervene to guarantee a healthy system which, as mentioned, deals with the nation's savings as well as the long-run growth of the economy, ultimately through investment flows.

Securities Valuation: Term Structure of Interest Rates

Discussing supply and demand and the way prices are formed brings up the issue of interest rates. Whether they are surplus units or deficit units, anyone who deals with financial instruments continuously faces risks associated with financial transactions.[228] These risks can be related to the default of the issuer of a security or to external shocks, such as the result of a presidential election in the United States, that can affect the potential market values of securities through the variation of interest rates. An interest rate can be simply defined as the price that a surplus unit would offer to the market for its available funds, or the price that a deficit unit is willing to pay in order to

---

[224] http://economictimes.indiatimes.com/definition/tick-size.
[225] Tick Sizes | Euronext https://euronext.com/en/trading/tick-sizes.
[226] https://www.sec.gov/oiea/investor-alerts-bulletins/ia_ticksize.html; Madura, *Financial Markets and Institutions*.
[227] Larry D. Wall, "The role of Liquidity in the Financial Markets," Federal Reserve Bank of Atlanta, 2015, https://www.frbatlanta.org/cenfis/publications/notesfromthevault/1511.aspx.
[228] Joseph Daniels and David Vanhoos, *International Monetary and Financial Economics*, South Western College Publishing, 1999.

obtain funds. In other words, interest rates are "prices for loanable funds – prices of funds invested, lent out or borrowed for various periods of time. The supplier or lender of funds normally wants to earn an income and the user or borrower will generally be prepared to pay for the right to use the accumulated funds."[229]

The holding of securities means an extension of credit. The credit that is purchased through the issued security is called principal, and payments from the issuer to the buyer of funds calculated in percentage terms represent the interest rate. For instance, the amount of an annual interest rate regarding a simple interest loan is obtained through dividing the amount of interest by the principal. Slightly different from the interest rate is the interest yield. If the interest rate is the amount that banks charge on funds that they lend, the interest yield is the amount that an investor will receive and seek to obtain from investments made through stocks or bonds. Therefore, the owner of a financial instrument considers interest payments as a kind of income yield generated by the security that was purchased. Interest yields can be measured in different ways. For instance, the nominal yield is calculated through the formula below. It is a coupon return on a hypothetical bond, which is divided by its face value.

RN=C/F

"RN" represents nominal interest yield, "C" is the coupon return and "F" is the face amount of the bond. Supposing that a government issues a bond in an amount of $500,000 that bears $45,000 in interest yearly, which is the bond's annual coupon return too. If we go through the formula, the nominal interest rate would be RN=45,000/500,000=0.09 or simply 9%. However, because the face value of a bond most of the time is not the same as its current value on financial markets, the coupon yield is considered a better indicator of a bond's performance. It is calculated through the formula:

RC=C/PB

Here again, "C" represents the return on the coupon, "PB" is the current price of the bond and "RC" represents the current yield on the bond. Therefore, if the market price of our bond with a face value of $500,000 is down to $450,000, the coupon yield will be 10%: RC=45,000/450,000=0.10.

While these two measures are easy to calculate, other measures such as yield to maturity, which is the rate of return on an instrument that is supposed to be held until its maturity, is slightly more complicated.[230] This

---

[229] The Banking Association, South Africa, http://www.banking.org.za/consumer-information/conventional-banking/what-are-interest-rates.

[230] Daniels and Vanhoos, *International Monetary and Financial Economics.*

will reflect the market price, the coupon return and the gain from holding a bond until it matures. To measure the yield to maturity we need to know how to determine the price of our instrument. Discounted present value is one of the techniques that we can use to determine a payment that will be received at a given time in the future. Because whoever issues a bond sells it at a discount (that is, at less than the face value), the automatic capital gain that goes to the buyer must be taken into consideration when calculating the yield to maturity. This is also why we first need to calculate the price of a bond and secondly its yield to maturity. There is a relationship between coupon returns and capital gains, which is illustrated through the case below.

A bond with a maturity of 3 years and a face value of $10,000 offers a coupon return of $600, and as such has a nominal rate of 6%. In order to calculate the yield to maturity we need to compute its market price. It is obvious that with payments of $600 at the end of each year and $10,600 at the end of the third year, the amount that a buyer is willing to pay for this bond must equal the value of these payments from the buyer's perspective at the future date. This would happen through discounted present value: today's value of payments supposed to be received at the future date given the current market interest rates. Supposing that the current interest rate on the market is 7%, the formula below will give the discounted present value.[231]

Discounted present value=n payments from now/$(1+R)^n$

The discounted present value of the bond=$10,600/$(1+0.7)^3$ =$8,652.76. This would be today's value of $10,600 received at the end of the third year. However, in the hypothesis that transaction costs and risk do not exist, the price of the three-year bond must be the amount that a potential investor considers it to be worth on the purchase date and with a 7% interest rate. This is calculated by summing up each yearly discounted present value.[232] The price of the 3-year bond=$600/(1.07)+$600/$(1.07)^2$+$600/ $(1.07)^3$=$9,737.57.

Interest rate movements affect a wide range of policies and the performance of all types of financial institutions and this is well understood within developed economies. Theories such as the loanable funds theory, which explains interest rate movements, affirm that interest rates are determined by supply and demand for loanable funds.[233] The theory identifies the main sectors for demand and supply of loanable funds, and by combining the two wings of the market it explains changes that occur continuously in

[231] Hassan Mansoor, lecture notes, American Graduate School of Business and Economics in Paris, 2011; Madura, *Financial Markets and Institutions*; A.M.S Fatemi, lecture notes on international financial markets and institutions, American Graduate School of Business and Economics in Paris, 2010.

[232] Daniels and Vanhoos, *International Monetary and Financial Economics.*

[233] Madura, *Financial Markets and Institutions.*

interest rates. Through this theory, foreign demand and supply for loanable funds are also studied. For instance, the French government can go for financing through issuing French bonds targeted to the American markets and investors. That would be considered a French demand for American funds. This can have a significant impact on demand in any given country since it is influenced by the other country's interest rate, among many other factors. Thus, for a given French interest rate, if it is less than the American interest rate for loanable funds, demand for American loanable funds will decrease and firms and other deficit units will increase their demand for the French loanable funds. The graph below confirms the shift in demand.[234]

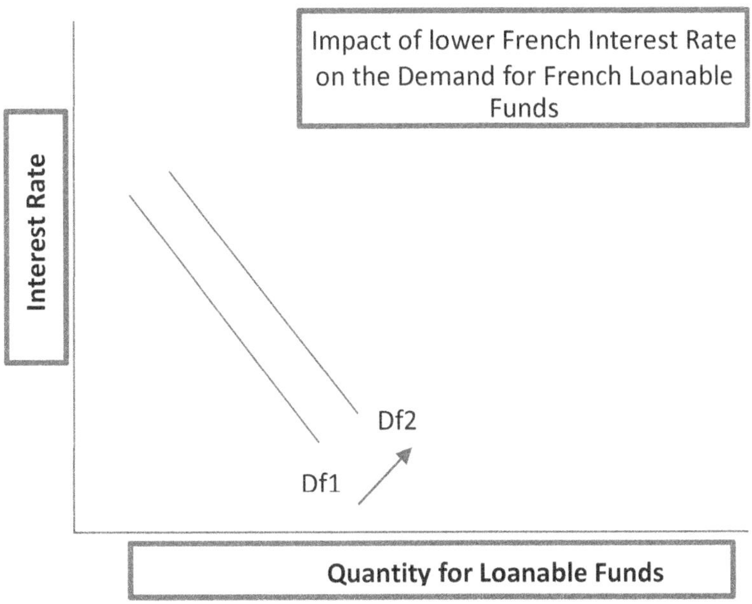

By integrating the aggregate demand for loanable funds, which is the sum of the demand in each sector, such as household, government, foreign, etc., with the aggregate supply of the loanable funds, the equilibrium interest rate is obtained.[235] Considering five sectors for each wing of the market, the algebraic presentation of the equilibrium would be:

---

[234] Fatemi, lecture notes on international financial markets; Mankiw and Taylor, *Economics*; Robert G. King and Andre Kurmann, "Expectations and the Term Structure of Interest Rates: Evidence and Implications," Federal Reserve Bank of Richmond, Economic Quarterly, 88(4), 2002.

[235] Madura, *Financial Markets and Institutions*.

$$D_A=D_h+D_b+D_G+D_m+D_f$$

D_h = Gross household demand for loanable funds
D_b = Gross business demand for loanable funds
D_G= Gross government demand for loanable funds
D_m= Gross municipal demand for loanable funds
D_f = Gross foreign demand for loanable funds

$$S_A=S_h+S_b+S_G+S_m+S_f$$

S_h = Gross household supply for loanable funds
S_b = Gross business supply for loanable funds
S_G= Gross government supply for loanable funds
S_m= Gross municipal supply for loanable funds
S_f = Gross foreign supply for loanable funds

In case of an equilibrium ($D_A=S_A$), if there were an increase in aggregated demand while aggregated supply remains intact, the shortage of loanable funds would cause the interest rate to rise until additional loanable funds come in to accommodate the market. In case of a surplus of aggregate supply, the interest rate would fall and aggregate demand would increase.

The equilibrium interest rate would change with demand and supply. Optimism among economic actors and market players can be translated into a greater demand for loanable funds. However, this would not automatically affect the supply curve.[236] The result depends on other factors, and as long as the shortage persists the market would deal with a higher interest rate.

Another theory of interest rates is the one of Irving Fisher. It does not contradict the previous theory, and adds an additional explanation to interest rate movements within the financial markets. The theory argues that nominal interest payments will offset savers through purchasing power. It states that they compensate savers' reduced purchasing power through an additional premium for the lost present consumption. They would forego consumption if premiums received on the savings were above the anticipated rate of inflation. The relationship between the interest rate and inflation is called the Fisher effect. The real return will be the difference between the nominal rate and the expected inflation rate. This is how the real interest rate is calculated.[237]

$$i_r=i_n-E(I)$$

[236] *Ibid.*
[237] Jeff Madura, *International Financial Management*, Cengage Learning, 2008; Mankiw and Taylor, *Economics*.

In the hypothesis that the normal rate is equal to inflation, the real interest rate would be zero and the purchasing power of savings would stay untouched.[238]

To conclude, interest rates and interest rate movements are considered as a major issue concerning the financial markets and institutions. These movements can influence any decision-making process and the performance and growth of business units that interact with the financial markets. In the real economy, macroeconomic factors such as the inflation rate can affect the interest rates within the financial markets. A government's deficit or any foreign interest rate movement within the global markets and within the developed world can alter the movement of these rates. A huge amount of activity and interactions take place behind the scenes of a functional financial market. They take place in a continuous, highly organized way. Professional monitoring confirms how important financial markets are in developed countries and the important role that they have played in helping European economies to integrate.[239]

Efficiency

Efficiency in economics is a term that can be used in different circumstances while embracing different definitions. It can be mainly considered as an economic state within which resources are allocated in a way that are put to their best use. Therefore, in the circumstance that resources are not allocated optimally, we would witness inefficiency. If an economy does not produce the maximum possible from its resources – in other words, if the economy cannot touch its production possibility frontier – there would be a case for inefficiency. As Vilfredo Pareto offered his definition of the concept, "a position from which it is not possible by any reallocation of inputs or outputs to make anyone better off without causing at least one person (to be) worse off." Pareto defined the social optimum as a position from which no change could be made that would make everybody better off. Thus, the Pareto Optimum is a position not only of maximum efficiency but also of maximum welfare. In short, any change that improves the well-being of at least one individual, without lowering the well-being of anyone else, is a desirable change and is known as a Pareto Efficient Change. According to Pareto's criteria, an action is beneficial to society if it helps someone to be better off without hurting anyone else. There are five first-order marginal conditions that, if met, would guarantee the maximization of social welfare:

---

[238] *Ibid.*

[239] Bankim Chadha and Daniel Tsiddon, "Inflation, Nominal Interest Rate and Variability of Output," International Monetary Fund, 1996; Robert L. Sexton, *Exploring Economics*, Cengage Learning, 2015; Madura, *International Financial Management*.

1. Marginal Social Benefit = Value of Marginal Product (MSB = VMP)
2. Value of Marginal Product = Marginal Private Revenue (VMP = MPR)
3. Marginal Private Revenue = Marginal Private Cost (MPR = MPC)
4. Marginal Private Cost = Value of Marginal Factor (MPC = VMF)
5. Value of Marginal Factor = Marginal Social cost (VMF = MSC)

The combined equation of the above conditions can be given as follows:

MSB=VMP=MPR=MPC=v<f=MSC

These conditions can be satisfied in a perfectly competitive market. Five marginal first-order conditions are:

1. The optimum condition of exchange
2. The optimum condition of production
3. The optimum condition for the composition of output
4. The optimum condition for the intensity of factor use
5. The optimum inter-temporal conditions

These five conditions can he summed up as follows: Between any two goods, the subjective and objective marginal rate of substitution (MRS) must be equal for all households and all production units respectively, and these ratios must be equal to each other.[240] Therefore, an allocation of resources is efficient if an action makes someone better off and will not cause someone else to be worse off.[241] The graph on the next page shows Pareto's frontier, within which there is no "dead weight" and resources are efficiently allocated.[242]

Since all financial instruments have their prices determined through market interactions, favorable or unfavorable characteristics are supposed to be reflected in their prices. This means, for instance, that if a particular security were considered to be undervalued by the market, its price would increase and adjust to the demand. The same is valid for those securities that are overvalued, which consequently would be sold, and a fall in the price will follow. Thus, whenever prices of securities reflect all the information available, the market is considered efficient.

---

[240] Fatemi, lecture notes on international financial markets.
[241] Megan Martorana, "Pareto Efficiency," Federal Reserve Bank of Richmond, 2007: https://www.richmondfed.org/~/media/richmondfedorg/publications/research/region_focus/2007/winter/pdf/jargon_alert.pdf.
[242] Jeffery Carte, "Points and Figures," http://pointsandfigures.com/2013/02/11/microeconomics-monday efficiency-vs-equity/.

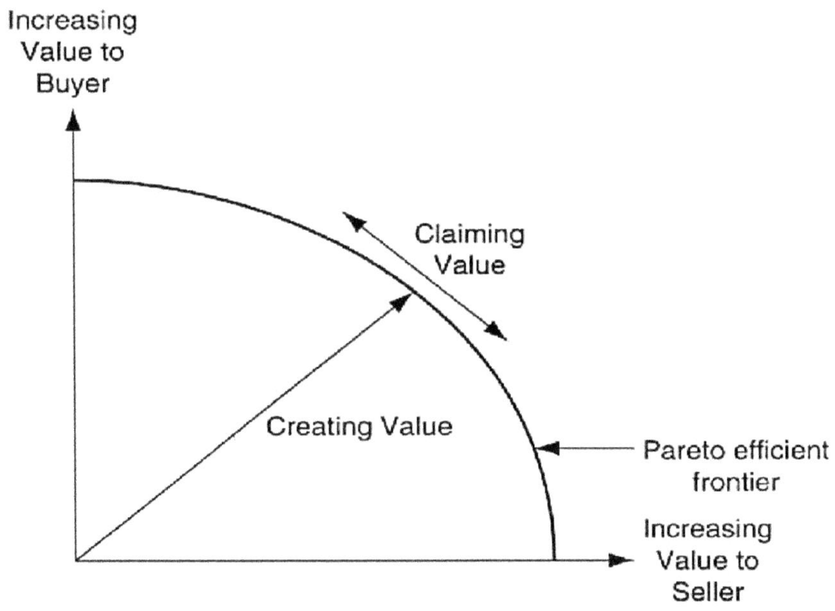

Within financial systems, investors have their own particular preferences. They try to reach their desired objectives in terms of high returns from the investments made, based on factors such as financial assets liquidity, the risk associated with their choices and surely subjective factors such as how risk-averse an investor is in general. When financial markets are efficient, information pertinent to risk, economic conditions and performance of a corporation, firm or government are reflected in the price. This is why in financial markets both surplus units and deficit ones would respond quickly to the potential changes perceived and understood. As they react, changes occur in prices and a new equilibrium will be attained. However, if the information is not offering something valuable and interesting, there will not be a response from the market and those interacting within the market. It is worth mentioning that market participants are also capable of predicting and anticipating their responses. If, for instance, there is an announcement that the central bank is injecting money to the markets, since investors in the bond market react so quickly to this kind of information, prices adjust rapidly to it. Thus, market participants are able to predict announcements or similar information that may affect their short-term and long-term objectives.

The concept of market efficiency is very important. It can measure the efficiency of the financial system as a whole. Therefore, for a considerable understanding of financial markets, it would be helpful to develop this a little more. Market efficiency would explain the relationship that exists between information and the prices in the market. In general, with the help of the theory of efficient markets, we can evaluate whether prices at any point in time "fully reflect" the available information.[243] Supposing that the information is not only financial but includes a wide range of different types such as political, economic and social, the decision that an investor would make is ultimately based on how all these details concerning, for instance, a particular stock are perceived. In addition to this, based on the Efficient Market Hypothesis (EMH), the fact that all participants are considered to have access to the same information results in no one making others worse off, respecting the "fair games" model.[244] In fact, the Efficient Market Hypothesis assumes the efficiency of markets as given and categorizes it into weak, semi-strong and strong forms. Within the weak form, current prices fully reflect all the past information up to that point, and none of the participants can profit from the others based just on past patterns. In this form, returns are not correlated and would have a constant mean.

A semi-strong efficient market is made in a way that prices instantly reflect any fresh announcements or newly revealed details that are made public. Finally, within the strong efficient form, prices reflect all the information whether publicly or privately made available, and therefore no one can gain above the average investor. The EMH also offers tests that help to identify the three aforementioned forms. Testing the weak form through autocorrelation tests would confirm or reject the assumption made in regards to returns being uncorrelated, ultimately affirming that rates of return are independent. Tests for the two other forms also provide helpful details on the form of the efficiency. Concerning the semi-strong form, tests such as regression or event tests would clarify it. Accepting the fact that a market is semi-strong and prices reflect all publicly available information, a test based on regressions would confirm the idea that an investor cannot make a profit through this approach.[245]

Finally, a test for a strong form would be done through people that should have more access than others to information, based on their positions. In other words, those insiders to a business unit, by having access to an extra set of information, can reap benefits. Exchange specialists, because they may have access to the orders, consequently could also profit above the average.

To summarize, market efficiency is very important mainly because:

> The only way to have resources allocated correctly is through the fact that prices and other available information obtained would perfectly give the required tools to assess the performance of, for instance, a business unit or government that is present within the

[243] Eugene F. Fama, "Efficient Capital Markets: A Review of Theory and Empirical Work," *Journal of Finance*, 25(2) 1969.

[244] *Ibid.*

[245] *Ibid.*; Stefan Palan, *The Efficient Market Hypothesis and its Validity in Today's Market*, GRIN Verlag, 2007; Colin Read, *The Efficient Market Hypothesists: Bachelier, Samuelson, Fama, Ross, Tobin and Shiller*, Springer, 2012.

financial markets. Therefore, prices must reflect the reality on the ground.

If prices do not reflect the reality of the markets and participants within it, and thus is inefficiently formed, investments would also be affected and will not flow where they should go. For instance, those unqualified firms that need to pay a higher price for obtaining resources would end by having it at a lower cost, and the opposite is valid for qualified business units that merit paying less but in fact pay at a higher rate.

The cost of inefficiency is higher, and can go beyond financial markets. Social consequences would be one of the costs and the society as whole would pay for it.[246]

Financial Markets Regulation

Regulation

Another important phenomenon that can affect the way markets function is regulation. Markets and market participants are concerned with this phenomenon. The American Heritage Dictionary defines regulation as either "a principle, rule, or law designed to control or govern conducts" or "a governmental order having the force of law." Put simply, regulation is the state of being regulated or the act of regulating. However, it is worth mentioning that the term "regulation" can embrace different definitions and have different meanings in different contexts. In regards to financial markets, Nobel Prize-winning economist Joseph Stiglitz related the importance of regulation to the well-being of society as a whole. He states that

> markets are at the center of every successful economy. Nevertheless, unfettered markets often do not serve society well. Over the past 200 years, economic theory and historical experience have shown that financial markets often fail to perform their essential functions of managing risk and allocating capital well, with disastrous social and economic consequences.[247]

The regulating of business and commerce existed in ancient civilizations, and concepts such as standardization or having measures to monitor activities and interactions have existed since the eras of the Egyptians

---

[246] Mircea Trandafir, http://mirceatrandafir.com/teaching/econ435/Chapter_12.pdf.

[247] Joseph Stiglitz, "Regulation and Failure," in *New Perspectives on Regulation*, ed. David Moss and John Cisternino, Cambridge, Mass.: The Tobin Project, 2009, p. 21.

and Romans.[248] In our recent history, government regulations concerning financial systems were introduced once the importance of financial markets and the role they play within the economy became known. The idea of regulating markets was first proposed for the sake of protecting market participants from fraud and fraudulent business and investment schemes.

For as long as there have been regulations, businesses and individuals have complained that they are against freedom and would hurt the efficiency of markets. However, statistics confirm that regulatory costs in many fields are justified and paid back by the results obtained. The wide range of benefits from regulatory policies and regulations in general cover everything from the environment to health, while regulations on industry confirm that new jobs created offset the cost of regulation. Yearly studies conducted by the Office of Management and Budget in the United States, in which it analyzes cost-benefit reports, affirm that between 2000 and 2010, on average, the value of benefits was almost seven times higher than the costs.[249] Others studies, for instance one by Wells Fargo and Gallup, showed that while 9% of small businesses complained about the regulations in their area of business, 14% confirmed that they have benefited from regulation and gained new customers.[250] The list of the benefits is also supported by data from the U.S Bureau of Labor Statistics. It confirms that job losses resulting from environmental regulations were offset by other jobs needed to achieve the objectives.[251]

Regulation and the Free-Market Economy

The definition of a free market can be ambiguous, mainly because it sounds like a market without a regulatory mechanism or simply a market within which prices freely reflect the law of supply and demand. Sometimes it can mean a competitive market without any form of oligopoly or monopoly.[252] Regulation is able in some circumstances to increase the economic efficiency and help avoid external costs to offset the value created. We also need to confirm that governments' interventions to regulate the

---

[248] John Braithwaite and Péter Drahos, *Global Business Regulation*, Cambridge University Press, 2000.

[249] Darryl F. Jackson, "Is government regulation really so bad for business?" *Business Journal*, 2016: http://www.bizjournals.com/bizjournals/how-to/growth-strategies/2016/03/is-government-regulation-really-bad-for-business.html.

[250] Wells Fargo, "Small Businesses Enter 2016 with More Optimism," https://www.wellsfargo.com/about/press/2016/small-business-optimism_0216/.

[251] U.S. Bureau of Labor Statistics, news release, http://www.bls.gov/news.release/mslo.t02.htm.

[252] Paul Craig Roberts, "The Case for Regulation: The Failure of Free Market Economics," Center for Research on Globalization, 2011.

economy and markets as important social institutions are not always welcome. In the United States, for example, there has been a tendency over many years toward increased regulation.[253] Thus, regulating different aspects of the economy must be done in a way that marginal costs and benefits are respected.

Finance and Regulation

Financial systems are regulated in different ways and with measures that can vary in terms of efficiency and intensity. As mentioned above, many of the regulations put in place concerning financial markets were designed because increasing fraudulent practices were considered as harmful to the markets' healthy functioning. For example, in the United States, the Securities Act of 1933[254] was mainly aimed at reducing fraudulent activities by obliging the complete disclosure of all the information that is relevant to securities issued and offered to the public.[255] Acts such as manipulating market prices, issuing misleading financial statements or any others that are deceptive and could affect participants' perceptions were declared as illegal. However, these measures could not prevent decisions poorly made by market participants and would not guarantee them the desired results. In fact, organizations that exist in all the developed economies around the globe, such as the Securities and Exchange Commission in the United States, are there to enforce the laws regarding markets and the free flow of information. They guarantee the disclosure of the information, monitor the system and facilitate the implementation of additional laws over time when deemed necessary.

Regulations can be different from one type of institution to another; however, the principle remains the same. The performance of financial markets and institutions are sensitive to regulations, and their impact can go beyond the markets themselves. For example, recent financial crises had devastating consequences in some countries and the intervention of their respective governments to save their financial systems augmented the public debt through creating money without anything to back its value. The result was that confidence in the financial systems was undermined and the social costs were not easy to face. On the one hand, the lack of regulation created dysfunctional systems, and on the other hand, authorities' interventions worsened the situation. The group Better Market, a nonprofit financial reform

---

[253] Columbian College of Art and Sciences, Regulatory Studies Center, https://regulatorystudies.columbian.gwu.edu; https://regulatorystudies.columbian.gwu.edu/sites/regulatorystudies.columbian.gwu.edu/files/downloads/Pages-in-the-federal-register-2014.png.

[254] https://www.sec.gov/about/laws/sa33.pdf.

[255] https://www.sec.gov/about/laws/sea34.pdf.

advocacy group, estimated the cost of the 2008 financial crisis at about $12.8 trillion, affirming that the economic costs were not possible to measure.[256]

Therefore, if we accept the fact that financial crises not only cause output to decline but cause economic downturns that can last for long periods and that can be experienced in various forms such as unemployment, the disappearance of retirement investments, lost educational opportunities and much more, the dilemma is evident: How much regulation would guarantee the safety of markets and participants without undermining efficiency or reducing the competition? Such an issue, in modern days, must be faced rigorously, based on knowledge and through independent institutions that are not ideologically motivated and put in place to serve the citizens first by guaranteeing a well-functioning system. Considering the United States as a monetary union, the way it functions can be a tool for analyzing monetary union projects such as the one of the GCC, where, clearly, the institutional conditions required to guarantee the system are not met. The U.S. regulatory structure includes 12 specialized agencies of the national government, and many activities in the financial sector are subject to regulation by more than one of them. In addition, regulators at the level of U.S. state governments exist for banking, insurance and securities trading.[257]

Financial Markets and Globalization

In the aftermath of World War II, developed nations were eager to achieve more trade, and toward that end decided to go for more liberalization. That was how the General Agreement on Tariffs and Trade (GATT) was launched. The GATT later became the World Trade Organization. As barriers to trade were reduced and different costs such as transportation diminished, the greater flow of goods and services within the international trade and business system could not be sustained without more liberalization within the international financial system. The role that a financial system plays within a country, the international financial system plays at the global level.[258] It consists of a full range of interest- and return-bearing securities, banks and other financial institutions. It includes various financial markets that trade and by doing that form prices. It is also a place for transactions such as private equity and/or hedge funds' joint ventures. It is worth mentioning that the international financial system cannot function without the presence of sound

---

[256] Eleazar David Melendez, "Wall Street Reporter," Huffington Post, 2013: http://www.huffingtonpost.com/2013/02/14/financial-crisis-cost-gao_n_2687553.html.

[257] http://www.gao.gov/products/GAO-13-180; U.S. Government Accountability Office: http://www.gao.gov/products/GAO-16-175.

[258] Gail D. Fosler, "International Monetary System vs. International Financial System – and the Significance for Policy Makers," Chatham House, 2011.

currencies, which must be there to make the payments system work properly through the international monetary system.

Considering that after World War II nations were able to conduct more trade with each other, mainly due to the reduction of national barriers, the process of regulating and managing the flow of goods and services could not be done without the crucial role that the international financial and monetary system has played and continues to play. We accept the fact that the global economic system, in theory, is out there to allocate resources such as land, labor and capital in the most efficient way, to produce the goods and services that societies demand. This is a highly complicated task. To combine the aforementioned factors of production, including capital, with the aim of creating outputs, the flow of goods and services produced would later need to be compensated through generating an adequate flow of payments and investments. This is done through the financial system.[259]

The crucial role of the global financial system can be explained through seven functionalities:

1. The global financial system is considered as a mechanism that provides a conduit for public savings. Securities that are sold within markets such as bonds, stocks, etc., give necessary tools to surplus units to associate profits with their savings. This is how, through investments, productivity will rise and ultimately increase the world's living standard.

2. If current savings are considered like a flow of funds, savings that are accumulated over years represent wealth. Global markets in fact provide the opportunity of storing wealth. They would preserve the value of securities until they are needed to become available for spending. Unlike other ways of storing wealth that would depreciate rapidly, the risk of loss is considered less than in the other forms of stored wealth. Here it is worth mentioning that wealth is defined as the sum of the values of all assets held at any point of time, as demonstrated through the formula below, in which W_t is the sum of the values of all individual assets (A_{it}) held over time (t).[260]

$$\mathbf{W_t = \sum_i A_{it}}$$

---

[259] F.J. Fabozzi, F. Modigliani, Frank J Jones and M. G. Ferri, *Foundations of Financial Markets and Institutions*, Prentice Hall, 2002; Claudia M. Buch, *Globalization of Financial Markets: Causes of Incomplete Integration and Consequences for Economic Policy*, Springer, 2004; Madura, *International Financial Management*; Mankiw and Taylor, *Economics*.

[260] Mankiw and Taylor, *Economics*, *ibid.*

Consequently, wealth that is accumulated over years will be calculated through the formula below, where ΔW_t is the change in wealth at t, S_t is current savings, r_t represents the average rate of return on accumulated securities and W_{t-1} is wealth accumulated a year before.

$$\Delta \mathbf{W}_t = \mathbf{S}_t + \mathbf{r}_t . \mathbf{W}_{t-1}$$

This is how the financial wealth of a society can be calculated, and it represents the wealth of a nation in terms of securities that are held. In developed economies, financial wealth grows over time. For instance, in 2003 and before the financial crisis, foreign investors held $8 trillion in securities issued in the United States and Americans themselves held $80 trillion, which was ten times bigger. Although we must subtract from the $80 trillion the debt owed by market participants in order to obtain the net value of financial wealth in the U.S., this accumulated wealth offers future purchasing power. Moreover, as such, it is also considered a source of income. Thus, the income generated this way would increase consumption and at the same time be a source for new savings. All these would result in a higher standard of living. Mathematically, wealth-created income is presented through the formula below, where Y_t is income created that would be considered earned by the rate of return at time t (r_t) through wealth currently held at time t (W_t).[261]

$$\mathbf{Y}_t = \mathbf{W}_t . \mathbf{r}_t$$

3. The other issue of importance concerning the global economy and trade is the concept of liquidity, which financial markets offer. In developed economies, financial markets can turn securities into cash immediately and with little risk of loss. The fact that cash and money in general, in comparison with other financial instruments, offer the lowest return and purchasing power is eroded rapidly due to inflation cause surplus units to prefer other instruments than cash. However, thanks to financial markets, whenever liquidity is needed, the markets will make securities liquid.

4. In connection with liquidity comes the concept of credit. The international financial system, in addition to directing the flow of savings toward investment opportunities around the globe, also performs the task of directing and facilitating access to funds for deficit units, which can be in the form of both consumption and

---

[261] *Ibid.*

investments. As mentioned earlier, with the globalized world, businesses and individuals try to expand and go beyond their borders, constantly facing the issue of credit, and are well aware of how it is of vital importance to their businesses.

5. The international financial system also provides a payment mechanism by including the international monetary system, made of a network of money flows and institutions. These are either governmental or not, and are responsible for establishing the quantity of money that would circulate, as well as for setting the basis for currency exchanges. Moreover, the system defines requirements that would guarantee payment obligations across countries. This is simply a mechanism that facilitates transactions and finalizes payments due. Checking accounts, for instance, have long served as a medium of exchange, but today technology has helped the system enormously. A buyer can pay immediately and electronically from a remote place, debiting her/his account, or obtain credits whenever her/his account is short of resources. Today one can pay from China to buy products in Europe. All these are managed efficiently through the international financial and monetary system.

6. Another important function of the international financial system is to provide insurance and offer shelter to those exposed to different kinds of risks. These risks can vary in type and intensity and can cover life, health, property and income, among many others. Life insurance companies operating in the markets offer compensation against possible loss of these items, which can damage the well-being and the daily rhythm of people's lives. In fact, the system makes it possible for people to transfer their risks to those that are willing to accept them, and by doing that they share the risk.

7. The international financial and monetary system also serves as a tool in the hands of policymakers around the world, to intervene when it is necessary, with the aim of, for instance, stabilizing the economy or controlling inflation. Therefore, governments and central banks separately (since in developed economies they are independent of each other) can use interest rates or other policies to affect the way the economy functions.

The chart on the next page highlights how the financial system contributes to the real economy of different countries.[262]

---

[262] Anjan Thakor, "International Financial Markets: A Diverse System Is the Key to Commerce," Center for Capital Markets, 2015.

Today, the international financial system is as integrated as it has ever been in history. Even small countries with their small national financial systems are part of an integrated global one. Technologies have made the impossible possible, and financial systems around the world are tied together in different ways. In addition, the deregulation of financial systems in general has fostered the integration of financial markets and institutions, mainly through the initiatives of developed and industrialized countries.

For less developed countries, being part of the global system as well as being able to reap the benefits of globalization is primordial. However, the structure that exists in developed countries is not only the result of technological progress, because it is knowledge-based. In addition, it is also the result of a certain way of thinking, living and working achieved over time. Therefore, for less developed countries, before being connected to others, experiences and methods of the developed countries must be studied in detail.

In a highly connected world, the integrated financial system is not an exception. In 1997, the stock exchanges in East Asia fell rapidly right after a selloff by investors. When Hong Kong's Hang Seng index declined more than 23% in almost one week, the decline affected the performance of markets in China, Europe and the U.S. In one week, a dramatic decline was experienced around the world, and 27 October 1997 was dubbed "Black Monday."

Without entering into the details of the 1997 crisis, it is worth mentioning a few critical particularities of it. Markets in the region were underdeveloped, and with a heavily managed exchange rate policy, the inflow of capital and assets could not be allocated efficiently and caused buildups of available resources within national markets. Risks associated with these flows were enormous and not shared globally. Therefore, risk management that was poorly done contributed to what happened to the Thai currency and later the tremendous pressure on the Hong Kong dollar, bringing down the markets.[263]

As seen through the table below, East Asian countries were able to recover, however, the risks of being contaminated is always there. Some markets are not well-developed but are connected to the wider global networks. As mentioned, due to technologies, new investment techniques and financial instruments created out of nothing that are heavily traded, fostered interdependencies between markets and the actors within markets make them integrated in a way that a disturbance in the Far East can affect investors in the Far West. Therefore, financial markets, as important as they are in bringing prosperity and growth to economies, can turn the other way and create disasters.[264]

East Asian GDP
Average annual percentage growth

	1987-1996	1997-1999	2000-2006
Hong Kong	5.2	-0.8	4.7
Indonesia	7.1	-6.4	4.9
Korea	8.1	1.0	4.6
Malaysia	9.5	-0.8	4.7
Philippines	3.6	1.4	4.6
Singapore	9.2	2.8	4.6
Taiwan	7.2	5.1	3.3
Thailand	9.5	-3.3	5.1
East Asia*	**7.6**	**0.0**	**4.5**

* Excluding China and Japan
Source: IMF, CEIC, RBA

The system can affect easily macroeconomic aspects of a country, such as economic growth, GDP and living standards of each citizen. The way the international financial system connects different markets and institutions functions as a facilitator of resource allocation. It guarantees the flow of available resources from surplus units to deficit units while creating opportunities for businesses and households. This is how businesses can obtain resources they need at lower cost through a wider range of funds available to them. Individuals benefit from investment opportunities and eventually employment increases. As we have seen, the international financial

---

[263] Glenn Stevens, "The Asian Crisis, A Retrospective," Reserve Bank of Australia, 2007: http://www.rba.gov.au/speeches/2007/sp-gov-180707.html.
[264] Richard Carnery, *Lessons from Asian Financial Crisis*, Routledge, 2009; Nadin Poser, *The Asian Financial Financial Crisis and Institutional Change in East Asia Crisis*, GRIN Verlag, 2008; Jikon Lai, Springer, 2012.

system is vast and manages a flow of resources that are widely used across countries, impacting the global economy and ultimately having consequences for national economies. The increasing interconnectivity that does not know boundaries needs to be monitored through a set of harmonized regulations agreed at international level, so the complexities created through this interconnectedness will not lead to crises that can cause devastating outcomes in different places around the world.

Europe is a case that must be studied and restudied. Between 1980 and 1990, many regulations were eliminated, resulting in the expansion of markets. A series of privatizations saw state-owned companies sold to individuals and helped Europe go through the integration process and ultimately share the same currency, monetary policy and a fully integrated financial market. There were also few crises. More recently, there has been the Greek crisis, while the consequences of Brexit are still unknown, raising the question of how much regulation would guarantee the safety of markets and participants without undermining efficiency and without harming the global economy. Other questions remain to be answered also, for instance, whether Greece would be better off unilaterally or as part of a regional bloc.[265]

Financial Markets and Foreign Exchange

Within the world economy, countries buy and sell goods and services from each other. In addition, based on the concept of the allocation of resources, nations that are in surplus lend to those that are in deficit, and at the same time, based on investment opportunities available, they invest abroad or accept the investments made by other countries within their own territories. If we exclude foreign aid and other politically motivated economic exchanges, it is seen that the same principles governing national businesses govern also businesses and economic activities conducted internationally. Thus, nations buy goods and services from each other based on their needs and prices offered to them. Evidently, if circumstances change, there would be a shift in demand, supply, or perhaps both of them. Subsequently, prices would be affected as well, and ultimately the pattern would change. Countries take actions and change their decisions accordingly. Since nobody can just live by borrowing and being a deficit unit forever, they need to adjust themselves to the reality of economics; therefore, they need to reduce consumption or increase production in order to face the coming payments. Countries with different currencies must know the price of their currencies in terms of those of other countries. An exchange rate is simply the price of one currency in terms of another. Currencies are traded in the foreign exchange ("forex")

[265] Detlev Hummel, *The Euro Financial Crisis: Impacts on Banking, Capital Markets, and Regulation*, Potsdam University Press, 2013.

market. Being an institutional arrangement that regulates buying and selling of different foreign monies, it is considered as a kind of money market within the financial system.

In the presence of integrated and connected financial markets that manage the increasing flow of international trade and investments every day, the need for exchange currencies also must be addressed. The foreign exchange market represents a global network that functions as an intermediary for such transactions.[266] Therefore, affirming the fact that a national economy is tied to other nations through international trade and capital flows, countries must go through the foreign exchange market in order to regulate these flows. Speculation on the value of currencies based on interest rate differentials takes place within this market as well.

The forex market also offers a wide range of other financial instruments such as swap and spot. Being connected to the concept of sovereignty, a decentralized mechanism that is functional 24 hours a day makes it possible to confirm that the foreign exchange market is the largest market and the most liquid one. In April 2016, the average amount of foreign exchange traded was $5.1 trillion on daily basis. Although this was down from the $5.4 trillion that had been traded daily in 2013, it gives an idea of how huge the forex market is. Besides so-called dealers, the financial institutions that are the main drivers for the growth of the forex market are small banks, institutional investors, insurance companies and hedge funds.[267]

Among the many currencies traded in the market, the United States dollar is still considered as the vehicle currency. In more than 85% of the market's total activity, the dollar was on one side of the transaction. A vehicle currency is one that dominates international contracts made by parties that are not residents of the country that issued the currency. As we noted previously, with the ways that markets are connected and respond to new information, the effects are rapidly seen through supply and demand, and are ultimately reflected in prices. This is why, for instance, the euro lost value right after the Greek debt crisis began, declining almost 8% since 2010.[268] As the foreign exchange market can be considered a competitive market, changes occur rapidly as circumstances change. On the one hand, trading of euro currency

---

[266] Ian H. Gidday, *Global Financial Markets*, D.C. Heat and Company, 1994.

[267] Kostyantyn Kondakov, *How to View and Forecast the Market: Forex Fundamental Indicators*, Bookbaby, 2013; Adam Kritzer, *Forex for Beginners: A comprehensive guide to profiting from the global currency market*, Apress, 2013; Madura, *International Financial Management*.

[268] Bank for International Settlements, "Triennial Central Bank Survey: Foreign exchange turnover," 2016: http://www.bis.org/publ/rpfx16fx.pdf.

pairs such as USD/EUR experienced a decline in turnover of about $119 billion. On the other hand, trading of EUR/SEK and EUR/NOK increased.[269]

The foreign exchange market is very dynamic and this is why it is also liquid. It is highly sensitive to changes across nations and around the world. During 2016, currencies of developed economies such as Australia (Australian dollar) or Switzerland (franc) saw their share of the market diminish respectively by 3.4% and 2.1% while Canada and Norway were able to gain greater shares of the turnover. The foreign exchange market is not an exclusive club of developed economies. Emerging countries compete as well. By 2016, the Chinese renminbi had an average turnover of $202 billion on a daily basis, registering a 2% rise from 2013. In connection with the Chinese currency, the USD/CNY pair was among the most traded pairs, reaching sixth place. The renminbi's rise in the share of global forex turnover was mainly achieved through trading against the US dollar.

Other Asian countries, mainly emerging economies, are also part of the foreign exchange market's dynamics. The Indian rupee, Korean won and the Thai baht gained better positions and saw their shares of the market increase. However, countries such as Russia and Mexico experienced substantial declines in their shares of the market. The foreign exchange market reflects the weight of national economies. The more a national economy is solid and competitive, the more the currency's position and consequently its share of the market is higher.[270]

It is very important to consider the market turnover by both instruments as well as counterparties. Concerning financial instruments, as was the case for other markets, there are instruments that are also used within the forex market. Among others, spot and swap were the most exploited ones:[271]

A spot transaction involves a direct transaction between the currencies involved. In terms of timing, it is the most rapid one and would deliver and finalize the transaction within 48 hours. It is a direct exchange that takes place, and the medium of exchange is cash. Other types of contracts are not involved, and as such it is not an interest-bearing instrument.

A Swap is not considered a standardized contract, and as such the parties involved agree to exchange currencies for a period, at the end of which the transaction must be considered reversed.

[269] Madura, *International Financial Management*. Andrew Sheng, "A Strong US Dollar, Global Trade and Crisis," The Straits Times, 2015: http://www.straitstimes.com/opinion/a-strong-us-dollar-global-trade-and-crises.

[270] Madura, *International Financial Management*; Gidday, *Global Financial Markets*; George Mangus, "China's currency policies need an overhaul," Bloomberg.

[271] Bank for International Settlements, "Triennial Central Bank Survey."

Spot and swap being the main categories of foreign exchange instruments, in 2013 they experienced growth according to the growth of the market's turnover. The spot market grew by 38%, reaching $2 trillion per day. Between 2010 and 2013, it was considered a driver that contributed to around 40% of the rise that occurred within the entire market in that period. The same is almost the case for the swap market, where $2.2 trillion per day of swap contracts accounted for 42% of the transactions that took place. Foreign exchange trading activities are also conducted over-the-counter (OTC), in the derivatives market and through forward contracts.[272]

The traded volume of the two categories registered opposing trends in 2016. While the spot market fell by 19% and the amount traded decreased to $1.7 trillion on a daily basis, the swap market experienced a 6% increase in 2016 and trades amounted to $2.4 trillion per day. In 2016, swap was confirmed as the most traded tool within the forex market.[273]

Another important aspect of the foreign exchange market is the counterparty – "an individual or a bank that deals with international financial exchange and ultimately is considered as the guarantor of the contract."[274] In other words, a counterparty means "the opposite party in a currency transaction. If you are the buyer, the counterparty is the seller, and vice versa."[275] Contrary to other financial markets, the foreign exchange market can be considered as a hierarchal one. The largest commercial and investment banks form the interbank foreign exchange market. These account for almost 51% of the total amount transacted. Right after them come smaller banks and businesses, and the extent of their activities reaches many countries. Other financial institutions such as pension funds, insurance companies and mutual funds have participated increasingly within the market since early 2000.[276] Central banks also participate in the market. These banks decide money supply, interest rates and how inflation must be managed; they have access to foreign exchange reserves and can use them to stabilize economies, so the way they behave can affect the forex market and its participants.

A big share of the market involves financial institutions other than reporting dealers – a term that refers to institutions or participants within the market that report details and information on their activities to monetary

---

272 Madura, *International Financial Management*; Gidday, *Global Financial Markets.*

273 Gidday, *Global Financial Markets*, *ibid.*

274 Forex Glossary: http://www.cmsfx.com/en/forex-education/Forex-Glossary/counterparty/.

275 Forex Trading Charts.com: http://forex.tradingcharts.com/glossary/Forex%2BTrading/Counterparty.html.

276 Gabriele Galati and Michael Melvin, "Why has FX trading surged? Explaining the 2004 triennial survey," Bank for International Settlements, 2004: http://www.bis.org/publ/qtrpdf/r_qt0412f.pdf.

authorities.[277] Trading by non-financial entities such as governments or corporations was modest, at about 7% of the market.

Exchange Rate Quotations and Decision-making Tools

Information related to major currencies is available continuously through different portals and means of communication. This is essential for a market economy since participants cannot make decisions efficiently without having details and transparency. Today, as technology has made tremendous contributions to the growth and development of any market, online quotations are available within few clicks of the mouse.[278]

In addition to currency tables, currency charts increase the efficiency of the markets for a better allocation of resources. The currency chart is a graphical reproduction of historical data of quoted currencies through sophisticated software that has manifold options which ultimately enable participants to make decisions for achieving a better trading performance. Historical trade patterns and details are not the only things that are graphically observable; indicators that signal abnormalities or statistical details such as momentum, volatility or ultimate oscillator are also put in place this way to work for the market's efficiency.[279]

Exchange Rate Systems

The international financial and monetary system has witnessed different types of exchange rate systems. After World War II and until the beginning of the 1970s, through the Bretton Woods system, governments maintained specific rates for their currencies, which could vary within a 1% limit. Afterwards, mainly to avoid the overvaluation of currencies, major countries in the world decided in 1971 to augment the range of variation for exchange rates from 1% to 2.15%. This gave a range of oscillation to exchange rates while still respecting their fixed nature. It was in 1973 that a system called dirty floating was put in place – boundaries were eliminated and currencies of major economies could float. Exchange rates then became market-determined, although governments could still intervene to influence their currencies.[280]

A freely floating system is a type of exchange rate system in which markets are generally free from government manipulation. There are also

---

[277] Reuters, Financial Glossary, http://glossary.reuters.com/index.php?title=Reporting_Dealer.
[278] Madura, *International Financial Management*; Forex Glossary: http://www.cmsfx.com/en/forex-education/Forex-Glossary/counterparty/.
[279] Reuters, Currencies Quote: http://www.reuters.com/finance/currencies/quote.
[280] Madura, *International Financial Management*; Ross P. Buckley, *International Financial System: Policy and Regulation*, Kluwer Law International, 2009.

currencies whose value is pegged to other currencies, or, as was the case for the European countries before the euro, their currencies were pegged to a multi-currency unit of account called the European Currency Unit (ECU). Therefore, European currencies were also pegged to each other. This type of system is known as an exchange rate mechanism (ERM).[281] ERMs are necessary for any monetary union project. As shown below, different types of exchange rate systems can be created, assuming the exchange rate is flexible and based on variables that can affect many aspects of a country and its economy such as macroeconomic factors and the reliability of its financial system.[282]

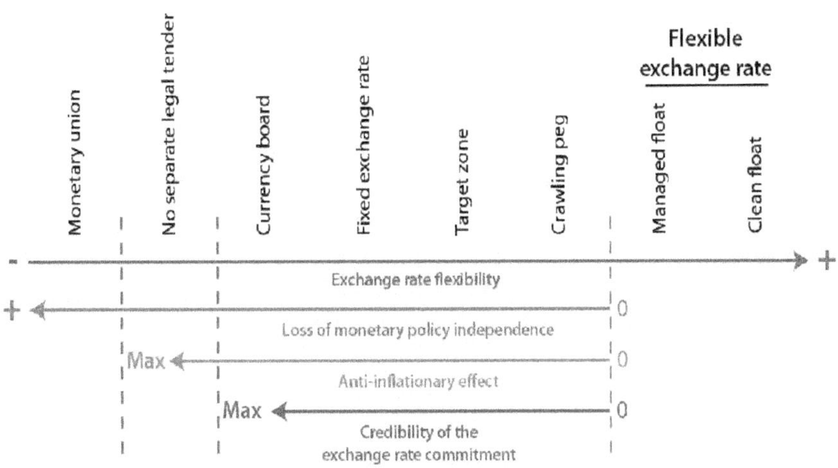

Exchange Rate Mechanism (ERM)

The exchange rate mechanism was the main factor that facilitated European integration. The European exchange rate mechanism was launched years before the monetary union was considered complete. In 1979, countries that were part of the European Community introduced it in order to control fluctuations of exchange rates and to guarantee their monetary stability. This prepared the community for the complete and successful economic and monetary union and for the introduction of the common currency, the euro.

---

[281] European Commission, "What is ERMII?" http://ec.europa.eu/economy_finance/euro/adoption/erm2/index_en.htm.

[282] Policonomics, 2012: http://www.policonomics.com/flexible-exchange-rate/; Madura, *International Financial Management.*

In 1992, the European countries experienced economic conditions that were not of the same kind or origin, and many of them were in recession.[283] Germany, in order to control inflation, introduced a tight monetary policy, and consequently interest rates increased. Capital flew to Germany from other members that were trying to stimulate their economies through lower interest rates. As this reduced their supplies of funds, their interest rates increased and aggregate spending diminished.[284] This confirms the degree to which European Community members' economies were integrated.

The associated risks were limited mainly because the ERM required European central banks to maintain exchange rates among themselves within already defined ranges of movement.

The European countries were not able to stimulate their economies. Though they attempted in different ways, such as direct intervention in the foreign exchange markets, the result was not satisfactory and tensions rose. As they had different and conflicting objectives of reducing unemployment and reducing inflation at the same time, the British and Italians were forced to suspend their participation in the exchange rate mechanism and preferred to take care of high unemployment at home rather than accommodating inflation in Germany.

The Maastricht Treaty[285] was a proposal for a single currency. The European countries wanted to facilitate the flow of capital and trade among themselves through the elimination of exchange rate risks. An ERM functions on the basis of prefixed margins that allow exchange rates to oscillate, and the European exchange rate mechanism was done in that way, functioning through a weighted average of participating countries' currencies. With the exception of the Italian lira, the currencies had to fluctuate within a margin of 2.25%. The euro's value was established in 1998, and in 1999 the EMR2 replaced the EMR and currencies were allowed to oscillate within a range of 15% to try to ensure economic stability within the region.[286] The Deutsche mark of Germany was acting as an anchor and was a source of stability for the system.[287]

---

[283] Spanish Economic Association, "1992, Crisis in Europe," http://asesec.org/CFCweb/Desc_Rec_ingles/european_11Mar2015.pdf.
[284] Lars Jonung and Thomas Hegberg, "European Economy," European Commission, 2005: http://ec.europa.eu/economy_finance/publications/publication692_en.pdf.
[285] European Union, Treaty on European Union, https://europa.eu/european-union/sites/europaeu/files/docs/body/treaty_on_european_union_en.pdf.
[286] European Commission, "What is ERM2?" http://ec.europa.eu/economy_finance/euro/adoption/erm2/index_en.htm.
[287] Brandon Mitchener, "An Anchor Begins to Drag as the Tide Tests the Mark," *New York Times*, 1993: http://www.nytimes.com/1993/06/26/business/worldbusiness/26iht-anchor.html.

Over-the-Counter Markets

Over-the-counter markets are considered as opaque because buyers and sellers do not trade through a centralized system in order to aggregate bids and offers. Instead, all terms and details are negotiated privately. Sometimes counterparties are not even aware of the terms of trade and prices that are negotiated elsewhere. This is why many details on OTC markets are not publicly available. The securities that are traded over-the-counter are of different types and available within other markets too – government and corporate bonds, derivatives, asset-backed securities as well as currencies. Activities that take place within an OTC market are done by a dealer. Some OTC markets function through intermediaries called brokers; contrary to a dealer that trades on its own account, a broker helps negotiations go through between sellers and buyers while respecting the anonymities of the counterparties.[288] The table below gives a sense of the magnitude of OTC trading.[289]

OTC foreign exchange turnover

Net-net basis,[1] daily averages in April, in billions of US dollars

Instrument	2001	2004	2007	2010	2013	**2016**
Foreign exchange instruments	1,239	1,934	3,324	3,971	5,355	**5,088**
Spot transactions	386	631	1,005	1,488	2,046	**1,654**
Outright forwards	130	209	362	475	679	**700**
Foreign exchange swaps	656	954	1,714	1,759	2,239	**2,383**
Currency swaps	7	21	31	43	54	**96**
Options and other products[2]	60	119	212	207	337	**254**
Memo:						
Turnover at April 2016 exchange rates[3]	*1,381*	*1,884*	*3,123*	*3,665*	*4,915*	***5,088***
Exchange-traded derivatives[4]	*12*	*25*	*77*	*145*	*145*	***115***

[1] Adjusted for local and cross-border inter-dealer double-counting (ie "net-net" basis). [2] The category "other FX products" covers highly leveraged transactions and/or trades whose notional amount is variable and where a decomposition into individual plain vanilla components was impractical or impossible. [3] Non-US dollar legs of foreign currency transactions were converted into original currency amounts at average exchange rates for April of each survey year and then reconverted into US dollar amounts at average April 2016 exchange rates. [4] Sources: Euromoney Tradedata; Futures Industry Association; The Options Clearing Corporation; BIS derivatives statistics. Foreign exchange futures and options traded worldwide.

288 Over the Counter Markets, http://press.princeton.edu/chapters/s9623.pdf; Darrell Duffile, Nicolae Garleaun and Lasse Heje Pederson, "Over the Counter Market," *Econometrica*, 73(6), 2005.

289 Bank for International Settlements, "Triennial Central Bank Survey."

Most of the OTC markets' forex turnover takes place in the U.S., the U.K., Japan, Singapore and Hong Kong. Within the European Union, forex turnover has been highest in France, followed by Germany. Within the GCC countries, the Kingdom of Saudi Arabia has the largest OTC market for forex.[290]

As mentioned previously, spot transactions and foreign exchange currency swaps are the most exploited instruments on the OTC markets. The data confirm that the main currencies are the US dollar, followed by the euro and the Japanese yen. Reporting dealers and non-reporting banks are among the main counterparties, after local and cross-border financial institutions.[291]

Although many financial products that are relatively standardized are offered and traded in large quantities within the OTC markets, the increasing use of these markets can also be explained through the fact that there is also a range of products that are traded in relatively small quantities, which lack liquidity and transparency.[292] These are preferably offered and accepted within the OTC markets mainly because tailoring products to the needs of participants is easily done. It is worth mentioning that reforming the OTC markets is among the priorities of financial authorities.[293]

Types of Exchange Rates

To further clarify exchange rates, prices of currency are formed through nominal and real exchange rates.[294] The latter is simply defined as the rate at which goods and services of different countries are traded. Pricing on foreign exchange markets is done through the former, nominal exchange rates. This is the quantity of a currency exchanged for a unit of another country's money, or the value of currency A in terms of currency B.[295] For instance, if we assume that the British pound's value is $1.535, it implies that $1 equals 0.651 of a British pound.

The real and nominal rates are closely related, since countries trade goods and services with different currencies. To know the real exchange rate, we need to use the nominal exchange rate to figure out prices expressed in a common currency. This is important because it affects trading of goods and services among countries. If a producer in one country must buy a raw material elsewhere, it needs to know where it can find the cheapest price. The real exchange rate would help the producer during the decision making process. It is a variable to not only the nominal rate, but also to prices of goods

290 *Ibid.*
291 *Ibid.*
292 Over the Counter Markets, http://press.princeton.edu/chapters/s9623.pdf.
293 *Ibid.*
294 Mankiw and Taylor, *Economics.*
295 Madura, *Financial Markets and Institutions.*

and services produced and offered in other countries around the world. The calculation can be simply done through the formula below:

Real Exchange Rate =
(Nominal Exchange Rate x Domestic Price) / (Foreign Price)

Since each currency can buy many other currencies, the result is that nominal exchange rates are also many. Changes in the rates are mainly studied through indices that are averaged and often used in calculations.

Purchasing Power Parity

Exchange rates change constantly over time *vis-à-vis* other currencies; for instance, the euro can gain value against one currency and at the same time lose value against another currency. The simplest theory of exchange rates, called purchasing power parity (PPP), explains the way they are affected in the long-run. The theory is based on the concept of "one price," and it means that a product must be sold at the same price in any market in order to avoid profit opportunities being unexploited, since differences in the prices of the same product in different markets create arbitrage opportunities. Thus, if product Z is cheaper in country A than in country B, traders can go to country A to buy the Z and sell it in country B. Athough this can continue until the prices are the same in both countries, the law of one price suggests that a currency must buy the same quantity of product Z all around the globe. In other words, purchasing power parity states that the real value of a currency must be the same everywhere. Therefore, a currency must have the same purchasing power everywhere.[296]

Purchasing power parity proposes that the nominal exchange rate between countries is connected to the level of the prices formed in each of them. Therefore, if, one unit of country A's currency can buy the same quantity of product Z in country B, the number of country B's currency units in terms of country A's currency must reflect the price of product Z in country A. Otherwise, the purchasing power of country A's currency would not be the same in both countries A and B.

Expressed mathematically, P is the price of a basket of goods in country A as measured in terms of its currency; P* is the price of a basket of goods in country B and measured in terms of its currency, and *e* is the nominal exchange rate, which is the value of country B's currency for buying one unit of country A's currency. Since in country A the price level is P, the purchasing power of A's currency within A itself would be 1/P. Abroad, country A's currency can be exchanged into *e* units of country B's currency which has a

---

[296] Mankiw and Taylor, *Economics*.

purchasing power of e/P^*; therefore "1/P" must equal "e/P^*." Thus, the equation **1/P = *e*/P*** once rearranged, is **1=*e*P/P***.[297] To sum up, if the purchasing power parity of a currency is the same at home and elsewhere, the real exchange rate would not change and the relative prices of goods and services would remain unchanged as well. Rearranging again our previous formula gives us the equation for obtaining the nominal exchange rate:

$$\mathbf{e = P^* / P}$$

According to the purchasing power parity theory, this rate reflects the price level within the two countries, and would indicate nominal interest rate movements in the future if it is based on changes that occur in price levels.

This theory has limitations. Foremost, many goods are not easily traded across borders. Secondly, tradable goods and services are not always perfect substitutes when produced and offered in different places. These two reasons offer an understanding of why nominal rates change continuously. Due to the limitations of the purchasing power theory, the model cannot be a perfect theory of exchange rate determination, however it does offer an easy understanding of exchange rates by affirming that large and consistent movements of nominal rates give clues to changes that occur in price levels.

Empirical evidence shows that there is a relationship between changes in nominal exchange rates and inflation rates. Countries with a decline in purchasing power experience a deterioration of their foreign exchange values.[298]

In open market macroeconomics, the PPP theory has allowed for analysis in regards to evaluating nominal exchange rates through price ratios, and has served to explain if a currency is undervalued or overvalued. Taking several large developed countries as examples, the following graphs show the relationship of nominal and real exchange rates and price levels.[299]

It is clear that the real exchange rate is not constant and does not move upward or downward for long periods. The rate of Canada with respect to those of both the United Kingdom and the United States is an exception. The absence of a trend for real exchange rates explains the fact that the equilibrium value of the exchange rate moves up and down through time. However, during the period when the nominal exchange rate was fixed, the price ratio and real

---

297 *Ibid.*

298 Pearson, Modern Corporate Finance: http://www.prenhall.com/divisions/bp/app/finflash/html/onlinehtml/topicf/topicf2.html; Craig S. Hakkio, "Is purchasing power parity a useful guide to the dollar?" *Federal Reserve Bank of Kansas Economic Review*, 1992; Paul Schreyer and Francette Koechlin, "Purchasing power parities – measurement and uses," OECD, 2002.

299 University of Toronto, Department of Economics, https://www.economics.utoronto.ca/jfloyd/modules/ppar.html.

exchange rate of Canada with respect to the United States and United Kingdom registered a high correlation.

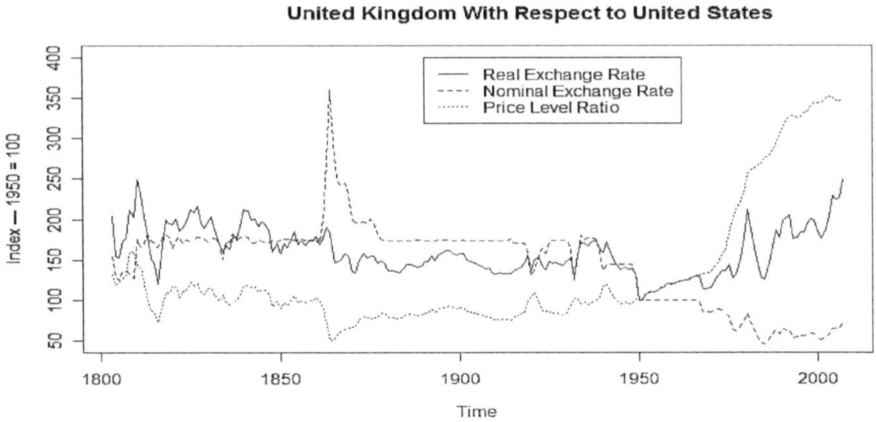

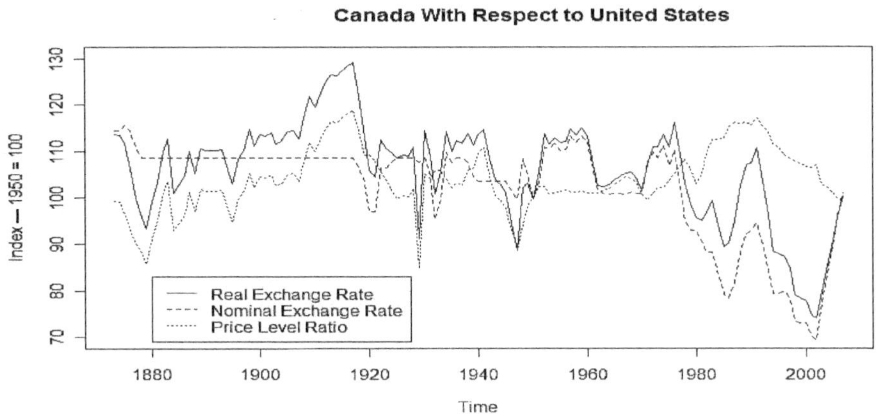

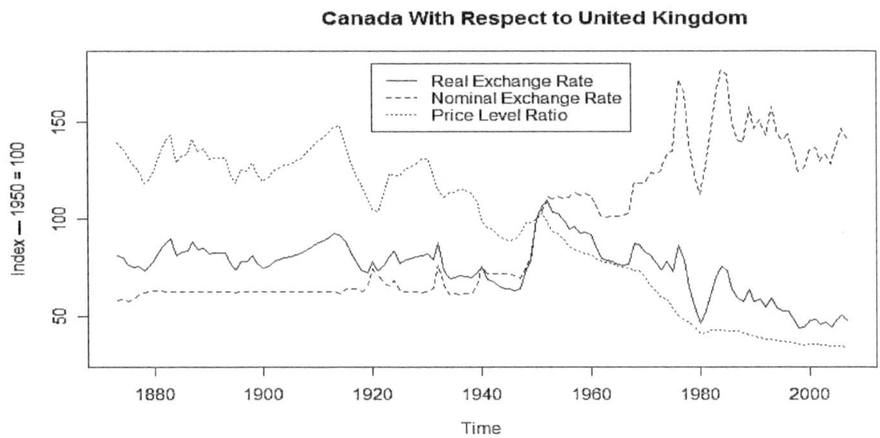

From the 1970s onward, nominal and real exchange rates were highly correlated and price levels experienced much regulated changes. Based on the empirical analysis made concerning the purchasing power parity theory and historical aspects, it can be concluded that, on the one hand, during the time exchange rates were fixed there was a strong and significant correlation between real exchange rates and price levels; however, on the other hand, whenever the nominal exchange rate was flexible, a strong correlation between the two exchange rates had been registered. Therefore, based on plotted graphs, a constant real exchange rate equilibrium cannot be retained. Real exchange rate movements are changes in the equilibrium level, and occur continuously due to shifts in investment flows, technological progress or economic growth.

Despite being an imperfect theory, PPP can still serve as a tool for policy and decision makers around the world. Both purchasing power parity and real exchange rates can lead to different conclusions. For instance, calculating PPP based on the producer price index, which measures the average change over time on final prices received by domestic businesses, is considered by many as more reliable than a calculation based on consumer prices. *The Economist*'s "Big Mac Index,"[300] based on purchasing power parity and consumer prices, suggests that in the long run exchange rates must change in order to equalize the price of the same goods and services everywhere. For example, through the Big Mac index, we learn that the Swiss franc is overvalued by up to 62%. Therefore, the exchange rate that equalizes the price of a Big Mac in Switzerland with an American one is 1.55 francs to the dollar. However, different studies using other methods of calculation can suggest other results.[301]

Finally, the theory of purchasing power parity confirms several things:

A unit of a hypothetical currency must be able to buy the same quantity of a hypothetical product all around the world.

Nominal exchange rates between countries must reflect the price levels among them.

Countries experiencing higher inflation would have a more depreciated currency and countries with relatively lower inflation would experience a more appreciated currency.

[300] "The Big Mac Index," http://www.economist.com/node/2154 2840/print.

[301] George Dorgan, "Purchasing Power Parity: Swiss franc overvalued?" SNBCHF.com, 2016; UBS: https://www.ubs.com/global/en/wealth_management/chief-investment-office/investment-views/swiss-economic-forecast.html; https://snbchf.com/fx-theory/real-effective-exchange-rate/.

Foreign Direct Investments

Foreign direct investment (FDI) is considered as one of the key features of international economic integration. It can foster "regional integration project" initiatives by guaranteeing financial stability, promoting growth and ultimately bringing prosperity to society.

A foreign direct investment is made when a resident of one country invests in a business in another country with the aim of establishing a durable interest within the economy of that foreign nation. The latter is called the "direct investment enterprise [302] and the former is called the "direct investor."[303] One of the main motivations for investing in an enterprise on foreign soil is to have a long-term strategic relationship with the direct investment enterprise, with the objective of ensuring the presence and influence of the direct investor in the business organization. Establishing a durable interest within the economy of a foreign nation, in other words a "lasting interest," is made clear and considered as evident when the direct investor owns at least 10% of the voting power within the business organization.[304]

Direct investment enterprises are both corporations and quasi-corporations. In case of corporations, they can exist either as subsidiaries or as associates. Within the latter, 10% to 50% of the voting power can be held, and within the former, 50% of the voting power is held. In regards to quasi-corporations, although they are unincorporated enterprises, they function like other corporations: they produce goods and services within a foreign economy, but without establishing separate legal entities in the host country. Quasi-corporations, such as branches, are owned 100% by the parent corporation. The relationship between the direct investment enterprise and the direct investor is considered as complex, and it plays an indispensable role in implementing the foreign direct investment concept. Before entering into more detail, it is worth mentioning that some relationships may be evident among enterprises that also exhibit characteristics of direct investment, though there are no links that would ultimately qualify them as such. Therefore, these cases are not treated as direct investments.

Statistics are very important in order to study, evaluate and finally understand foreign direct investment. They are presented on both an aggregate and a directional (inward and outward) basis. The latter can be broken down into geographical and industrial categories, and the former can be in terms of assets and liabilities. In addition, statistics cover whole transactions and

---

[302] International Monetary Fund, Glossary of Foreign Investment Terms: http://www.imf.org/external/np/sta/di/glossary.pdf.

[303] *Ibid.*

[304] OECD Benchmark Definition of Foreign Direct Investment, OECD 4th ed, 2008: https://www.oecd.org/daf/inv/investmentstatisticsandanalysis/40193734.pdf.

positions that mainly take place among the enterprises of the same group. That would include positions such as equity and debt, income flows such as distributed earnings, interest income, etc., and financial flows. Methodologies such as Benchmark, offered by groups such as the Organization for Economic Cooperation and Development (OECD), reflect and help the understanding of the reality of foreign direct investment transactions in a world that is more and more integrated.[305]

Direct Investment Relationships

Any discussion on direct investment relationships should be based on the assumption that the institutional units involved are residents of different economies and of course in a direct investment relationship. The direct investment must include the initial equity-based transaction, respecting the limit of 10% of voting power, and all the positions and financial transactions that follow between the aforementioned institutional units.[306] As a foreign direct investor, an institutional unit can be the following:

- An individual
- A group of related individuals
- An incorporated or unincorporated enterprise
- A public or private enterprise or group of related enterprises
- A governmental body
- An estate, trust or other social organization
- Any combination of the above

For the sake of calculations, different statistical approaches may measure direct investment differently. Therefore, based on the aforementioned definitions of direct investor and direct investment enterprise, the legal structures of enterprises involved can create complex and different ownership chains. Defining and clarifying structural aspects and the way entities are connected are crucial for any analysis. Moreover, in statistics, this would be done through the framework for direct investment relationships (FDIR), which is a generalized methodology and would ultimately identify and determine the extent and the nature of direct investment relationships. In a hypothetical economy, the FDIR method would identify all the enterprises that are linked to a particular enterprise.[307]

---

[305] Olivier De Schutter, Johan F. M. Swinnen and Jan Wouters, *Foreign Direct Investment and Human Development: The Law and Economics of International Investment Agreements*, Routledge, 2013.

[306] *Ibid.*

[307] Stephen D. Cohen, *Multinational Corporations and Foreign Direct Investment: Avoiding Simplicity, Embracing Complexity*, Oxford University Press, 2007; *Theodor H. Moran,*

As an example of these links, if enterprise A in country X owns 80% of the voting power in enterprise B in country Y, and if enterprise B owns 80% of enterprise C in country Z, the result would be that enterprise A, through its control of enterprise B, indirectly controls enterprise C. In another type of case, an institutional unit may be a direct investor in more than one foreign business: enterprise A in country X may own 80% of the voting power in enterprise B in country Y while simultaneously owning 20% of the voting power in enterprise C in country Z. Although enterprise B has nothing to do with enterprise C in terms of participation, the transactions and positions between the two is important for FDI statistics.[308]

In a third type of relationship, enterprise A in country X may own 70% of enterprise C in country Z, while enterprise B in country Y may own another 20% of enterprise C. Being controlled through the participation of enterprises A and B, enterprise C is in the middle of two overlapping direct investment relationships.[309]

FDI and Free Capital Flows

The issue of free movement of capital is a long-debated one. The movement of capital across borders can allow its owner to reach the highest rate of return, but the advantages of free capital movement go beyond that.[310] They include:

Diversification: capital that can freely circulate around the globe offers the opportunity to reduce risks associated with investments and savings that both surplus and deficit units regularly face.

The idea of globally integrated capital markets would reinforce and nurture best practices that are essential and would guarantee important and constructive outcomes at the international level within fields such as corporate governance, accounting and legal practice.

Foreign Direct Investment, Wiley Online Library, 2012; E. Borensztein, J. De Gregorio, J-W. Lee, "How does foreign direct investment affect economic growth?" *Journal of International Economics*, 45(1), 1998.

[308] OECD Benchmark Definition of Foreign Direct Investment.

[309] Cohen, *Multinational Corporations and Foreign Direct Investment.*

[310] Martin Feldstein, "Aspects of Global Economic Integration: Outlook for the Future," Federal Reserve Bank of Kansas City, 2000, https://www.kansascityfed.org/publicat/sympos/2000/feldstein.pdf; OECD Benchmark Definition of Foreign Direct Investment.

Limited government: having capital freely flow would also limit governments' abilities to introduce policies that are not efficient and can affect the growth and consequently the economy as a whole.

For a nation that is also the host economy of direct investment enterprises, benefits from free movement of capital in the form of FDI, in addition to those aforementioned, can be realized in other forms, too:[311]

Technology: Foreign direct investment would be accompanied by new technologies. FDI can offer new technology to a host economy through direct investment enterprises. This can be in the form of capital goods, such as equipment, machinery, etc.

Competitiveness: In connection with the previous point, competition would be encouraged as well. Local markets and producers witnessing newcomers trying to reap their market shares and exploit their resources would start probably to modify their business models.

Human resources: New businesses and new technologies would also bring in the need for more skilled and qualified work forces. This is realized through training and other educational and professional programs and courses.

Government revenues: direct investors and direct investment enterprises, once they reap the profits and created value they sought through foreign direct investments, must also respect the fiscal policies and rules of the host country.

Foreign direct investment can differentiate itself clearly and perhaps more affirmatively from other types of capital flows such as short-term debt flows that by many are considered not as beneficial as FDI. The main argument is that the short-term borrowing from others would be driven by speculative considerations such as interest rate spreads and expectations rather than long-term objectives, which can ultimately create boom and bust cycles. On the other hand, other evidence suggest that although capital normally moves toward where financial markets and institutions are safer and more advanced, the share of foreign direct investment out of total capital flow is much higher in countries that are riskier with less-developed financial markets and institutions.[312] During the last years of the nineteenth century, although capital inflows toward Latin America decreased, the continent witnessed an

[311] Assaf Razin and Efraim Sadka, *Foreign Direct Investment: Analysis of Aggregate Flows*, Princeton University Press, 2007.
[312] *Ibid.*

increase in its share of foreign direct investment out of total capital inflow. Therefore, the question that can be raised is how things developed as a result of an increase in the share of FDI, and if that brought stability, growth and development.[313]

FDIs have been important drivers that have helped economies to integrate, fostering globalization through different means such as mergers and acquisitions. Data related to developed countries show that despite the growing[314] importance of emerging economies as hosts to direct investors, the European Union has been both the largest investor and the largest recipient of foreign direct investment. As shown through the next graph, in 2013 foreign direct investment inflows into the European Union registered an increase of 14%, reaching $246 billion. This increase guaranteed the European market's position and fostered the consolidation of the European single market.[315]

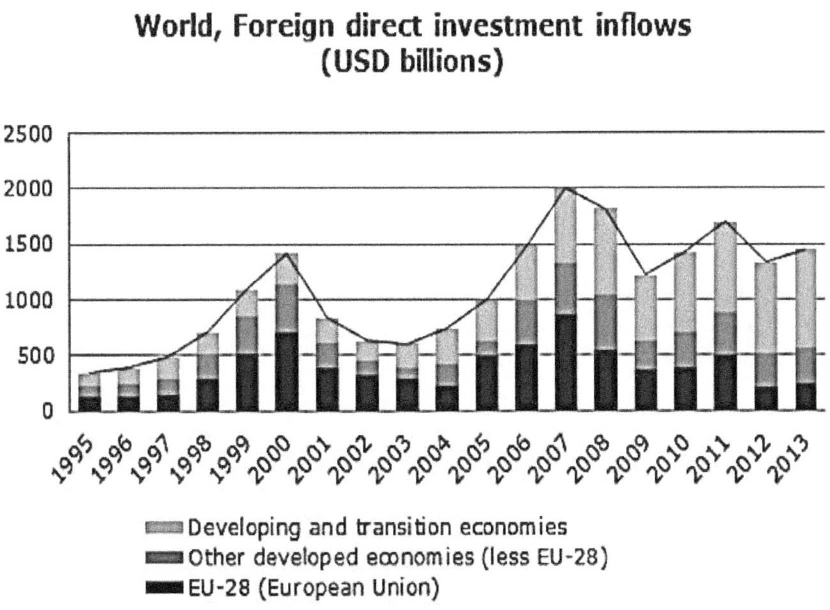

Debates continue to exist on whether foreign direct investments are circulating more within developed and organized economies or within those less developed and with riskier profiles. Since data and statistics change over

[313] *Ibid.*; Ricardo Hausmann and Eduardo Fernandez Arias, "Foreign Direct Investment: Good Cholesterol?" Inter-American Development Bank, no 348.

[314] Assaf Razin, "The contribution of FDI flows to domestic investment in capacity and vice versa," University of Chicago, 2004.

[315] European Commission, "Foreign Direct Investment," 2014.

time, being prudent and taking time to study opportunities for economies to be affected through foreign direct investment can be considered as an essential time-saving and cost-saving strategy for less developed countries.[316] However, considering the reality of FDI and the way ownership is transferred in addition to voting power requirements, foreign direct investment can also be seen as a corporate governance mechanism. During crises, for instance, how would issues such as a "fire sale" be dealt with? Having access to information and details that a local investor may not possess can be considered problematic as well.[317]

Other arguments against FDI for the host economy can be discussed. Issues include the consequences of excess advantage, damage to local competition, and, in some cases – since a significant share of FDI is intercompany debt – the ability of the parent company to recall a portion of its investment. In any case, the rise in foreign direct investment is not a bad phenomenon *per se*. Less-developed countries must reform their institutional frameworks in order to support and guarantee investments, finance and risk-sharing mechanisms.

FDI: The First Flow

Among other forms of capital flow such as portfolio investments or financial flows like bank loans, foreign direct investment can guarantee a one-for-one increase in domestic investments while the other forms would not contribute to the same extent. If we hold the idea that conceptualized "foreign direct investment" is an extension of corporate control over international boundaries, then we also need to confirm that foreign direct investment flows play a crucial role in so-called high-productivity projects and as such contribute enormously to local investments in terms of both quality and quantity.[318] Data analysis concerning interactions between capital inflows and investment in capacity confirm that FDI has a larger effect on domestic investment in capacity and growth than loan or portfolio inflows, and *vice versa.*[319]

---

[316] Ralph Setzer and Massimo Suardi, "Determinants of Capital Flows to the New EU Member States Before and During the Financial Crisis," *Economic Papers*, 425, 2010.
[317] Robert E. Lipsey and Jean-Louis Mucchielli, *Multinational Firms and Impacts on Employment, Trade and Technology: New Perspectives for a New Century*, Routledge, 2003.
[318] Razin, "The contribution of FDI flows to domestic investment."
[319] Borensztein, J. De Gregorio, J-W. Lee, "How does foreign direct investment affect economic growth?"; Economy Watch, "Disadvantages of Foreign Direct Investment," 2010: http://www.economywatch.com/foreign-direct-investment/disadvantages.html; "FDI in Green Buildings in China: A solution for its affordable housing problems?" *China Business Review*, 2016: http://www.chinabusinessreview.com/fdi-in-green-buildings-in-china-a-solution-for-its-affordable-housing-problems/; Razin, "The contribution of FDI flows to domestic investment."

In regards to developing countries, the contribution of foreign direct investment in comparison with the other forms of capital, mainly portfolio and loans, is definitely higher. In recent decades, capital flows in general into developing countries would be used to finance current account deficits, and the share of FDI on domestic investment has had enormous beneficial effects. The graph here captures the pattern of capital inflows between 1978 and 1995.[320]

Capital Inflows to Industrial and Developing Countries, 1978–95

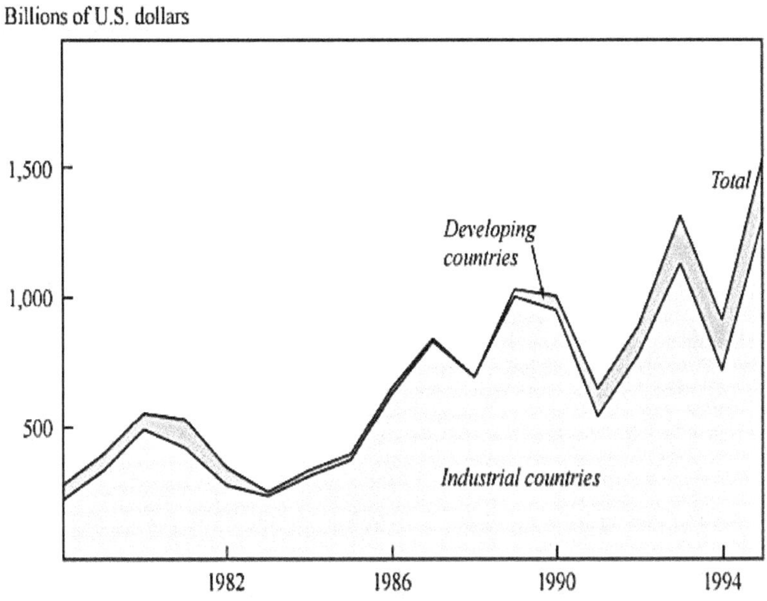

- Inflows

Based on theories of FDI[321] and empirical studies, its importance for host economies are confirmed despite the risks such as reversion through financial transactions, adverse selection problems, benefits that are limited by leverage or even consideration of a high share of FDI within a host country as

---

[320] Barry P. Bosworth and Susan M. Collins, "Capital Flow to developing Economies: Implications for Investment and Savings," Brookings Paper on Economic Activities, Brookings institute, 1999.

[321] Vintila Denisia, "FDI theories: An overview of the main theories of FDI," *European Journal of Interdisciplinary Studies*, 2, 2010.

a sign of weakness.[322] Although developed countries enjoyed a greater but more volatile share of global FDI inflows,[323] developing countries also registered steady increases over time and accounted for 55% of the global total.

In 2014, the total amount of foreign direct investment in the world amounted to about $1.23 trillion, a 16% decrease from the total registered in 2013, which was $1.47 trillion. However, as shown in the table, the decline of FDI, caused by mainly a fragile world economy and elevated political risks and instability, was offset by growth in other parameters such as GDP and trade.[324]

Growth Rates of Global GDP, Trade, Gross Fixed Capital Formation, Employment and FDI, 2008-2016 (%)

Variable	2008	2009	2010	2011	2012	2013	2014	2015ᵃ	2016ᵃ
GDP	1.5	-2.0	4.1	2.9	2.4	2.5	2.6	2.8	3.1
Trade	3.0	-10.6	12.6	6.8	2.8	3.5	3.4	3.7	4.7
GFCF	3.0	-3.5	5.7	5.5	3.9	3.2	2.9	3.0	4.7
Employment	1.2	1.1	1.2	1.4	1.4	1.4	1.3	1.3	1.2
FDI	-20.4	-20.4	11.9	17.7	-10.3	4.6	-16.3	11.4	8.4
Memorandum									
FDI value (in $ trillions)	1.49	1.19	1.33	1.56	1.40	1.47	1.23	1.37	1.48

Source: UNCTAD, FDI/MNE database for FDI in 2008–2014; United Nations (2015) for GDP; IMF (2015) for GFCF and trade; ILO for employment; and UNCTAD estimates for FDI in 2015–2016.

ᵃ Projections.

Note: FDI excludes Caribbean offshore financial centres. GFCF = gross fixed capital formation.

Regional patterns of FDI confirm that developing Asia got the biggest share of inflows and Latin America experienced a decline in its share.[325] Data from the U.N. Conference on Trade and Development show that FDI flows to developed countries decreased by 28%. FDI inflows to both United States and Europe fell and European economies within themselves experienced both decreases and increases (inflows to United Kingdom and Finland increased but France and Belgium experienced declines).[326] For the rest of the world, with the exception of Africa, inflows of FDI remained stable. FDI inflows to transition economies decreased by 52% mainly because of regional conflicts and the instability of host economies. However, FDI inflows to developing economies, with an increase of 2%, reached $681 billion in 2014. The largest

[322] Prakash Loungani and Assaf Razin, "How beneficial is foreign direct investment for developing countries?" *Finance and Development*, 38(2), International Monetary Fund, 2001.
[323] Timothy Taylor, "Snapshots of Foreign Direct Investment," *Conversable Economist*, 2014: http://conversableeconomist.blogspot.fr/2014/06/snapshots-of-foreign-direct-investment.html.
[324] U.N. Conference on Trade and Development, *World Investment Report 2015*: http://unctad.org/en/PublicationsLibrary/wir2015_en.pdf
[325] *Ibid.*
[326] *Ibid.*

portion went to those located in Asia, which experienced a 9% increase in their share of FDI, to $465 billion.

Liberalizing investments and reducing barriers and restrictions to the free flow of capital can lead to an increase in FDI inflows. Foreign direct investments foster the regional integration process, and the decline in FDI inflows in 2014 slowed this. Long-term projects such as economic integration, by creating new opportunities within the economies as well as harmonizing policies in regards to both surplus units and deficit units, must augment the FDI inflows, while short- and medium-term policies and coordination initiatives as listed below are essential to attract more foreign direct investment inflows to regional blocs and groups:[327]

- Extending and deepening the common market within the region
- Promoting and enforcing competitiveness
- Harmonizing as well as balancing regulations
- Developing and upgrading infrastructure and the scientific base

In 2014, as total world foreign direct investment declined, the countries negotiating the Transatlantic Trade and Investment Partnership and those negotiating the Trans-Pacific Partnership experienced falls in their share of global FDI inflows, while other groupings such as the Association of Southeast Asian Nations saw increases. The impact of regional integration on intraregional and extra-regional inflows of FDI can vary from one bloc to another, but coordinated efforts and a larger market size would improve the inflows of FDI.[328] The chart on the next page shows the distribution of FDI inflows based on regional groups.[329]

---

[327] European Commission, "Foreign Direct Investment," 2014, http://ec.europa.eu/economy_finance/international/globalisation/fdi/index_en.htm; Bogdan Bogdanov, "Liberalized Capital Accounts and Volatility of Capital Flows and Foreign Exchange Rates," *Economic Papers*, 521 2014.

[328] Michael Czinkota and Valbona Zeneli, "Why the Transatlantic Trade and Investment Partnership Is More Important Than TPP," *The Diplomat*, 2016: http://thediplomat.com/2016/01/why-the-transatlantic-trade-and-investment-partnership-is-more-important-than-tpp/; Natasha Turak, "U.S Secretary of Commerce Lauds TPP and Free Trade," *FDI Intelligence*, 2016: http://www.fdiintelligence.com/Locations/Americas/USA/US-secretary-of-commerce-lauds-TPP-and-free-trade; Thomas McEvoy, "Brexit: Uncertain times ahead, but let's focus on what we can manage," *Drogheda Independent*, 2017; Robert McHugh, "Irish job creation and employment: Growth set to continue in 2017," *Business World*, 2017; "Why Foreign Investment Makes Sense," *The National*, 2016: http://www.thenational.ae/opinion/comment/why-foreign-investment-makes-sense.

[329] U.N. Conference on Trade and Development, *World Investment Report 2015*.

FDI inflows to selected regional and interregional groups, 2013 and 2014
(Billions of dollars and per cent)

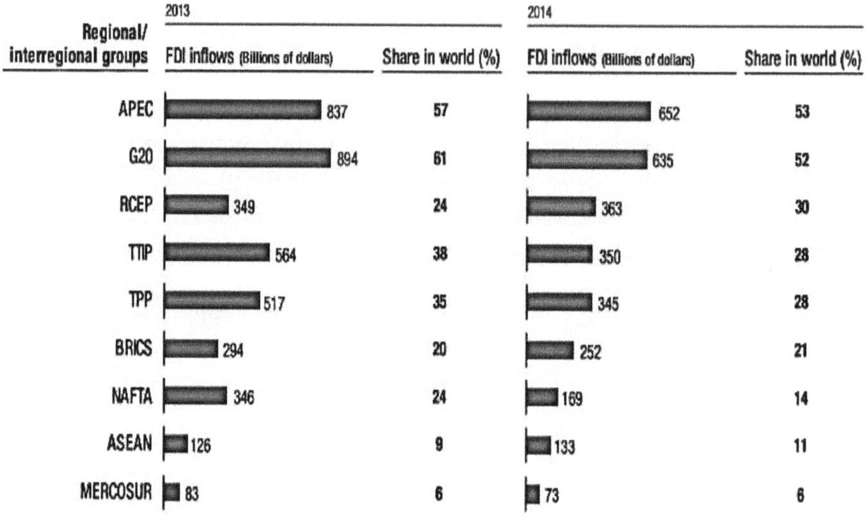

Source: UNCTAD, FDI/MNE database (www.unctad.org/fdistatistics).
Note: Ranked in descending order of 2014 FDI flows. G20 = only the 19 member countries of the G20 (excludes the European Union); APEC = Asia-Pacific Economic Cooperation; TTIP = Transatlantic Trade and Investment Partnership; TPP = Trans-Pacific Partnership; RCEP = Regional Comprehensive Economic Partnership; BRICS = Brazil, Russian Federation, India, China and South Africa; NAFTA = North American Free Trade Agreement; ASEAN = Association of Southeast Asian Nations; MERCOSUR = Common Market of the South.

- Outflows

Evaluating outflows of foreign direct investment is important as well. In 2014, despite the fall in total world FDI, such investments by multinational enterprises from developing and transition economies continued to grow. Within the developing economies, more than 50% of the total outflows of $468 billion in investments were in equities. Multinational enterprises in Asia increased their investments and became the world's largest investing group, and their share of world FDI outflows reached almost one-third of the total. The following graphs show the developing countries' share of FDI outflows, and a breakdown of FDI outflows by type.[330]

[330] *Ibid.*

Developing economies: FDI outflows and their share in total world outflows, 2000–2014

(Billions of dollars and per cent)

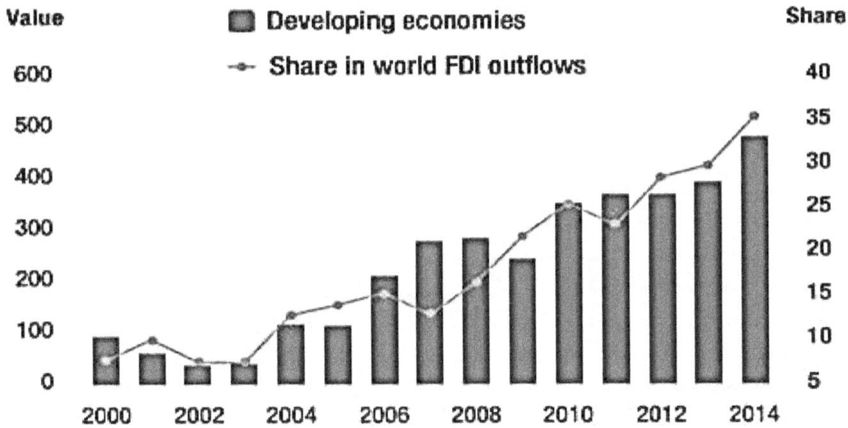

Source: UNCTAD, FDI/MNE database (www.unctad.org/fdistatistics).

FDI outflows by component, by group of economies, 2007–2014

(Per cent)

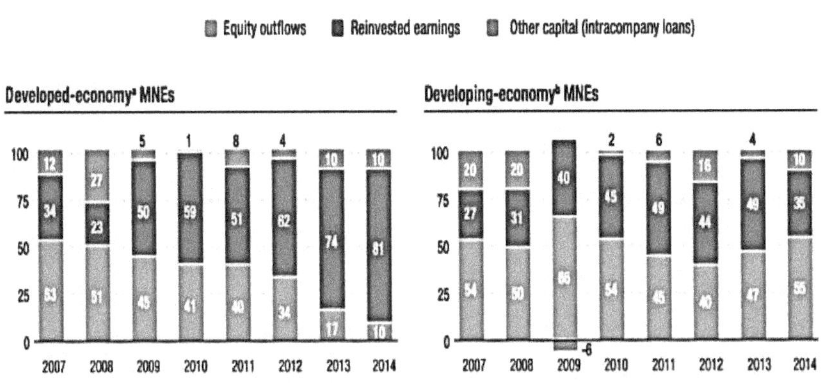

Source: UNCTAD, FDI/MNE database (www.unctad.org/fdistatistics).

Despite the uncertainties that existed in 2014, international production increased and most of the indicators of multinational enterprises' foreign affiliates showed gains. These entities collectively registered a 7.6% rise in sales, while the rate of return on their inward FDI reached 6.4%.[331] They also created 75 million jobs. Also in 2014, the top 100 multinational enterprises moved toward a higher degree of internationalization as a series of major merger and acquisition deals took place.[332]

In addition to the high degree of internationalization among multinational enterprises, the major ones also maintained high cash balances. The 100 largest experienced decreases in their cash, confirming that they spent money on new investments, mainly through mergers and acquisitions, although they also used a portion of their cash to buy back some of their shares and pay dividends.[333]

A larger sample of 5,000 multinational enterprises confirms the achievement of high cash reserves. With the aim of relying less on debt and to protect themselves from undesirable events in the future, they held $4.4 trillion in cash at the end of 2014. The cash they did spend went toward capital expenditures and/or acquisitions.[334] Meanwhile, multinational enterprises that made foreign direct investments in 2014 registered a stable and high level of profitability.[335]

Monetary Policy and Integration

In order to close the chapter, we need to clarify the role of central banks and central banking tools that are essential to the proper functioning of any financial and monetary system. The issue discussed here is important as it plays a crucial role in regards to regional integration projects and monetary unions. Here we examine the Federal Reserve System, the "Fed," which is the central bank of the United States of America. The Fed is recognized as an independent institution that cannot be affected by any political authority or political will. Its objectives are clear, and are based on the Federal Reserve Act passed by Congress in 1913:[336]

---

[331] *Ibid.*
[332] *Ibid.*
[333] *Ibid.*
[334] *Ibid.*
[335] "FDI generated 12.037 new jobs in 2016," PR Newswire, 2016: http://www.prnewswire.com/news-releases/fdi-generated-12307-new-jobs-in-2016-300378621.html; "Foreign firms in Spain generate 28% out of national turnover, employ near 3 million people," *The Corner*, 2016: http://thecorner.eu/spain-economy/foreign-firms-spain-generates-28-national-turnover/60670/.
[336] Board of Governers of the Federal Reserve System, "What are Fed objectives in conducting monetary policy?" https://www.federalreserve.gov/faqs/money_12848.htm.

- Maximum employment
- Price stability
- Moderate long term interest rates

Since 1791, when the First Bank of the United States was created, several tentative efforts were made with the aim of maintaining the stability of the U.S. economy through supervising commercial banks. Finally, the Federal Reserve Act established requirements for the reserves of commercial banks that wanted to be part of the system. Twelve districts were defined and a city within each district was selected to host the Federal Reserve district bank in that part of the United States. Each Federal Reserve district bank was allowed to sell and buy U.S. government securities with the aim of manipulating the supply of money whenever needed, while remaining focused on its own district.[337]

Besides its district banks, the Federal Reserve System has four main components:[338]

- Member Banks
- Board of Governors
- Federal Open Market Committee
- Advisory Committees

Purchasing stock offered by a Federal Reserve district bank is considered as a requirement for those commercial banks that want to join the Fed system. Although these are not tradable stocks within the secondary market, they do give a dividend of up to 6% per year. The Federal Reserve district banks are mainly there to facilitate the operations of the banking system through clearing checks, providing loans and replacing worn currency with new banknotes. They also monitor commercial banks' activities as well as conduct research on the economy. Three out of the nine directors[339] of each Federal Reserve district bank are appointed by the Federal Reserve Board of Governors and the other six are elected by member banks.[340] In the United States, national banks must by law be members of the Fed. Banks that are

---

[337] Federal Reserve Board, "Federal Reserve Districts," https://www.federalreserve.gov/otherfrb.htm.
[338] Madura, *Financial Markets and Institutions.*
[339] Federal Reserve Board, "Directors of Federal Reserve Banks and Branches," https://www.federalreserve.gov/aboutthefed/directors/about.htm.
[340] Federal Reserve Board, "Procedures for Elections of Class A and Class B Directors," https://www.federalreserve.gov/aboutthefed/directors/PDF/procedure-for-elections-classes-a-b.pdf.

chartered by their respective states are not required to be members, but they may join if they meet certain requirements.[341]

The Federal Reserve Board[342] has seven members who are selected for fourteen-year terms by the president of the United States and confirmed by the Senate. It has two main responsibilities: regulating commercial banks and controlling monetary policy. The Board of Governors oversees and intervenes within the wide range of Fed district banks' activities as well as decides on reserve requirements and confirms changes in the discount rate – the interest rate charged on funds. The committees of the Federal Advisory Councils, whose members are elected by the board of directors of each Fed district bank, meet four times a year and make recommendations about banking and economic-related issues. There are two main Advisory Councils. The Consumer Advisory Council, which represents financial institutions and their consumers, has the objective of addressing consumer-related issues. The Thrift Institutions Advisory Council discusses issues that are concerned with savings banks, loan associations and credit unions.

Finally, the most important component of the Federal Reserve System is the Federal Open Market Committee. Composed of the Board of Governors and five out of the 12 presidents of the Fed's district banks, its objectives are:

- Promoting high employment
- Fostering economic growth
- Ensuring price stability

These objectives, when met, can stabilize financial markets, foreign exchange rates and interest rates, among other things.[343] They are mainly achieved through controlling the money supply. The monetary measures that the Fed monitors in order to manipulate the supply of money must have two main characteristics: first, the Fed must be able to control them, and second, it must be able to predict and evaluate the impacts and consequences that any manipulation of them would bring to economic variables. The most rigid form of money, lacking flexibility, is known as M1 and includes currency held by the public and checking deposits, accounts and automatic transfer balances. Another form that is a broader and more flexible measure is M2; it includes M1 plus saving accounts and minor deposits that are usually below $100,000. The third form is known as M3, and in addition to M1 and M2 it includes those deposits above $100,000. The fact that new services and different

[341] Federal Reserve Bank of Dallas, "Becoming a Member Bank of the Federal Reserve System," http://www.dallasfed.org/banking/apps/faq.cfm.

[342] Federal Reserve Board, "Board of Governors," https://www.federalreserve.gov/aboutthefed/bios/board/default.htm.

[343] Madura, *Financial Markets and Institutions.*

deposit accounts can be created means that consumers can change their preferences. During the deregulation phase in the 1980s, for instance, transfers of funds from demand deposit accounts to money market deposit accounts reduced the base of M1. That happened without any intervention from Federal Reserve authorities. It is useful to note that money supply measures can be slightly different in other region of the world. The table below shows how M1, M2 and M3 are defined in the eurozone.[344]

Definitions of Eurozone M1, M2, and M3 Stocks (Source: European Central Bank)

	M1	M2	M3
CURRENCY IN CIRCULATION	X	X	X
OVERNIGHT DEPOSITS	X	X	X
DEPOSITS WITH AN AGREED MATURITY UP TO 2 YEARS		X	X
DEPOSITS REDEEMABLE AT A PERIOD OF NOTICE UP TO 3 MONTHS		X	X
REPURCHASE AGREEMENTS			X
MONEY MARKET FUNDS, SHARES			X
DEBT SECURITIES UP TO 2 YEARS			X

Monetary Policy Tools

The different three tools available to Federal Reserve Bank in managing the money supply are:

- Open Market Operations
- Discount rate
- Adjustment of reserve requirements

Each of these interventions can in a different way decrease or increase the money supply's growth. The Fed does not need to use the three policies simultaneously and usually uses open market operations, although it can use

[344] Hyun Kim, Hyun Shin and Jaeho Yun, "Monetary Aggregates and Central Bank Financial Stability," Federal Reserve Board, 2012.

the other two whenever it is deemed necessary. The main reason of opting for the open market policy is that the other two alternatives are less convenient. For instance, a change in reserve requirements can produce erratic shifts in the money supply that would ultimately end in missing the targeted money supply level. The same goes for the discount rate adjustment, because it depends on the response from depositary institutions to the adjustment and, in any case, the adjustment in reserves would be temporary.[345]

Open market operations do not have these problems and are not restricted or dependent on the response to, or the timing of, the interventions. In addition, the intentions of the Fed are not revealed when such operations occur, avoiding the loss of credibility by causing concerns within the public. Therefore, once the target money supply growth level is decided and specified in terms of an annualized growth rate and a target range, for instance 3% or 6%, the buying and selling of government securities would start. Once started, it continues throughout the year in order for the Fed to remain responsive to ongoing changes and to ultimately remain within the target range.

The table below compares the different monetary tools available to the Federal Reserve as it implement its monetary policies.

Comparison of Monetary Policy Tools		
Monetary Policy Tool	**To Increase Money Supply Growth**	**To Decrease Money Supply Growth**
Open Market Operations	Purchasing of government securities in the secondary market	Sale of government securities within the secondary market
Discount Rate	Lowering the discount rate to encourage borrowing through the discount window	Raising the discount rate, discouraging people from borrowing
Reserve Requirement	Lowering the reserve requirement ratio, multiplying money at a higher rate	Raising the reserve requirement ratio to cause money to multiply at a lower rate

In establishing the Federal Reserve System, the 12 districts were based on trade patterns among regions of the United States in 1913 and the

345 Madura, *Financial Markets and Institutions.*

respective economic factors and interests. The fact that the 12 Federal Reserve district banks were independent in implementing their policies was because the idea of national economic policy-making was not well defined and developed. As the American economy became more and more integrated and complex, a more integrated financial system was required, and subsequently revisions[346] of the first Act of 1913 were decided in 1933 and 1934 to serve the public interest within an integrated economy.

In the United States, the Federal Reserve System can be considered an excellent model through which an independent monetary policy is conducted. This is an important and inseparable feature of any integration project which cannot be neglected. The central bank in any country needs to be completely separate from political pressures and groups that push for advancing their own interests which can be unrelated to monetary policies and objectives. It is very important to achieve objectives such as price stability, economic growth and promoting high employment through the financial system of a country with an independent central bank as its core institution. If a central bank is dependent, it would easily become a tool of politicians in order to help them to achieve their short-term interests. Important aspects of a healthy economy would be affected and a high price would be paid by the public. This is why the way the Federal Reserve System was created is important. In the larger picture, with democratically elected bodies and national monetary objectives that are well defined within a decentralized system that is also integrated economically, the public interest is the ultimate goal and is served in a best possible way.

[346] Federal Reserve Bank of Philadelphia: https://www.phil.frb.org/-/media/publications/economic-education/first-100-years.pdf?la=en.

CHAPTER 6

ISLAMIC BANKING AND FINANCE

Sharia'ah

Muslims, comprising the second largest religious group on earth, account for about 25% the global population, and in 2015 this reached the number of 1.7 billion individuals.[347] The main concentrations are in the Middle East, northern Africa and southwestern Asia. All aspects of Muslims' lives must be in accordance with Sharia'ah law, which comes from a combination of three sources: first is Qur'an, the holy book of Muslims; next are the sayings and conduct of the Prophet Muhammad, called "Hadith;" and the third are the rulings of Islamic scholars, called "Fatwas."[348] Qur'an says, "To each of you we prescribed a law and a method. Had Allah willed, He would have made you one nation [united in religion], but [He intended] to test you in what He has given you; so race to [all that is] good. To Allah is your return all together and He will [then] inform you concerning that over which you used to differ."[349]

بِسْمِ ٱللَّهِ ٱلرَّحْمَٰنِ ٱلرَّحِيمِ

وَأَنزَلْنَآ إِلَيْكَ ٱلْكِتَٰبَ بِٱلْحَقِّ مُصَدِّقًا لِّمَا بَيْنَ يَدَيْهِ مِنَ ٱلْكِتَٰبِ وَمُهَيْمِنًا عَلَيْهِ ۖ
فَٱحْكُم بَيْنَهُم بِمَآ أَنزَلَ ٱللَّهُ ۖ وَلَا تَتَّبِعْ أَهْوَآءَهُمْ عَمَّا جَآءَكَ مِنَ ٱلْحَقِّ ۚ لِكُلٍّ جَعَلْنَا
مِنكُمْ شِرْعَةً وَمِنْهَاجًا ۚ وَلَوْ شَآءَ ٱللَّهُ لَجَعَلَكُمْ أُمَّةً وَٰحِدَةً وَلَٰكِن لِّيَبْلُوَكُمْ فِى مَآ
ءَاتَىٰكُمْ ۖ فَٱسْتَبِقُوا۟ ٱلْخَيْرَٰتِ ۚ إِلَى ٱللَّهِ مَرْجِعُكُمْ جَمِيعًا فَيُنَبِّئُكُم بِمَا كُنتُمْ فِيهِ
تَخْتَلِفُونَ ﴿٤٨﴾

---

347 "Christianity 2015: Religious Diversity and Personal Contact," gordonconwell.edu, 2015: http://www.gordonconwell.edu/resources/documents/1IBMR2015.pdf.
348 https://quran.com/5:48.
349 *Ibid.*

For Muslims, life does not start with birth. In fact, God already created everybody's soul and asked of his created souls, "Am I not your Lord?"[350] And, everybody responded yes. Each soul has a time on earth that is already decreed by God, and after completion of their lifetimes they would be judged and sent to either a destination of endless bliss or one of everlasting grief. As such, this life on earth is considered as a short journey that also offers to its wayfarers different and multiple paths; however, the only one that is clear and straight is the one of Sharia'ah.[351]

Sharia'ah is considered a divine guidance, and in Arabic it means "the clear and well-trodden path to water;" therefore the meaning of Sharia'ah echoes in its usage within daily life. As essential and vital as water is to human life during one's journey on earth, likewise Sharia'ah is to soul and mind. Although many messengers had been sent by God, the Prophet Muhammad is considered the last one and the Sharia'ah is the final manifestation of God and divine mercy.[352] Sharia'ah is structured and regulates the everyday aspects of Muslims' lives in the following ways:

I. Obligatory
II. Recommended
III. Permitted
IV. Disliked
V. Forbidden

The first category must be observed and performed, and if it is done with good intentions, people are rewarded. The opposite of this category is the last category of "forbidden." The category of "recommended," the second one, is opposite to the fourth category of "disliked" and includes actions that should be done. Finally, the category of permitted actions is where acts are neither encouraged nor discouraged. Therefore, Sharia'ah sets rules for women and men that cover all aspects of human life, from personal acts of worship to laws regulating commerce and businesses, and from laws covering marriage and divorce to those of crimes. In fact, as stated in Qur'an, this life under Sharia'ah is the objective of God. God sent the Prophet and the Book to show humanity how to be happy in this life as well as the way that must be taken in order to guarantee success and happiness in the other life. As shown on the next page, Qur'an says, "Our Lord, give us good in this life and good in the next, and save us from the punishment of the Fire."[353]

---

[350] Ruqaiyyah Waris Maqsood, *Teach Yourself Islam*, Teach Yourself Books, 2003.
[351] Faraz Rabbani, "Sharia," BBC, 2009:
http://www.bbc.co.uk/religion/religions/islam/beliefs/sharia_1.shtml.
[352]Asmak ab Rahman, "Exploring Sharia'ah views on the practice of Takaful Company reinsuring with Reinsurance Company," Department of Sharia'ah and Economics, Academy of Islamic Studies, University of Malaya: http://www.kantakji.com/.
[353] https://quran.com/2:201.

بِسۡمِ ٱللَّهِ ٱلرَّحۡمَٰنِ ٱلرَّحِيمِ

وَمِنۡهُم مَّن يَقُولُ رَبَّنَآ ءَاتِنَا فِي ٱلدُّنۡيَا حَسَنَةٗ وَفِي ٱلۡأٓخِرَةِ حَسَنَةٗ وَقِنَا عَذَابَ ٱلنَّارِ ٢٠١

As legal philosophers confirm about Islam, the main objective of Sharia'ah is to promote human welfare.[354] The desired welfare of each individual and the society as a whole, all around the world, is considered as achieved through the fulfillment of necessities, needs and comfort. In Islam, necessities[355] are those issues that religious and daily aspects of life are based upon and as such if neglected, the consequences would be in terms of facing difficulties in this life and bearing punishments in the other one. These necessities are categorized into five categories:[356]

I. Preservation of religion
II. Life
III. Intellect
IV. Lineage
V. Wealth

These necessities are guaranteed and assured through preserving them once they are established. That means belief and worship are obligatory since they would ensure the establishment of religion. Later, to ensure its preservation, rulings were made in regards to the obligation of learning and conveying. In regards to intellect, for instance, God permitted that knowledge and science be promoted, while whatever can be harmful such as drugs or

---

[354] Muhammad al-Ghazali, *The Socio-Political Thought Of Shah WaliAllah*, Adam Publishers, 2004; Nabil Nofal, "Al-Ghazali's Theory of Education," Muslim Heritage: http://muslimheritage.com/article/al-ghazalis-theory-education; Hunt Janin and Andre Kahlmeyer, *Islamic Law: The Sharia from Muhammad's Time to the Present*, McFarland & Company, 2007.

[355] Abdul Kareem Zaidan and Hakam Bin Adel Zummo Al-Nuwairy Al-Aqily, "The Legislation Guarding the Five Necessities," Islam House, 2009: https://islamhouse.com/en/articles/228515/.

[356] Atique Tahir, Atiq uz Zafar Khanm Ataullah and Khan Mahmood, "Right to Basic Necessities of Life in Islam: Meaning and Concept," Qurtuba University: http://www.qurtuba.edu.pk/thedialogue/The%20Dialogue/11_2/Dialogue_April_June2016_202-212.pdf.

alcohol must be forbidden, and punishments are legislated to prevent people from consuming them. In connection with establishing and preserving wealth, God made it obligatory for people to support themselves and those who are responsible for supporting others. In addition, God provided laws that regulate issues such as commerce, fair dealings and economic justice.

The other two concepts related to welfare are "needs" and "comforts."[357] These are considered as not essential even though people seek to guarantee a good life through them. The spirit of Sharia'ah in regards to needs and comforts is in Qur'an itself:[358] "He has not placed any hardship for you in religion," and "God does not seek to place a burden on you, but that he purifies you and perfects his grace on you, and that you may give thanks. Thus, everything that guarantees human happiness within the spirit of Divine Guidance is permitted in Sharia'ah."

بسم الله الرحمن الرحيم

وَجَاهِدُوا فِي اللَّهِ حَقَّ جِهَادِهِ ۚ هُوَ اجْتَبَاكُمْ وَمَا جَعَلَ عَلَيْكُمْ فِي الدِّينِ مِنْ حَرَجٍ ۚ
مِلَّةَ أَبِيكُمْ إِبْرَاهِيمَ ۚ هُوَ سَمَّاكُمُ الْمُسْلِمِينَ مِنْ قَبْلُ وَفِي هَٰذَا لِيَكُونَ الرَّسُولُ شَهِيدًا
عَلَيْكُمْ وَتَكُونُوا شُهَدَاءَ عَلَى النَّاسِ ۚ فَأَقِيمُوا الصَّلَاةَ وَآتُوا الزَّكَاةَ وَاعْتَصِمُوا بِاللَّهِ هُوَ
مَوْلَاكُمْ ۖ فَنِعْمَ الْمَوْلَىٰ وَنِعْمَ النَّصِيرُ ﴿٧٨﴾

بسم الله الرحمن الرحيم

يَا أَيُّهَا الَّذِينَ آمَنُوا إِذَا قُمْتُمْ إِلَى الصَّلَاةِ فَاغْسِلُوا وُجُوهَكُمْ وَأَيْدِيَكُمْ إِلَى الْمَرَافِقِ
وَامْسَحُوا بِرُءُوسِكُمْ وَأَرْجُلَكُمْ إِلَى الْكَعْبَيْنِ ۚ وَإِنْ كُنْتُمْ جُنُبًا فَاطَّهَّرُوا ۚ وَإِنْ كُنْتُمْ مَرْضَىٰ
أَوْ عَلَىٰ سَفَرٍ أَوْ جَاءَ أَحَدٌ مِنْكُمْ مِنَ الْغَائِطِ أَوْ لَامَسْتُمُ النِّسَاءَ فَلَمْ تَجِدُوا مَاءً فَتَيَمَّمُوا صَعِيدًا
طَيِّبًا فَامْسَحُوا بِوُجُوهِكُمْ وَأَيْدِيكُمْ مِنْهُ ۚ مَا يُرِيدُ اللَّهُ لِيَجْعَلَ عَلَيْكُمْ مِنْ حَرَجٍ
وَلَٰكِنْ يُرِيدُ لِيُطَهِّرَكُمْ وَلِيُتِمَّ نِعْمَتَهُ عَلَيْكُمْ لَعَلَّكُمْ تَشْكُرُونَ ﴿٦﴾

---

[357] Lights: the Middle Eastern Studies Students' Association's Subcommittee of Publications at The University of Chicago, Spring 2013: https://lucian.uchicago.edu/blogs/messa/files/2013/08/Lights-Spring-2013-FINAL.pdf; Rabbani, "Sharia."

[358] https://quran.com/22/78; https://quran.com/5:6.

Sharia'ah Sources

The primary sources of the Sharia'ah are Qur'an and the life of Prophet Muhammad, the way he behaved and lived. Qur'an, whose principal message is establishing the uniqueness of God and the fact that humanity needs God in terms of both spirituality and morality, became revealed directly to the Prophet over a period of almost 23 years.[359] The aforementioned "needs" will be achieved only through worship and submission to God's will. Qur'an is considered to be words of God and as such it assures people welfare both during their lifetimes on earth as well as in the life after death. As confirmed below in his own words, "Lo! This Qur'an guideth unto that which is straightest, and giveth tidings unto the believers who do good works that theirs will be a great reward."[360] "Verily this Qur'an doth guide to that which is most right (or stable), and giveth the Glad Tidings to the Believers who work deeds of righteousness, that they shall have a magnificent reward."[361]

بِسْمِ ٱللَّهِ ٱلرَّحْمَٰنِ ٱلرَّحِيمِ

إِنَّ هَٰذَا ٱلْقُرْءَانَ يَهْدِى لِلَّتِى هِىَ أَقْوَمُ وَيُبَشِّرُ ٱلْمُؤْمِنِينَ ٱلَّذِينَ يَعْمَلُونَ ٱلصَّٰلِحَٰتِ أَنَّ لَهُمْ
أَجْرًا كَبِيرًا ﴿٩﴾

Qur'an says, "O people of the Book! There hath come to you our Messenger, revealing to you much that ye used to hide in the Book, and passing over much (that is now unnecessary): There hath come to you from Allah a (new) light and a perspicuous Book."[362] "O People of the Scripture! Now hath our messenger come unto you, expounding unto you much of that which ye used to hide in the Scripture, and forgiving much. Now hath come unto you light from Allah and plain Scripture."[363]

The other source that is also considered as the primary one are the examples of Prophet Muhammad. These are known as Sunnah, a set of customs and beliefs that are simply presented as tradition.[364] Within the legal

---

359 Beginning of Revelation, Mission Islam: https://www.missionislam.com/quran/beginrevelation.htm; Mohammad Shafi, "The Qur'an: How it was revealed and compiled," Daralislam: http://www.daralislam.org/.

360 Pickthall English translation.
361 https://quran.com/17:9; Yusuf Ali English translation.
362 Yusuf Ali English translation.
363 Pickthall English translation.
364 "The Islamic World: Past and Present," Oxford Islamic Studies.

and religious domains, Sunnah refers to sayings, actions and teachings of Prophet Muhammad. As Prophet Muhammad's role and presence in Qur'an are explained in detail, his actions and sayings became a model for Muslims' conduct, thus affirming them as one of the primary sources of Islamic Law and the legal system. However, applications of Sunnah go beyond public matters. The role of the Prophet within Qur'an is given below as a sample: "We have revealed the remembrance to you that you may explain to people that which was revealed for them." "[We sent them] with clear proofs and written ordinances. And we revealed to you the message that you may make clear to the people what was sent down to them and that they might give thought.[365]

بِسْمِ ٱللَّهِ ٱلرَّحْمَٰنِ ٱلرَّحِيمِ

بِٱلْبَيِّنَٰتِ وَٱلزُّبُرِ ۗ وَأَنزَلْنَآ إِلَيْكَ ٱلذِّكْرَ لِتُبَيِّنَ لِلنَّاسِ مَا نُزِّلَ إِلَيْهِمْ وَلَعَلَّهُمْ يَتَفَكَّرُونَ ﴿٤٤﴾

In connection with the Sunnah of Prophet Muhammad, Qur'an itself, explained succinctly and in detail, clarifies this as follows: "O you, who believe, obey God and obey the messenger, and verily, in the Messenger of God you have a beautiful example for those who seek God and last day, and remember God much."[366] "O you, who have believed, obey Allah and obey the Messenger and those in authority among you. And if you disagree over anything, refer it to Allah and the Messenger, if you should believe in Allah and the Last Day. That is the best [way] and best in result. The prophet himself instructed, "I have left two things with you which if you hold on to, you shall not be misguided: the book of God and my example."[367]

بِسْمِ ٱللَّهِ ٱلرَّحْمَٰنِ ٱلرَّحِيمِ

يَٰٓأَيُّهَا ٱلَّذِينَ ءَامَنُوٓا۟ أَطِيعُوا۟ ٱللَّهَ وَأَطِيعُوا۟ ٱلرَّسُولَ وَأُو۟لِى ٱلْأَمْرِ مِنكُمْ ۖ فَإِن تَنَٰزَعْتُمْ فِى شَىْءٍ فَرُدُّوهُ إِلَى ٱللَّهِ
وَٱلرَّسُولِ إِن كُنتُمْ تُؤْمِنُونَ بِٱللَّهِ وَٱلْيَوْمِ ٱلْءَاخِرِ ۚ ذَٰلِكَ خَيْرٌ وَأَحْسَنُ تَأْوِيلًا ﴿٥٩﴾

---

[365] https://quran.com/16:44.
[366] Rabbani, "Sharia."
[367] https://quran.com/4:59.

Besides the two main sources of Sharia'ah, there are two derived sources [368] and there is consensus about them. These two sources are categorized into scholarly consensus, or in Arabic "ijma'," and the legal analogy, which is known as "qias." [369] The basis for the latter, which is considered as a strong tool that serves to formulate new rulings, is in the term itself, legal analogy. For instance, drugs are prohibited because of the analogy and the prohibition of alcohol that is established in Qur'an. Therefore, through legal analogy, underlying reasons and causes that exist in Qur'an or Sunnah can be understood and later provide new rulings applicable to changing the way of life and time of people. The former, ijma', is a way to resolve controversies and legal cases through consultation. The basis for ijma' is Qur'an itself. As noted below, "those who answer the call of Allah, established prayer, and whose affairs are by consultations. Here the scholarly consensus is defined as when all those Muslim scholars agree at the level of reasoning in one age on a given legal ruling. It is worth mentioning that in fact its objective is limited to issues that are in accordance with Qur'an and Sunnah.

To conclude, we need to affirm that Muslims submitting to Sharia'ah express their slavehood to their creator and believe that Sharia'ah does well for this entire world too. As reported by Sahih al-Bukhari, the divine statement conveyed by Prophet Muhammad himself is:[370]

بِسْمِ ٱللَّهِ ٱلرَّحْمَٰنِ ٱلرَّحِيمِ

وَٱلَّذِينَ ٱسْتَجَابُوا۟ لِرَبِّهِمْ وَأَقَامُوا۟ ٱلصَّلَوٰةَ وَأَمْرُهُمْ شُورَىٰ بَيْنَهُمْ وَمِمَّا رَزَقْنَٰهُمْ يُنفِقُونَ ٣٨

"My servant approaches Me with nothing more beloved to Me than what I have made obligatory upon him, and My servant keeps drawing nearer to Me with voluntary works until I love him. And when I love him, I am his hearing with which he hears, his sight with which he sees, his hand with which he seizes, and his foot with which he walks. If he asks Me, I will surely give to him, and if he seeks refuge in Me, I will surely protect him." (Prophet Muhammad, reported by Bukhari).[371]

---

[368] Caesar Farah, *Islam*, 7th ed., Barron's Educational Series, 2003, pp. 193-194.
[369] Shah Abdul Hannan, "Islamic Jurisprudence: Qiyas," http://www.muslimtents.com/aminahsworld/Islamic_jurisprudence_qiyas.html.
[370] https://quran.com/42:38
[371] Khalid al-Khazraji, Muhammad Ghoniem and M.S.M. Saifullah, "On The Nature Of Hadith Collections Of Imam Al-Bukhari & Muslim," Islamic Awareness, 1999:

Sharia'ah and the Economy

Here we analyze the framework offered by Sharia'ah that, after being applied to classical economics, gave birth to a field of study called Islamic economics. In fact, it is set forth and made operational through principles and rules directly derived from Sharia'ah and, as mentioned earlier, sources such as Qur'an and Sunnah. These rules and principles are applied to the economy considering the four-dimensional continuum conditions in addition to the economic problem at hand. These principles, as was the case for other aspects of human life, have had a key role in shaping the concept of Islamic economics, created around the concept of worshiping God. As previously mentioned, the concept of worship confirms that humankind was created on earth to worship God alone and then to make the planet flourish. This is how not worshiping God is considered as a defect in the basic condition of a human being, and is considered as kufr.[372] Since Islam is considered as a religion of an integrated life that includes both the one on earth and the hereafter, "it must possess an economic system distinct from all other economic systems. It is a divine system with regulated characteristics and components."[373] As the Islamic economic system serves the objectives of the aforementioned integrated system of life, it is not influenced or affected by individual wishes or desires, except that they also serve the overall objectives of the system. Therefore, if these principles are ignored, positive and negative results can follow.[374]

The Islamic economic system is constructed on principles and concepts that are offered and put in place by Sharia'ah. However, the objectives of this system are to achieve an equilibrium that ultimately would promote justice. Foremost among these, by rejecting and condemning any excessive behavior, the owner of all wealth is considered Allah. Humans are there to manage God's wealth in accordance with God's rulings. In connection with that, humans are allowed to obtain wealth and accumulate wealth, but within Sharia'ah-defined borders. In addition, wealth acquired through

---

http://www.islamic-awareness.org/; http://www.islamic-awareness.org/Hadith/bukhari.html; Sahih Al Bukhari, Sunnah.com: https://sunnah.com/bukhari; Sahih Bukhari, M. Mushin Khan, Islamhouse.com: https://d1.islamhouse.com/; Mohammad Shafi, "The Hadith: How it was collected and complied," Dar Al Islam Institute: http://www.daralislam.org/portals/0/Publications/TheHADITHHowitwasCollectedandCompiled.pdf.

[372] Ibn al-Qayyim, "Types of Kufr and Ruling by Other than What Allah has Revealed," in *Madarij us-Salikin*, Vol. 1, Salafi Publications, pp. 335-338.

[373] Elsiddig Talha M. Rahama, "Zakat, Waqf and Sadaqa and their Role in the Fight against Poverty: The Different Aspects of Islamic Culture," Islam in the world today, UNESCO, 2016.

[374] *Ibid.*

methods that are compliant with Sharia'ah must be also justified by an individual's social and spiritual necessities. Business activities conducted in Sharia'ah-complaint ways are considered as worshiping God. Although Islam does not restrict economic activities and allows a free-market economy, in order to establish and advance concepts such as justice, it imposes specific measures for such an economy.[375]

Restrictions in regards to the economy with different objectives such as advancing social justice or avoiding the accumulation of wealth are numerous; however, they are not observed and applied uniformly everywhere. The main body of limits and restrictions in that regard affects concepts such as the time value of money, property rights and the distribution of wealth. For instance, the time value of money is an important concept in finance. It simply means that the value of money is different in the future than today because it can be invested and earn interest. The principles discussed in the previous section, such as resource allocation and the transfer of resources from surplus units to deficit units, are not accepted or recognized in Islamic economics. Interest is an ancient concept that has been practiced since antiquity. Being considered as a form of sin during the medieval period, its questionable character started to vanish during the Renaissance when people understood that money can have value and borrowing money and investing money can improve their business and bring prosperity to their lives. However, within the Muslim world the concept of interest being regarded as a sin started to gain popularity. Toward the end of twentieth century, more and more Islamic countries started to have problems with the concept of interest on loans.

Interest in Islam

Interest is prohibited in Islam. The money earned through money itself is known as Riba. This literally means "increment or addition," and within Islamic economics it means any unjustified increment on money lent or borrowed, whether it is paid in kind or in terms of money itself. Therefore, whether it is an imposed increment by the lender or unilaterally offered by the borrower, since it is above the original amount it is considered Riba and can be categorized as debt usury or, if related to trade, trade usury. It is worth mentioning that other types of Riba also exist, even though the main categories are those just mentioned. This is mainly because in Islam, money as a medium of exchange does not have a value itself; it is there to define the value of other products. The issue of usury is also mentioned in Qur'an.

First of all God gives a warning on Riba: "That which ye give in usury in order that it may increase on (other) people's property hath no increase with

---

[375] Faleel Jamaldeen, *Islamic Finance for Dummies*, John Wiley & Sons, 2012.

Allah; but that which ye give in charity, seeking Allah's Countenance, hath increase manifold."[376]

بِسۡمِ ٱللَّهِ ٱلرَّحۡمَٰنِ ٱلرَّحِيمِ

وَمَآ ءَاتَيۡتُم مِّن رِّبٗا لِّيَرۡبُوَاْ فِيٓ أَمۡوَٰلِ ٱلنَّاسِ فَلَا يَرۡبُواْ عِندَ ٱللَّهِۖ وَمَآ ءَاتَيۡتُم مِّن زَكَوٰةٖ
تُرِيدُونَ وَجۡهَ ٱللَّهِ فَأُوْلَٰٓئِكَ هُمُ ٱلۡمُضۡعِفُونَ ٣٩

Secondly, Muslims are ordered and warned in regards to interest and the way it is calculated, specifically the compound rate:[377] "O ye who believe! Devour not usury, doubled and multiplied; but fear Allah; that ye may (really) prosper."[378]

بِسۡمِ ٱللَّهِ ٱلرَّحۡمَٰنِ ٱلرَّحِيمِ

يَٰٓأَيُّهَا ٱلَّذِينَ ءَامَنُواْ لَا تَأۡكُلُواْ ٱلرِّبَوٰٓاْ أَضۡعَٰفٗا مُّضَٰعَفَةٗۖ وَٱتَّقُواْ ٱللَّهَ لَعَلَّكُمۡ
تُفۡلِحُونَ ١٣٠

And finally, by Qur'an, Riba is not only definitely condemned as an act, but those that get involved with it face a holy war declared against them by Allah and his Messenger.[379] Considering the chronological aspect of Qur'an's revelation to the Prophet Muhammad, this is the third passage and the last one on usury: "Those who devour usury will not stand except as stand one whom the Evil one by his touch hath driven to madness. That is because they say, 'Trade is like usury,' but Allah hath permitted trade and forbidden usury. Those who after receiving direction from their Lord, desist, shall be pardoned for the past; their case is for Allah (to judge); but those who repeat (the offence) are companions of the Fire: They will abide therein (forever)."[380]

---

[376] https://quran.com/30/39-49.
[377] Abdel-Rahman Yousri Ahmad, "Riba, Its Economic Rationale and Implications," Institute of Islamic University, Pakistan: http://www.islamic-banking.com/iarticles_8.aspx.
[378] https://quran.com/3/130-140.
[379] Ahmad, "Riba, Its Economic Rationale and Implications."
[380] https://quran.com/2/275-285.

بِسۡمِ ٱللَّهِ ٱلرَّحۡمَٰنِ ٱلرَّحِيمِ

ٱلَّذِينَ يَأۡكُلُونَ ٱلرِّبَوٰاْ لَا يَقُومُونَ إِلَّا كَمَا يَقُومُ ٱلَّذِي يَتَخَبَّطُهُ ٱلشَّيۡطَٰنُ مِنَ ٱلۡمَسِّۚ
ذَٰلِكَ بِأَنَّهُمۡ قَالُوٓاْ إِنَّمَا ٱلۡبَيۡعُ مِثۡلُ ٱلرِّبَوٰاْۗ وَأَحَلَّ ٱللَّهُ ٱلۡبَيۡعَ وَحَرَّمَ ٱلرِّبَوٰاْۚ فَمَن جَآءَهُۥ مَوۡعِظَةٞ
مِّن رَّبِّهِۦ فَٱنتَهَىٰ فَلَهُۥ مَا سَلَفَ وَأَمۡرُهُۥٓ إِلَى ٱللَّهِۖ وَمَنۡ عَادَ فَأُوْلَٰٓئِكَ أَصۡحَٰبُ ٱلنَّارِۖ هُمۡ
فِيهَا خَٰلِدُونَ ٢٧٥

"Allah will deprive usury of all blessing, but will give increase for deeds of charity: For He loveth not creatures ungrateful and wicked."[381]

يَمۡحَقُ ٱللَّهُ ٱلرِّبَوٰاْ وَيُرۡبِي ٱلصَّدَقَٰتِۗ وَٱللَّهُ لَا يُحِبُّ كُلَّ كَفَّارٍ أَثِيمٍ ٢٧٦

"Those who believe, and do deeds of righteousness, and establish regular prayers and regular charity, will have their reward with their Lord: on them shall be no fear, nor shall they grieve."[382]

إِنَّ ٱلَّذِينَ ءَامَنُواْ وَعَمِلُواْ ٱلصَّٰلِحَٰتِ وَأَقَامُواْ ٱلصَّلَوٰةَ وَءَاتَوُاْ ٱلزَّكَوٰةَ لَهُمۡ أَجۡرُهُمۡ
عِندَ رَبِّهِمۡ وَلَا خَوۡفٌ عَلَيۡهِمۡ وَلَا هُمۡ يَحۡزَنُونَ ٢٧٧

"O ye who believe! Fear Allah, and give up what remains of your demand for usury, if ye are indeed believers."[383]

يَٰٓأَيُّهَا ٱلَّذِينَ ءَامَنُواْ ٱتَّقُواْ ٱللَّهَ وَذَرُواْ مَا بَقِيَ مِنَ ٱلرِّبَوٰٓاْ إِن كُنتُم مُّؤۡمِنِينَ ٢٧٨

"If ye do it not, Take notice of war from Allah and His Messenger: But if ye turn back, ye shall have your capital sums: Deal not unjustly, and ye shall not be dealt with unjustly."

---

381 *Ibid.*
382 *Ibid.*
383 *Ibid.*

فَإِن لَّمۡ تَفۡعَلُواْ فَأۡذَنُواْ بِحَرۡبٖ مِّنَ ٱللَّهِ وَرَسُولِهِۦۖ وَإِن تُبۡتُمۡ فَلَكُمۡ رُءُوسُ أَمۡوَٰلِكُمۡ لَا
تَظۡلِمُونَ وَلَا تُظۡلَمُونَ ٢٧٩

The attempts to justify interest within the Islamic world by Muslim economists themselves, such as M. Dwaleeby, for instance by asserting that interest on loans related to consumption are not justified but those charged on productive activities are not usury, were in vain.[384] All of the attempts to that end are considered as failed since "true Muslims" are not convinced. Schools of thought and institutions such as Al-Azhar of Egypt, the Council of Islamic Ideology in Pakistan and the Islamic Fiqh Academy of the Organization of the Islamic Conference firmly rejected any idea that would justify the concept of interest.[385] Fiqh is an institution and legal framework that also offers rulings and recommendations that prohibit interest or Riba:

> Any gain or profit made out of a loan is Riba. The only return for the lender and the money lent would be being grateful and the repayment.
>
> Based on Islamic finance, a capital owner instead is entitled to profit sharing if the potential loss of the capital is accepted. Profit sharing and guarantee on the capital lent cannot be combined. Therefore, it would be a profit sharing, accepting the loss or the fact that borrowed capital would be given back intact by borrower.

To conclude, we can affirm that money in Islam is not permitted to directly earn a return on the principal, since money is not considered an asset. Thus, interest can cause injustice and ultimately lead to exploitation of the society as a whole. Being treated as "Zulm" in Qur'an itself, it is regarded as unfair.[386]

Sharia'ah and Property Rights

From a general point of view, ownership of everything, from earth to heaven and all included within, belongs to Allah. However, in Islam, humans

---

[384] Sa'idu Sulaiman and Bashir S. Galadanci, *Islamic Banking and Finance: General Framework and Case Studies*, International Institute of Islamic Thoughts, Nigeria Office, 2003.

[385] Ahmad, "Riba, Its Economic Rationale and Implications."

[386] Institute of Islamic Banking and Insurance, "Prohibition of interest," http://www.islamic-banking.com/prohibition_of_interest.aspx; https://quran.com/2/279-289.

are considered as trustees. They are allowed to consume and to use for their own benefit and for the purposes assigned by God to them. Based on the Islamic concept of ownership, Muslims are allowed to have limited ownership over certain things, and over some other items joint ownership is allowed. Therefore, subject to Allah's will, Muslims are granted the right to own property since he/she is not the definitive owner, and the ways the property is utilized must reflect and respect the will of the real owner.[387] In other words, ownership belongs to God and people are allowed to exercise some rights under well-defined conditions in order to fulfill God's purposes. Therefore, once the will and purposes of Allah are respected, people have the right to buy and own property and other products as well as sell it or transfer it through lawful means.[388]

However, these are restricted and limited rights, and difficulties may occur due to specific traits of Islamic jurisprudence. For instance, the prohibition of interest, the obligation of redistributing wealth in different forms of charity and the issue of women's rights and inheritance all affect the definition of property rights compared to other legal systems.[389]

Islam and the Redistribution of Wealth

The concept of wealth distribution is treated differently in Islam. It has moral and ethical dimensions that are based on Allah's will. These address and encompass principles such as humanity, generosity and charity. In Islam, wealth distribution is categorized into two tiers, called primary and secondary. The primary tier considers the distribution of wealth among production factors and mainly those directly involved in the production process. Considering that interest is strictly forbidden in Islam, the factors of production remain land, labor and capital, where the return and reward on capital is based on profit/loss sharing. Therefore, if within the primary tier we see the distribution of wealth in the form of a different kind of reward such as rent for land, wages for labor or profit/loss sharing for capital, the second category is specifically called re-distribution of wealth. This second tier is related to the society and concerns those who are not participating in the production process. These individuals are in need of help. Therefore, to this end there are obligations for Muslims

---

387 Muhammad Akram Khan, *An introduction to Islamic Economics: Islamization of Knowledge*, International Institute of Islamic Thought and Institute of Policy Studies, 1994.
388 Masudul Alam Choudhury, *The Islamic World-System: A Study in Polity-Market Interaction*, Routledge, 2005; Siraj Sait and Hilary Lim, *Land, Law and Islam*, Zed Books, 2006.
389 François Facchini, "Islam and Private Property," Workshop of the European Network on the Economics of Religion, Granada, Spain, 16-17 November 2007; Amy Singer, *Charity in Islamic Societies*, Cambridge University Press, 2008.

that must be fulfilled. Among the many main obligations are Zakat, Waqf and Sadaqa.[390]

Zakat is a kind of obligatory alms, and is considered as the third pillar of Islam, the first pillar being that Allah is the only God and Prophet Muhammad is Allah's messenger, and the second pillar being the worship of Allah. Its placement as the third pillar confirms the importance of paying Zakat. Literally, it means prosperity that purifies and blesses. Consequently, the soul of someone who pays Zakat would be purified and his wealth would be increased. In technical terms, it is the part of individuals' riches which must be set apart for being redistributed to those in need within Muslim societies. That would facilitate the daily lives of those Muslims who are not active in the society since they do not participate in the production process and therefore do not produce any wealth. Muslim scholars figured out that both non-participating Muslims in the production process and those without sufficient income to live have got a marginal propensity to consume close to 100%, which would create a collective demand within the economy and ultimately through the multiplier effect positively affect macroeconomic factors such as investment and employment.[391]

This redistribution of wealth concerns eight categories of people within the Muslim societies who are eligible to receive Zakat:[392]

1. The poor, who cannot permit themselves to buy the basic necessities of daily life such as food, clothing and shelter
2. The needy, who can barely afford daily life's necessities
3. Those who collect Zakat and work to implement Zakat
4. Those whose hearts are considered as reconciled to truth, those who wish to be attracted to Islam or stop being aggressive toward Muslims
5. Those in bondage, these may be given Zakat in order to become free
6. Those in debt, who may receive Zakat in order to pay back their debt
7. Those fighting for Allah's purposes
8. Those who cannot afford their trip and cannot go back home

---

[390] Sayyid Qutb, *Social Justice in Islam*, Bookbaby, 2015; Omer Faruk Senturk, *Charity in Islam: A Comprehensive Guide to Zakat*, Tughra Books, 2007; Janine A. Clark, *Islam Charity and Activism*, Indiana University Press, 2004.

[391] Sulaiman D. Muhammad, Muhammad Usman, Abdul Majid and Ghulam Rasool Lakhan, "Distribution of Wealth: An Islamic Perspective: Theoretical Considerations," *World Applied Sciences Journal*, 23(8), pp. 1118-1124, 2013.

[392] *Ibid.*; Rahama, "Zakat, Waqf and Sadaqa."

The rationales behind promoting the obligatory nature of Zakat are summarized as follows:

- Poor people are the majority in most of the Muslim countries
- Fighting for the purposes of Allah strengthens the Muslims' stance
- Removing the resentment of the poor and reducing feelings such as hatred and animosity toward wealthy people
- Zakat leads to a rise in wealth and an increase in its blessing[393]

However, we need to affirm that being the third pillar of Islam, Zakat is redistributed in different countries through different mechanisms. For instance, in Pakistan, Sudan and Kuwait there are specific laws regulating the collection and redistribution of Zakat at a national level. In other countries such as Malaysia, the way Zakat is collected and distributed is different in each province. In many other places, Zakat is handled through private organizations.

To conclude, Zakat as an institutionalized religion-based aid system that requires Muslims to pay 2.5% of their available income to the eight categories aforementioned. The graph shown here, covering countries with official Zakat institutions, illustrates the increasing number of these institutions between 1971 and 2013.[394]

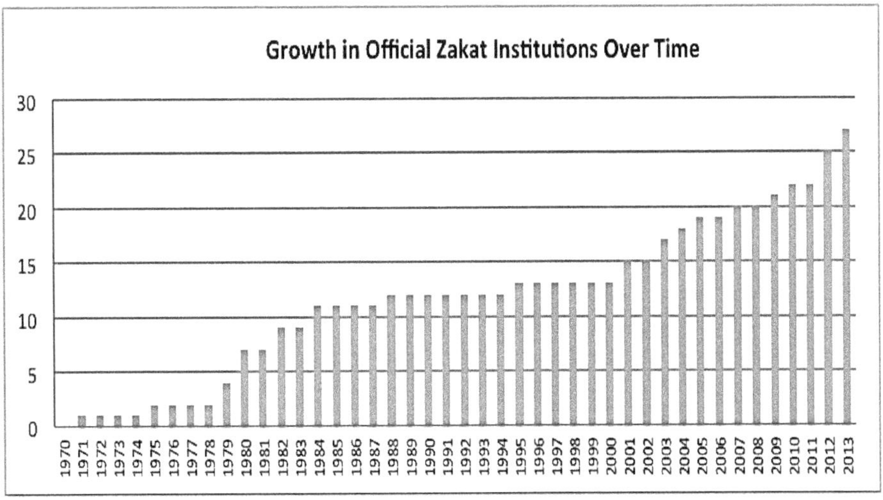

[393] *Ibid.*

[394] Allison Minor, "Zakat and Development Finance: Filling the Gaps," AidData, Open data for International Development, 2014: http://aiddata.org/blog/zakat-and-development-finance-filling-in-the-gaps.

It is worth mentioning that organizations dealing with Zakat, collecting/redistributing, manage billions of dollar each year. Studies are systematically being conducted with the objective of measuring the efficiency of the system.[395]

Another important concept in Islam that needs to be discussed here is the so-called Waqf. Translated from Arabic to English, Waqf simply means "literally stoppage, immobilization (of ownership of property), from waqafa come to a standstill."[396] In affairs related to Islamic economics, from a legal point of view, Waqf is defined as "an endowment made by a Muslim to a religious, educational, or charitable cause."[397] It is considered a religious endowment and can be presented as a voluntary and irrevocable dedication of an individual's riches or part of it, whether it is in kind or in cash, to be spent for Sharia'ah-compliant projects such as mosques, religious schools, etc.[398]

Waqf is considered as a permanent donation and, as such, once dedicated and created it cannot be redirected toward other projects or have its legal status modified. Therefore, being strict and unable to be modified, different types of Waqf are proposed for different purposes. For instance, family waqf would be when the endower gives it to his family and relatives. Charitable Waqf would be when the endowment is devoted to needy strata of the society. The legal status of Waqf is based on Qur'an, Sunnah as well as the scholars' consensus, ijma'.[399] Waqf is the act of taking public or private resources that are productive within an economy and using them with the aim of providing social welfare and improving a society's well-being.

Some of the contributions done through the institution of Waqf toward the growth and development of Muslim societies are:[400]

- Charitable acts becoming accountable institutions supported by private initiatives
- Improving social welfare
- Supporting and developing educational organizations that deal with the memorization of Qur'an and other centers dedicated to different fields of study such as applied and theoretical science, computing and languages
- Preserving the independence of religious centers and mosques

---

395 Mohamad Idham Md Razak, "Overview of Zakat Collection in Malaysia: Regional Analysis," *American International Journal of Contemporary Research*, 3(8), 2013: http://www.aijcrnet.com/journals/Vol_3_No_8_August_2013/17.pdf.

396 Oxford Living Dictionaries: https://en.oxforddictionaries.com/definition/waqf.

397 *Ibid.*

398 U.A.E. General Authority of Islamic Affairs and Endowments, "Definition of Waqf," 11/29/2016: http://www.awqaf.gov.ae/Waqf.aspx?Lang=EN&SectionID=13&RefID=857.

399 Razak, "Overview of Zakat Collection in Malaysia."

400 *Ibid.*; Majid Khadduri and Herbert J. Liebesny, *Origin and Development of Islamic Law*, Lawbook Exchange, 2010.

- Developing administrative and organizational capacity for long term purposes
- Disseminating the culture of Waqf and encouraging people to adopt it
- Tax exemption on Waqf fixed assets
- Creating legal formulas for management and supervision of Waqf institutions
- Integrating Waqf endowments into sources of funding to education and health services
- Creating an integrated network of information regarding Waqf

Waqf is considered a Sharia'ah-compliant charity, which is verified through both general and specific evidence. The general evidence is based on Qur'an itself:

> Allah – Exalted be He – in His revelation said about charity, including Waqf, "By no means shall you attain Al-Birr (piety, righteousness – here it means Allah's reward, *i.e.*, Paradise), unless you spend in Allah's cause. The Messenger of Allah (PBUH) said, 'When a son of Adam dies, his good deeds stop except for three things; ongoing charity, useful knowledge...'"[401]

The specific evidence is related to the Sunnah of the Prophet Muhammad:

> Further, Ibn Umar reported that "Umar acquired land in Khaibar. He approached Prophet Mohammad (PBUH) and sought his advice about it. He said to Allah's Messenger 'I have never acquired anything more valuable for me than this, so what do you command I do with it?' Prophet Mohammad (PBUH) said, 'If you like, you might keep the corpus intact and give its produce as Sadaqah Jariyyah (continuous charity).' So Umar made Sadaqah declaring that the property must not be sold or inherited or given away. The produce to be given the poor, to the needy, to the nearest of kin, to the emancipation of slaves, to wayfarers..."[402]

---

[401] U.A.E. General Authority of Islamic Affairs and Endowments, "Definition of Waqf."
[402] *Ibid.*

Therefore, Waqf is considered as lawful in Islam because it is a form of charity for the sake of Allah that contributes to the development as well as the strengthening of Muslim societies.[403]

Sadaqah, mentioned earlier in the context of Waqf, is another form of charity, the difference from the other two concepts being that Sadaqah is considered as a voluntary donation and the amount offered depends on the wishes of benefactors themselves. It is important because Allah ordered his Messenger directly in regards to Sadaqah as well.[404]

The last concept that may affect the way resources are redistributed is called Khums. Introduced by the Prophet Muhammad's grandfather, it is also mentioned in Qur'an. The related verse is: "And know that out of all the booty that ye may acquire (in war), a fifth share is assigned to Allah, – and to the Messenger, and to near relatives, orphans, the needy, and the wayfarer, – if ye do believe in Allah and in the revelation We sent down to Our servant on the Day of Testing, – the Day of the meeting of the two forces. For Allah hath power over all things."[405]

بِسْمِ اللَّهِ الرَّحْمَٰنِ الرَّحِيمِ

۞ وَاعْلَمُوا أَنَّمَا غَنِمْتُم مِّن شَيْءٍ فَأَنَّ لِلَّهِ خُمُسَهُ وَلِلرَّسُولِ وَلِذِي الْقُرْبَىٰ وَالْيَتَامَىٰ
وَالْمَسَاكِينِ وَابْنِ السَّبِيلِ إِن كُنتُمْ آمَنتُم بِاللَّهِ وَمَا أَنزَلْنَا عَلَىٰ عَبْدِنَا يَوْمَ
الْفُرْقَانِ يَوْمَ الْتَقَى الْجَمْعَانِ ۗ وَاللَّهُ عَلَىٰ كُلِّ شَيْءٍ قَدِيرٌ ﴿٤١﴾

As mentioned in Qur'an, it literally means one fifth, or 20%, however, today it legally represents 20% that must be paid on certain types of wealth

[403] *Ibid.*; Europe Trust : 11/29/2016: http://www.europetrust.eu.com/waqf-awaqf/waqf-concept-diagram/; Pascale Ghazaleh, *Held in Trust: Waqf in the Islamic World*, Oxford University Press, 2011; Peter C. Hennigan, *The Birth of a Legal Institution*, Brill, 2004.

[404] Elsiddig Talha M. Rahama, "Zakat, Waqf and Sadaqa and their roles in fighting poverty, UNESCO 2016; Muhammad Akram Khan, *Islamic Economics and* Finance: A Glossary, Routledge, 2004; Egbert Harmsen, Islam, Civil Society and Social Work, University Press, 2008.

[405] https://quran.com/8/41-51.

obtained by individuals.[406] In other words, it is considered as a tax levied on particular categories of items, which are:[407]

- Income surpluses that can be seen as profit
- The legitimate wealth which is mixed with some illegitimate types
- The precious minerals and natural resources obtained from the sea or soil of Islamic States
- Treasures found within the Islamic States and territories
- The land which a non-Muslim resident buys from a Muslim
- The spoils of war

These categories and policies for collecting Khums vary between the two major branches of Islam. Today, within the Shia branch, although generally Khums must be applied wherever gains and profits occur, it is mainly applied to business profits.[408] Within Shia Muslim countries, Khums is considered as one the major sources of revenue for the clergy. Within Sunni regions, Khums would be applied to the aforementioned categories and there are different points of view concerning whether it is also applicable to income as is the case within Shia countries.[409]

Islam and Finance

Islamic finance can be defined as financial services that are provided to economic actors, but based on and in respect of Sharia'ah law. Within Islamic finance, concepts such as interest known as Riba, uncertainties, short selling and in general activities considered as harmful to Muslims and Muslim societies are strictly prohibited. Therefore, speculation is not mentioned within the Islamic literature on finance. Nonetheless, different financial products have been created in order to meet the needs of Muslim societies in regards to the issue of resource allocations. These products can be organized into three categories:[410]

---

406 Abdulaziz Sachedina Al-Khums: "The Fifth in the Imami Shi i Legal System," *Journal of Near Eastern Studies*, 39(4), 1980, pp. 275-289.
407 "Khums in the Qur'an and History," Al-Islam.org: https://www.al-islam.org/khums-islamic-tax-sayyid-muhammad-rizvi/khums-quran-history; Zafar Iqbal and Mervyn Lewis, *An Islamic Perspective on Governance*, Edward Elgar, pp. 99-115.
408 Ibrahim F. I. Shihata, "Some Observations on the Question of Riba and the Challenges Facing 'Islamic Banking,'" *Internet Journal of the Centre of Energy, Petroleum and Mineral Law and Policy*, Dundee, 1998.
409 Robert W. McGee, *The Ethics of Tax Evasion: Perspectives in Theory and Practice*, Springer, 2001, p. 181.
410 Mumtaz Hussain, Asghar Shahmoradi and Rima Turk, "An Overview of Islamic Finance," International Monetary Fund, 2015.

- Debt like financing
- Profit and loss sharing instruments
- Saving deposits and agency contracts

Debt-like financing consists of products that regulate either sales with deferred payments, also known as Murabaha, or purchases with deferred delivery of the purchased items. This category also includes leasing contracts that offer different buying options at the end of the lease. The second category, profit-and-loss sharing, is designed to offer solutions mainly to investment projects. This is done through two different modalities. The first, also known as Mudarabah, takes place whenever a surplus unit provides the required resources for a project and the beneficiary or deficit unit offers skills and labor in return.[411] Consequently, profits are shared, but in case of loss, the surplus unit, whether it is a bank or an investor, will absorb it. Within Mudarabah types of contract, investors do not have any right of interfering in regards to management of the project. The second modality, known as Musharakah, is considered the pure version of profit-and-loss sharing contracts. Here, both profits and losses are shared by both parties. Finally, the third category, which is also the most common one, concerns services such as current deposits as well as those related to agency contracts. The latter is known as Wakalah and the former as Wadi'ah. A few important products are discussed and analyzed here.

Sukuk

Sukuk is roughly the equivalent of bonds offered in financial markets around the world. It is not considered as owning a debt. Rather, an investor obtains a share of an asset where risks and cash flows are proportional. Being a Sharia'ah-compliant instrument, interest payments do not exist. Returns are based on the cash flows that are created by the asset. As such, the problem of interest payments is circumvented and the benefits of debt financing perfectly distributed. The differences between an Islamic bond and the conventional one are identified below through the table on the next page.[412]

[411] *Ibid.*

[412] Mohamed Ariff, Munawar Iqbal and Shamsher Mohamad, *The Islamic Debt Market for Sukuk Securities: The Theory and Practice of Profit Sharing Investment*, Edward Elgar Publishing, 2012; Amana Bank, "Internet Banking," http://www.amanabank.lk/.

	Conventional Bond	Asset Backed Securities	*Sukuk*
Primary Level Relationship	Lending and borrowing transaction (loan); thus *haram*.	Sale of debt or income generating asset	Variety underlying Shariah contracts *('uqud)*
Return to Investors	Interest on loan.	Income generated from underlying asset	Profit elements in underlying contracts (sale, lease or partnership)
Recourse	To issuer	To asset	To the rights and obligations of the contracts.
Tradability in Secondary Market	Sale of debt	Sale of debt or income generating asset	Depends on nature of underlying assets. Majority scholars allow sale of tangible asset, some intangible asset and interest in ventures, except issues on receivables.

Sukuk is considered a Sharia'ah compliant debt instrument because:

- Funds raised through Sukuk are used for activities that are Halal
- Funds are directed toward needed tangible assets rather than an unspecified asset
- Cash flows are generated through tangible assets' profits
- Investors are considered as shareholders of the asset
- The parties involved are known
- There are no fixed returns on bonds

Although the way Sukuks are structured can be distinct from each other, the two principal building blocks they have in common are:

- The obligation created by the parties must be based on one of the Sharia'ah contracts, known and qualified as uqud-al-musamma
- The forms of Sukuk correspond to Sharia'ah contracts, in confirmation of the previous step[413]

Sukuks can be offered in different formats and differently structured. The main categories are sales-based, lease-based, agency-based and partnership. Each can encompass different types of instruments and financial tools, as seen in the following chart.[414]

---

[413] Mohd Nazri Bin Chik, "Sukuk: Shariah Guidelines for Islamic Bonds, Islamic Banking Operations and Regulatory Framework," Centre for Banking Studies, Central Bank of Sri Lanka, 2012.
[414] *Ibid.*

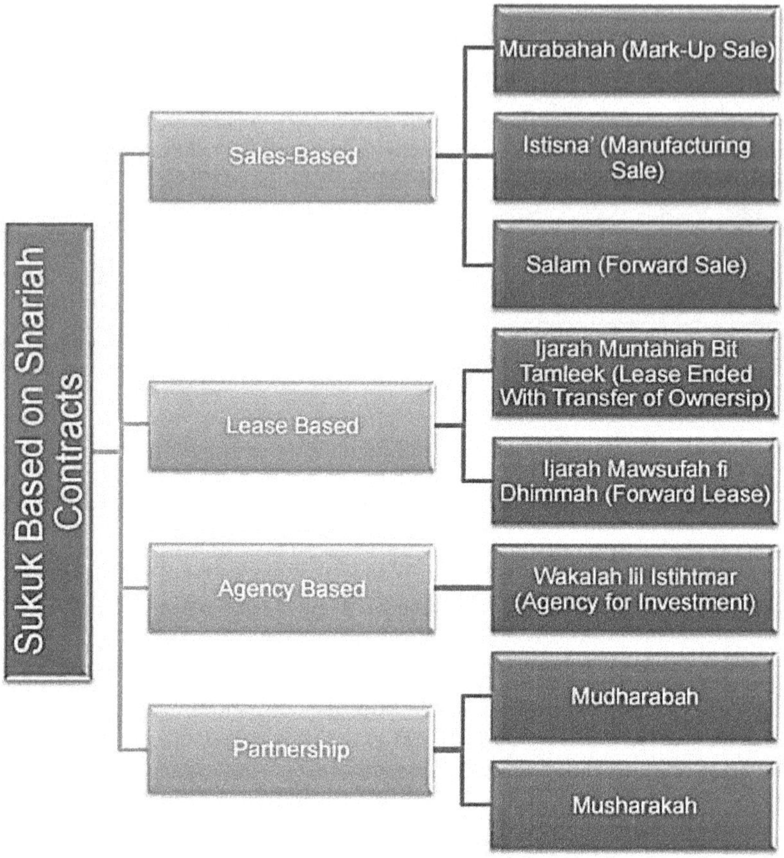

Sukuks can be differentiated through known features such as an issuer's objectives, the availability of an asset, a company's debt situation, a credit rating, and the tax and legal framework of a particular structure. However, the main distinctions between Sukuks can be identified and presented through four commonly used contracts available within Islamic capital markets: Ijarah, Murabaha and Istisna, Mudarabah and Musharakah.[415] They are described in the table on the next page.[416]

[415] Selim Cakir and Faezeh Raei, "Sukuk Vs. Eurobonds: Is There a Difference in Value-at-Risk?" International Monetary Fund, 2007.
[416] Bank Islam: http://www.bankislam.com.my/.

Nature of Sukuk	Contract	Feature
Represents ownership of asset, its usufruct or services (the "Underlying Asset")	Ijarah	▪ the sukuk are akin to trust certificates bearing undivided ownership in the leased asset and the rights to the cash flow stream arising from it as well as proceeds from sale of the assets
Evidences of indebtedness arising from sale of asset	*Murabahah* and *Istisna'*	▪ the claim is on the obligations arising from the applied contract of exchange. ▪ In this case, the sukuk does not represent ownership on the physical asset as the ownership of the asset has been transferred to the obligor, though in certain cases, depending on the credit strength of the obligor, assets are provided as collateral or security to the indebtedness.
Represents ownership of units of equal value in the equity and are registered in the names of holders on the basis of undivided ownership of shares in the scheme	*Mudharabah*	▪ Returns due to the holders as owners of capital are distributed according to the percentage of ownership. ▪ Losses are borne in totality by the sukuk holders in accordance to percentages of the shares owned unless the losses are attributed to the negligence and/or wilful misconduct of the *mudharib*, who will be responsible for the same.
Represents ownership of units of equal value in the equity and are registered in the names of holders on the basis of undivided ownership of shares in the scheme	*Musharakah*	▪ Returns and losses due to the holders as owners of capital are distributed according to the percentage of ownership.

The mechanisms that guarantee the functionalities of Islamic bonds may vary. However, those issued in the form of trust certificates, which are also the most common and have a more complicated structure, are comprehensible to nonprofessional investors because they are governed through non-Islamic laws. It is worth mentioning that the Western legal system is considered not supportive enough of the Sukuk market. The functioning of Sukuk is influenced by laws that are not Sharia'ah-compliant.[417] This is considered as an issue among Muslim investors and scholars as some specific features of Islamic securitization are not observed. As noted earlier, these features, such as riba, gharar and maysir, are firmly prohibited. Based on the Accounting and Auditing Organization for Islamic

[417] Umar A. Oseni and M. Kbair Hassan, "Regulating the governing law clauses in Sukuk Transactions," *Journal of Banking Regulations*, 2014; Jhorday Kashoogie Nazar, "Regulatory and Financial Implications of Sukuk's Legal Challenges for Sustainable Sukuk Development in Islamic Capital Markets," 8th International Conference on Islamic Economics and Finance, Hamed Bin Khalifa University, http://www.hbku.edu.qa/en/cis: http://webcache.googleusercontent.com/search?q=cache:v0XE0hIq9pcJ:conference.qfis.edu.qa/app/media/298+&cd=2&hl=en&ct=clnk&gl=fr#1.

Financial Institutions (AAOIFI), the specific categories of permissible Sukuk are as follows:[418]

هيئة المحاسبة والمراجعة للمؤسسات المالية الإسلامية
Accounting and Auditing Organisation for Islamic Financial Institutions

No	Securitization of/ Purpose	Contract
1	Existing or to be acquired tangible asset	Ijarah
2	Existing or to be acquired leasehold asset	Ijarah
3	Presale of services	Ijarah
4	To fund construction	Istisna'
5	Presale of the production of goods or commodities at a future date	Salam
6	To fund the acquisition of goods for future sale	Murabahah
7	To fund capital participation in a business or investment activity	Mudarabah/ Musharakah
8	To fund various asset, goods or services acquisition which are then entrusted to an agent to manage on behalf of the owners.	Wakalah
9	To raise funds for agricultural land cultivation, land management and orchard management activities	Muzara'ah

Securitization is a process that would ultimately end with a group of financial assets bound together which would be later introduced as a new security to the market. Cash flows are based on what is generated through underlying assets packed together and branded as the new security. Therefore, there would be an originator that gathers the assets together and sells or transfers this newly created security to an issuer. The issuer can be an entity called a special purpose vehicle (SPV) that exists for a limited time just to serve this purpose. Offshore special purpose vehicles can be created for the organizations and companies that are willing to issue Sukuks.[419] Once this occurs, trust certificates are issued and offered to qualified investors, who in return would share the profits generated though the asset.[420] The issue in

[418] Accounting and Auditing Organization for Islamic Financial Institutions, "Securitizations and permissible categories," http://aaoifi.com/?lang=en.
[419] Khairun Najmi Saripudin, Shamsiah Mohamad, Nor Fahimah Mohd Razif, Luqman Haji Abdullah and Noor Naemah Abdul Rahman, "Case Study on Sukuk Musharakah Issued in Malaysia," *Middle-East Journal of Scientific Research* 12(2), 2012, pp. 168-175.
[420] Bin Chik, "Sukuk: Shariah Guidelines."

regards to Sukuk is in the common form of a trust certificate. These are safer and offers a lower profit rate, but are complicated to analyze and are governed as mentioned by non-Islamic laws within the Western legal framework. Sukuk ijarah can be illustrated as below:[421]

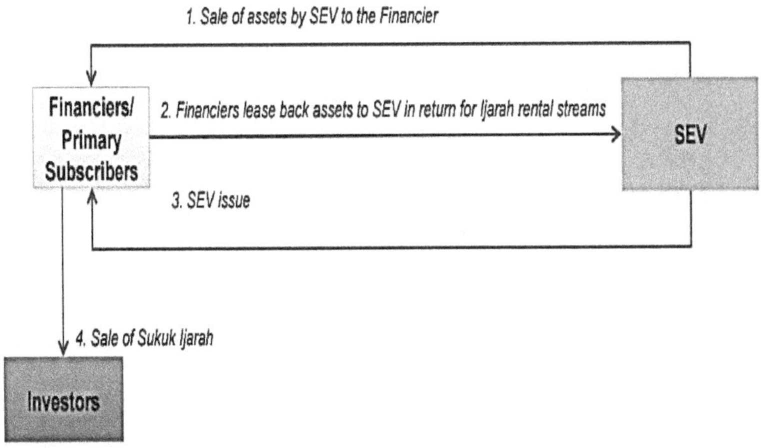

Within this framework, the issuer takes an asset originally belonging to the issuer itself on lease from the investor, called ijarah, and would sell it to investors, before it is leased back to the issuer for a rental. Through an SPV, the issuer issues Sukuk-type ijarah to the investor who can sell it to the secondary market, confirming that it is backed by a tangible asset.[422] Another Sukuk to be introduced is Sukuk Istisna. In this framework Sukuk are structured in order to finance projects that must be completed. As shown in the following diagram, the issuer accepts a project from its counterparty and enters into Istisna 1 with investors that are supposed to complete the project and deliver it back to the issuer. The costs and profit margin are paid later by creating a SPV. The investors enter into Istinsa 2 where the final payments would be done based on the agreed terms on the contract.[423]

---

[421] Salman Syed Ali, "Introduction to Ijarah Sukuk: Current Structures and Future Prospects," Monetary and Banking Research Institute: http://new.mbri.ac.ir/userfiles/file/Islamic%20Banking/%D8%A8%D8%A7%D9%86%DA%A9%20%D9%85%D9%82%D8%A7%D9%84%D8%A7%D8%AA/sukuk/introduction%20to%20ijarah%20sukuk%20current%20structures%20and%20future%20prospects.PDF.

[422] Rafe Haneef, "Retail Sukuk and SRI Sukuk: The Malaysian Experience," 1st Annual Islamic Finance Conference, Jakarta, the Islamic Research and Training Institute, 2016.

[423] Bin Chik, "Sukuk: Shariah Guidelines."

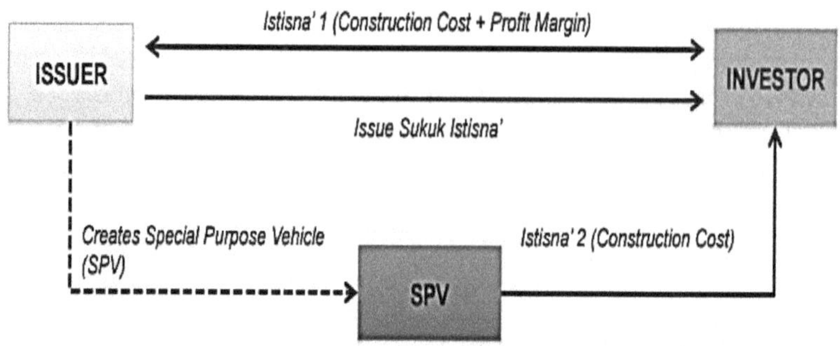

In such a contract, the sale price is represented under "Istisna 1," which is securitization of the obligation to pay the Istisna's price. It cannot be traded yet since the debt is not yet established. The following two real-life examples elucidate further the Sukuk in general and at the same time present two more different types of Sukuk, known as Sukuk Murabahah and Sukuk Musharakah.[424]

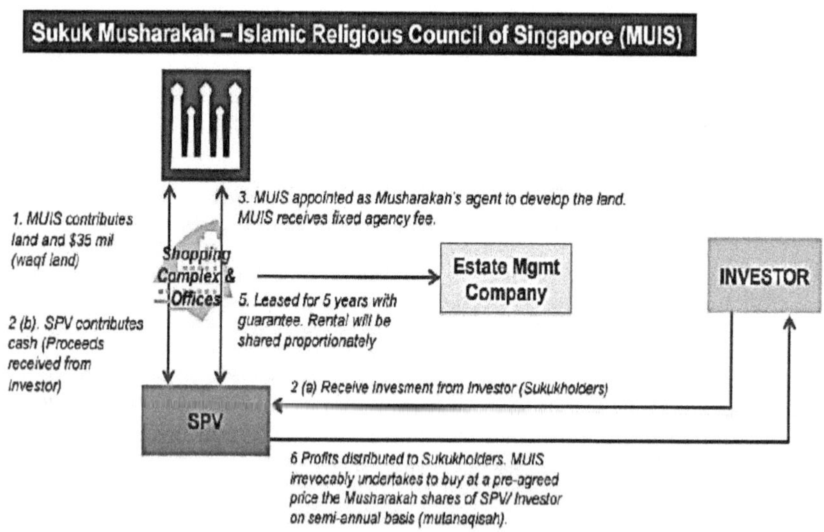

In this case, both parties represented by a special purpose vehicle participate in the project that can be also managed by a third organization. The issuer introduces Sukuk Musharakah based on capital injected by investors and a defined rate of profit which would be indicative and, if realized, would

[424] *Ibid.*

be shared between the parties based on the basis of agreed amounts. The difference with the usual Sukuk is that if losses occur, the parties will bear them together in amounts that are proportional to their participations.[425] The other type presented is known as Sukuk Murabahah, in which Malaysia's mortgage corporation assets that are Halal and that come from different financial institutions.

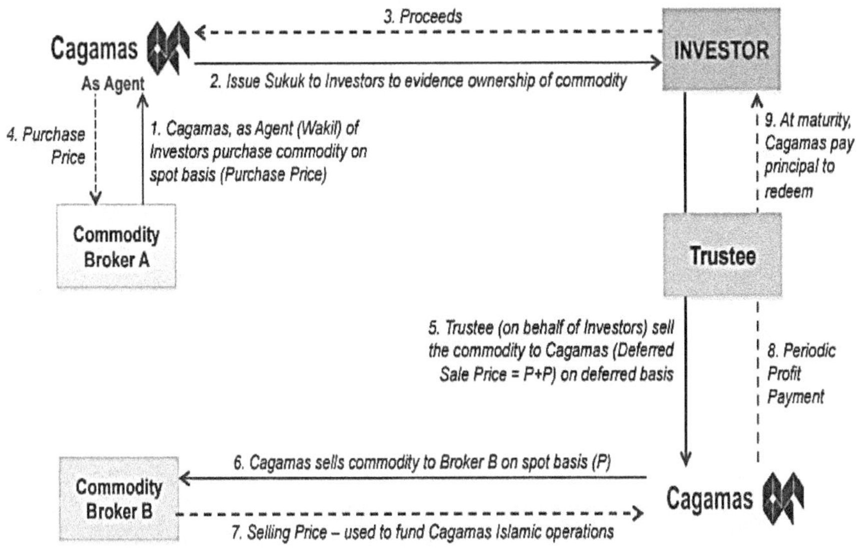

The Sukuk market, although it has performed well in its own right, has also been affected by the trends that occur within the conventional capital markets. Globally, Sukuk publicly issued and sold reached the threshold of $300.9 billion at the end of 2014.[426]

[425] Latham & Watkins LLP, "The Sukuk handbook: A Guide to Structuring Sukuk," https://www.lw.com/thoughtLeadership/guide-to-structurings-sukuk-2015.
[426] Islamic Financial Services Board, 2016 Report: http://www.ifsb.org/.

Global *Sukūk* Outstanding Trend (2003–11M15)

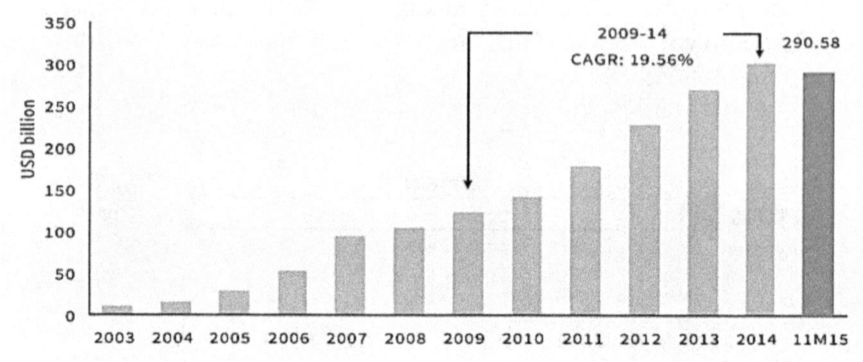

Source: Zawya, Bloomberg, IFSB.

The main cause of the growth within the Sukuk market was an increase of activity within the Sukuk primary market. As the following chart shows, government authorities have been the main issuers.[427]

Global *Sukūk* Issuances – Sovereign and Corporate (2004–11M15)

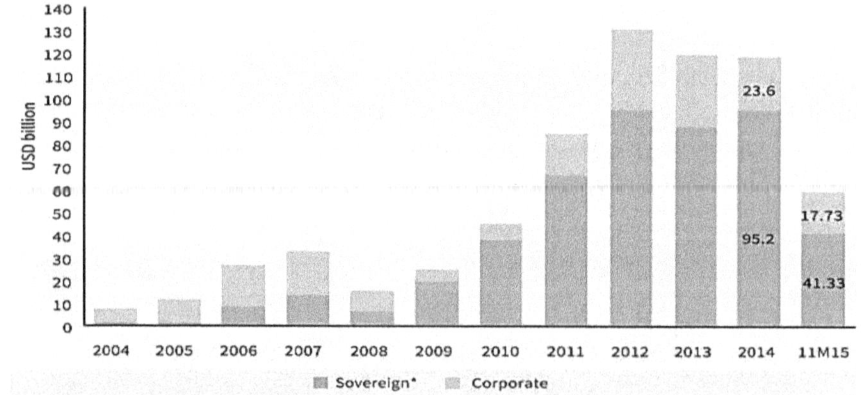

***Includes all GREs, multilateral development banks (MDBs) and international organisations (IOs).**
Source: Zawya, Bloomberg, IFSB.

[427] *Ibid.*; Bin Chik, "Sukuk: Shariah Guidelines;" Mohammad Hashim Kamali and A.K. Abdullah, *Islamic Finance: Issues in Sukuk and Proposals for Reform*, Kube Publishing Ltd, 2014.

Globally, the Sukuk issued and sold publicly has decreased 3.4% since 2014, and as of November 2015 the outstanding volume was valued at \$290.58 billion, mainly due to the absence of the Malaysian Central Bank (MCB) from the market. However, governments and state entities in 13 countries kept the market moving forward. Oman, one of the GCC members, issued a 5-year Sukuk known as al-ijarah, which amounted to \$650 million.[428] Sukuk were issued in order to provide investment options to institutions with excess funds that would consequently provide resources to the Sultanate of Oman for development projects.[429] Despite the MCB's absence in 2015, Malaysia remained the key player and Sukuk issuer. The main entities involved were those of the energy sector, such as Petronas; infrastructure builders such as Dana Infra; and Malaysia's sovereign wealth fund.[430]

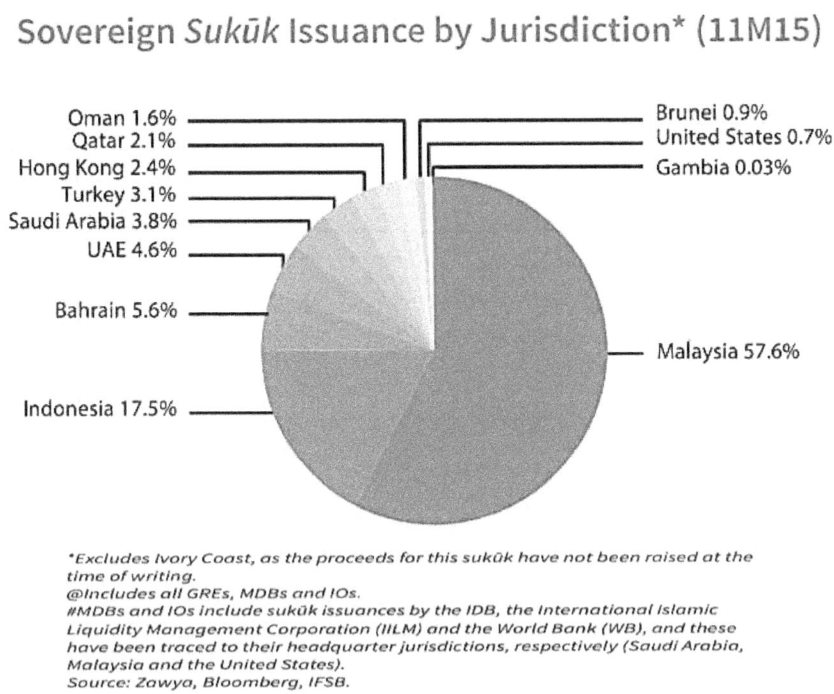

---

428 "Oman to issue first sovereign Sukuk by mid-2015," Reuters, 2015: http://www.reuters.com/article/oman-sukuk-idUSL5N0W30G420150301; Central Bank of Oman: http://www.cbo-oman.org/.

429 Central Bank of Oman, "Government development bond auction results," http://www.cbo-oman.org/circulars/2016/BM1144.pdf.

430 "Malaysia's Sukuk volumes will be stable, driven by corporate and sovereign refinancing," Moody's Investor Service, 2015: https://www.moodys.com/research/Moodys-Malaysias-sukuk-volumes-will-be-stable-driven-by-corporate--PR_325842; Islamic Financial Services Board, 2016 report: http://www.ifsb.org/.

Corporate issuers were also among the actors within the Islamic capital market. Their share of global Sukuk outstanding amounted to $17.7 billion, or approximately 30% of the market.[431] Despite challenges faced by global capital markets, mainly due to the American Federal Reserve Bank in regards to quantitative easing policies and other socio-political challenges in various areas of the globe, corporations within eight countries – the United Arab Emirates, Turkey, Saudi Arabia, Qatar, Bahrain, Pakistan, Indonesia and Malaysia – tapped the Islamic bond market, Sukuk.[432] As shown below, Malaysia and Saudi Arabia had the biggest shares. The Malaysian corporations that issued Sukuk were from different sectors of the economy, from agriculture and retail to real estate and health care services, and the maturities ranged from one month to 20 years. This is in contrast to the Gulf Cooperation Council countries, where Sukuk issuers were mainly those in the financial services sector and the maturities were limited to between five and ten years.[433]

Corporate *Sukūk* Issuance by Jurisdiction* (11M15)

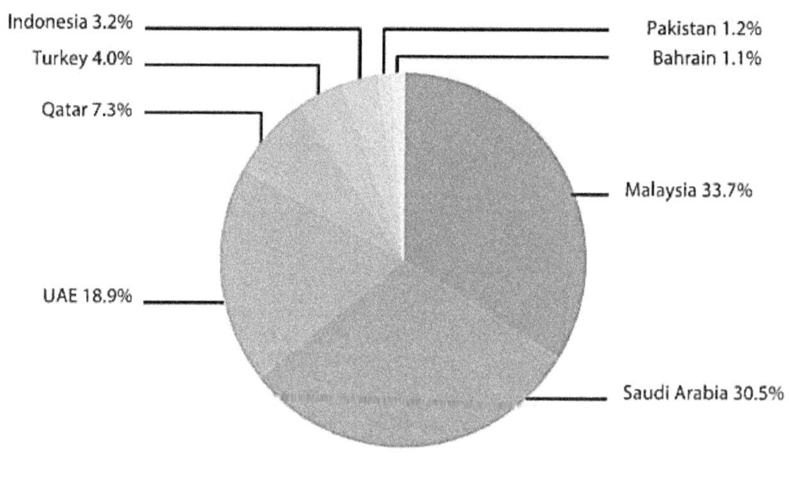

**Based on obligor's domicile.*
Source: Zawya, Bloomberg, IFSB.

---

[431] Islamic Financial Services Board, 2016 Report.
[432] *Ibid.*
[433] Rifaat Ahmed Abdel Karim and Simon Archer, *Islamic Finance: The Regulatory Challenge*, Wiley Finance, 2007.

Malaysia and Indonesia each accounted respectively for $29.8 billion and $7.8 billion of the total outstanding corporate and sovereign Sukuk. Collectively, the GCC countries accounted for 29.8% of the total volume.[434]

A sectoral breakdown of Sukuk issues in 2015 shows the financial sector's share increased to 34.43%, nearly the same as the 43.48% issued by governments. Other significant sectors included transportation (6.90%), power and utilities (4.45%) and construction (3.82%).[435]

Despite an increasing familiarity with Sukuk as an Islamic financial tool, the challenges that Sukuk and the Sukuk market in general face have proved insurmountable. Different Sharia'ah-based ideas concerning how the instrument must be traded, for instance, are one of the most important obstacles affecting liquidity.[436] The general tendency among investors to hold the instruments until maturity also adds to the problem of liquidity and the development of the secondary market. Islamic legislation has promoted standardized Sukuk, at least for the purpose of international markets, in order to overcome issues such as liquidity[437] and to adopt more harmonized and standardized infrastructures.[438]

Takaful

As is the case for Sukuk, which is considered as a conventional bond equivalent, Takaful is considered as a counterpart of conventional insurance. The term in Arabic means "joint guarantee," and it involves groups of individuals who form in order to support themselves whenever specified risks exist and losses can occur. The Islamic Financial Services Board offers a technical definition:

> In a Takaful arrangement participants contribute a sum of money as a "Tabarru[439]" commitment into a common fund that will be used

[434] Islamic Financial Services Board, 2016 Report.

[435] Abdou Diaw, Obiyathulla Ismath Bacha and Ahcene Lahsasna, "Incentive-Compatible Sukuk Musharakah for Private Sector Funding," *ISRA International Journal of Islamic Finance*, 4(1), 2012.

[436] Naveen Muhammad, "Sukuk and the problem of short term liquidity: Global home of the Sukuk industry," 2014: https://www.sukuk.com/article/sukuk-problem-short-term-liquidity-3508/.

[437] "Issues in Islamic Liquidity," *International Financing Review*, 2007: http://www.ifre.com/issues-in-islamic-liquidity/552713.fullarticle

[438] Sohail Jaffer, "Infrastructure Sukuk," World Bank, 2015: http://pubdocs.worldbank.org/en/109671448479782899/pdf/islamic-finance-2015-11-18-Sohail-Jaffer-Infrastrcture-Sukuk.pdf.

[439] Tabarru is the amount of contribution that the takāful/retakāful participants commit to donate in order to fulfil the obligation of mutual help in bearing the risks and paying the claims of eligible claimants; see http://www.ifsb.org/terminologies.php.

mutually to assist the members against a specified type of loss or damage. The underwriting in a Takaful is thus undertaken on a mutual basis similar in some respect to conventional mutual insurance. A typical Takaful undertaking consists of a two tier structure that is hybrid of a mutual and a commercial form of company which is a Takaful operator although in principle it could be a pure mutual structure.[440]

Takaful's features respect Sharia'ah law. Foremost, the concept of interest is never computed, since it is considered as an unfair and inequitable concept in Islam, as expressed several times in Qur'an itself. Secondly, Gharar or uncertainty does not exist. Uncertainty is part of conventional insurance products. Such products are offered and based on transfers of risk in return for premiums; concepts such as timing, severity and frequency are subject to uncertainty, and are not considered while computing or creating Takaful products. Thirdly, since gambling is prohibited in Islam, conventional insurance products that include speculative elements are Haram. Types of life insurance can be considered as gambling because one party benefits at the expense of another.[441] For instance, with a conventional term insurance contract, the risk is transferred to the insurer in return for a fixed premium and the payment of a small amount of money that could yield a disproportionate sum when the policyholders benefit at the expense of the insurer.[442]

Ultimately, the fact that insurance companies can invest their resources wherever they deem profitable is not accepted within the Muslim faith since they may be ultimately invested in activities that are considered as Haram. A comparison of Takaful with conventional insurance is given in the following table.[443]

---

440 Islamic Financial Service Board: http://www.ifsb.org/index.php

441 Debo Ajayi, *Takaful (Islamic Insurance): Concept, Challenges and Opportunities*, Milliman, 2010.

442 Simon Archer, Rifaat Ahmed Abdel Karim and Volker Nienhaus, *Takaful Islamic Insurance: Concepts and Regulatory Issues*, John Wiley & Sons, 2011; Kabir Hassan and Mervyn Lewis, *Handbook of Islamic Banking*, Edward Elgar Publishing, 2009; Mahmoud A. El-Gamal, *Islamic Finance: Law, Economics and Practice*, Cambridge University Press, 2006; Abu Umar Faruq Ahmad, *Theory and Practice of Modern Islamic Finance: The Case Analysis from Australia*, Universal Publisher, 2010; Abdulrahman Zuriah, "Takaful: Potential Demand and Growth," *Islamic Economic Journal*, 2010: http://www.kau.edu.sa/Show_Res.aspx?Site_ID=121&LNG=EN&RN=57694.

443 Mohammad Khan, "Takaful versus Conventional Insurance, Monetary and Banking," Research Institute: http://new.mbri.ac.ir/userfiles/file/Islamic%20Banking/%D8%A8%D8%A7%D9%86%DA%A9%20%D9%85%D9%82%D8%A7%D9%84%D8%A7%D8%AA/Takaful/Takaful%20vs%20Conventional%20Insurance.PDF.

CONVENTIONAL INSURANCE	TAKAFUL
A risk transfer mechanism whereby risk is transferred from the policyholder (the insured) to the insurance company (the insurer) in consideration of an 'insurance premium' paid by the insured.	Based on mutuality; hence the risk is not transferred but shared by the participants, who form a common pool. The company (takaful operator) acts only as the manager of the pool. In effect, the policyholders are both the insurer and the insured.
Contains the element of uncertainty, i.e., Gharar, which is forbidden in islam. The terms of the contract are unclear as to certainty of when any loss would occur and how much compensation would be payable.	The element of uncertainty, i.e., Gharar, is brought down to acceptable levels under shariah by characterising contributions as donations (Tabarru'), not obligations, and for a good cause, i.e., To mitigate the loss suffered by any one of the participants, as opposed to payments linked to definite expectation of insured benefits to be received.
Contains an element of gambling, i.e., Maisir, in that the insured pays an amount (premium) in the expectation of gain (compensation/payment against claim). If the anticipated loss (claim) does not occur, the insured loses the amount paid as premium. If the loss does occur, the insurer loses a far larger amount than collected as premium and the insured gains by the same.	The participant pays the contribution (Tabarru') in the spirit of ne'ea (purity) and brotherhood to cover mutual losses of members of the pool. Losses and gains are mutually shared by the pool members who contribute to the pool. That is, third parties (insurers or reinsurers) are not affected by the outcome of risk events.
Funds are mostly invested in fixed interest-bearing instruments such as bonds, fixed interest securities, etc. Hence these contain the element of riba (usury), which is forbidden in islam.	Funds are only invested in non-interest-bearing, i.e., Riba-free, instruments. Note that regular income investments are still possible (such as under Sukuk, Islamic bonds) as long as the income is not interest-based.
Surplus or profit belongs to both the shareholders and the with-profit policyholders. The insured is covered during the policy period but is not entitled to any return at the end of such period.	Surplus belongs to the participants and is accordingly returned to them.

The Takaful industry offers products[444] that are Sharia'ah-compliant, such as:

- Family Takaful: Since there would be an element of gambling on an individual's life, these products replace conventional life insurance. They provide life coverage in a way that is not interfering with Muslim religious beliefs.
- Sharia'ah-compliant assets: To avoid Riba, Gharar, Haram and Maisir, the Takaful market can turn toward Sukuk, creating regular income assets.
- Retakaful: Within a conventional insurance structure, insurance companies are able to share risks and gains and in general are able to benefit from a broader base of experience in regards to pricing and/or underwriting through signing reinsurance

[444]Abdul Rahim Abdul Wahab, Mervyn K. Lewis and M. Kabir Hassan, *Islamic Takaful: Business Models, Shariah Concerns, and Proposed Solutions*, Wiley, 2007; Nico P. Swartz and Pieter Coetzer, "Takaful: An Islamic insurance instrument," *Journal of Development and Agricultural Economics*, 2(10), 2010, pp. 333-339; Ajayi, *Takaful (Islamic Insurance)*."

contracts, where Islamic insurance is not allowed to do this. To overcome these limitations, the Retakaful market provides solutions such as allowing Takaful funds to share risk among other Takaful pools.

- Retro-Takaful: Here the idea is to offer market players the possibility of retroceding their businesses in order to reduce volatility.

The share of Takaful gross premiums in most Muslim countries is less than 15%.This is considered to have potential for further growth.[445]

Share of *Takāful* Gross Premiums to the Total Gross Premiums by Selected Countries (2014)

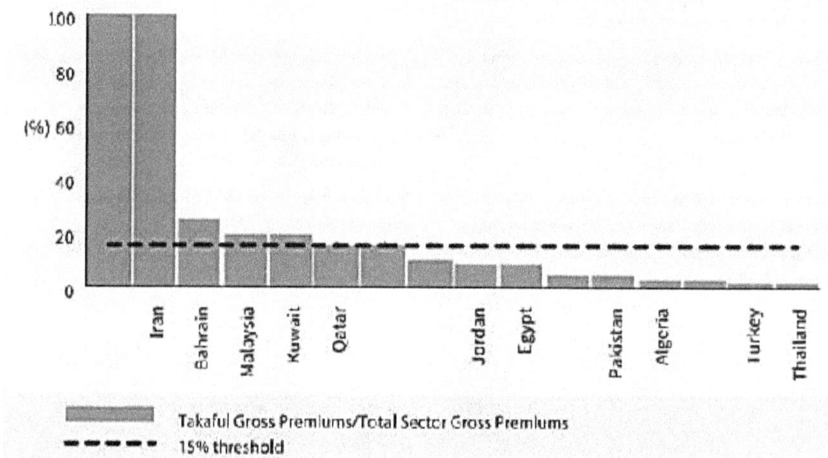

Source: Insurance Information Institute (2015), International Insurance Fact Book; Swiss Re (2015), Sigma-World Insurance Database; World Islamic Insurance Directory 2015.

Takaful products are offered and structured based on two key models known as Mudarabah and Wakalah.[446] Within the latter model, which is a kind of agency structure, the so-called Takaful operator is considered as an agent of participants that must manage the Takaful funds. The agent for these services is compensated through a regularly paid fixed fee. Here the operator

---

[445] Islamic Financial Services Board, 2016 Report; Wahab, Lewis and Hassan, *Islamic Takaful: Business Models*.

[446] "Takaful Models," Academy for International Modern Studies, Islamic Finance Training & Research Division: https://uaelaws.files.wordpress.com/2012/02/takaful-models.pdf.

would not face any risk since the risk, as mentioned earlier, is considered as a process of solidarity among the participants, known as a joint guarantee. Within the former model, known also as partnership model, the operator is considered as a business partner for the people involved. Based on the principle of profit-sharing, people provide funds and the operator invests and manages them. The operator can realize a profit if the business cost is less than the agreed sharing ratio.[447] The two models are shown here:[448]

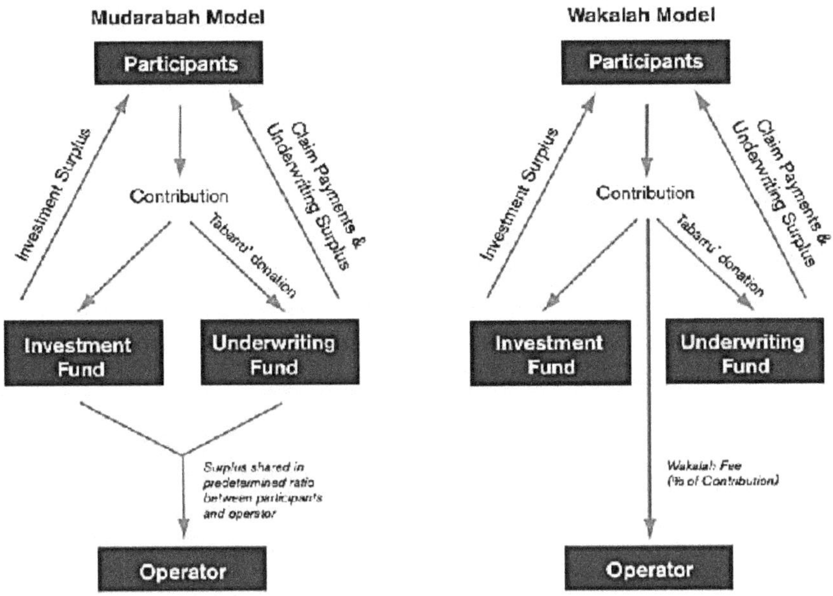

Although Muslims account for about 25% of the world's population, the Takaful market remains a tiny fraction of the global insurance market. However, the Takaful market is growing. The gross contribution of the Takaful industry reached an amount of $22.1 billion in 2014, with the Gulf Cooperation Council states being the second greatest contributor to its growth, after Iran.[449]

---

[447] Atiquzzafar Khan, "Takaful: Concepts and Models," https://zulkiflihasan.files.wordpress.com/2009/11/takaful-dlc.pdf; Khan, "Takaful versus Conventional Insurance;" Ajamal Bhatty, "The Growing Importance of Takaful Insurance," OECD: http://www.oecd.org/finance/insurance/46116115.pdf; Bank Negara Malaysia, "Annual Takaful Statistics," http://www.bnm.gov.my/index.php?ch=statistic&pg=stats_takaful; Islamic Financial Services Board, 2016 Report.

[448] Islamic Financial Services Board, 2016 Report, *ibid.*

[449] *Ibid.*; http://www.takaful-re.ae/.

The Industry's Development

Here we shall briefly compare the fields of finance and banking. Although the Sharia'ah-compliant bond market known as Sukuk is growing rapidly and the Sharia'ah-compliant insurance alternative known as Takaful is also increasingly used, banking represents four-fifths of total Islamic financial assets.

As Qur'an says Allah permitted trade but forbade Riba, Islamic scholars have offered other alternatives to their communities. Allah's will is expressed in the way Islamic banking and finance has been formed and forged. It is affirmed by Islamic economists that only a fixed, or predetermined, return on savings or transactions is forbidden, not an uncertain rate of return, such as the making of profit.[450]

Before briefly analyzing the development of the industry as a whole, it is important to emphasize that Mudarabah, as explained earlier, is considered by Muslim scholars as the basis of modern Islamic banking and finance that operates on a two-tier basis:

- First tier: Muslims put their money into the bank's investment accounts and agree on profit sharing. Thus, banks are fund managers.
- Second tier: Those in need of money for projects go to banks and agree on the proportion of profits to be shared. Losses would be borne by the banks. In this case, banks are providers of funds and the businessperson that obtained the financing is the manager of the funds.[451]

Muslim scholars defend the fact that the cost calculated for physical capital is not zero. The difference between the Islamic system and the interest-based system is based on the rationale that the cost of capital in the interest-based system is a predetermined fixed rate, while in Islamic banking it is expressed as ratio of profit.[452] In other words, on one hand the concept of the time value of money in Islam is considered an ex-post one, and on the other hand, for an ex-post return on capital in businesses, the time value of money

---

[450] Institute of Islamic Banking and Insurance, "Islamic Banking," http://www.islamic-banking.com/islamic_banking_principle.aspx.
[451] *Ibid.*
[452] *Ibid.*; Abu Umar Faruq Ahmad and M. Kabir Hassan, "The Time Value of Money Concept in Islamic Finance," Islamic Economics and Finance Pedia: http://iefpedia.com/english/wp-content/uploads/2009/11/The-Time-Value-of-Money-Concept-in-Islamic-Finance.pdf.

is considered as the purest one. Therefore, a predetermined fixed time value of money does not exist.[453]

As such, Islamic institutions, mainly banks, are created in a way that do not offer interest-bearing accounts but only accounts that are related to profit-sharing investments, where returns are ultimately deposited.[454] Consequently, as the banking system is not engaged in lending, assets are based on sales, leases, profit and loss sharing and/or services for which fees are charged.[455] The table here shows a typical Islamic bank's balance sheet:[456]

<table>
<tr><th>Assets</th><th>Liabilities</th></tr>
<tr><td rowspan="2">Cash and liquid securities</td><td>Demand deposits (qard al hasan, wakala)</td></tr>
<tr><td>Interbank murabahah</td></tr>
<tr><td>Interbank murabahah</td><td rowspan="2">Unrestricted profit-sharing investment accounts (mudarabah)</td></tr>
<tr><td rowspan="3">Inventory (real estate, automobiles, commodities, etc.)

Asset-backed transactions (murabahah, ijarah, salam, and istisna)</td></tr>
<tr><td>Restricted profit-sharing investment accounts (mudarabah) 1/</td></tr>
<tr><td>Reserves (PER, IRR)</td></tr>
<tr><td>PLS transactions (mudarabah, musharakah)</td><td rowspan="2">Shareholders' equity capital</td></tr>
<tr><td>Fee-based services (wakalah, kafalah) 2/</td></tr>
</table>

1/ Restricted profit sharing investment accounts are generally included off-balance sheet.

2/ Fee-based services include letters of credit, letters of guarantee, safekeeping of negotiable instruments and the collection of payments, internal and external transfer operations, hiring coffers, administration of real estate or projects, and administration of wills. Most of them are generally included off-balance sheet.

---

[453] Ahmad and Hassan, "The Time Value of Money Concept," *ibid.*; Bhatty, "The Growing Importance of Takaful Insurance;" Ismail Bin Abd Rahman and Arieff Salleh Bin Rosman, "Looking at an Islamic Investment: 'Cost of Capital' from Authentic Hadiths," https://www.wbiconpro.com/325-Ismail.pdf.

[454] Slaman Syed Ali and Ausaf Ahmad, *Islamic Banking and Finance: Fundamental and Contemporary Issues*, Islamic Research and Training Institute, 2004; Abdullah Saeed, "Islamic banking and finance: In search of a pragmatic model," http://www.abdullahsaeed.org/sites/abdullahsaeed.org/files/Islamic_Perspectives.pdf.

[455] Alfred Kammer, Mohamed Norat, Marco Piñón, Ananthakrishnan Prasad, Christopher Towe, Zeine Zeidane and IMF Staff Team, *Islamic Finance: Opportunities, Challenges, and Policy Options*, International Monetary Fund, 2015; Hassan and Lewis, *Handbook of Islamic Banking*.

[456] Hussain, Shahmoradi and Turk, "An Overview of Islamic Finance."

The global value of the Islamic financial industry, though affected by a series of events such as geopolitical conflicts, exchange rate depreciation and low oil and gas prices, reached $1.87 trillion during 2015. Within the system, the global Sukuk market and the assets of Islamic funds declined around 1.4% and 6.3% respectively, and the Islamic insurance and banking sectors expanded by 8.4% and 1.4%.[457] The causes of the slowdown and the modest results obtained in the Sukuk market and funds' assets are identified in terms of exchange rates' depreciation, mainly within key markets of major Muslim countries such as Iran, Malaysia, Turkey and Indonesia. The table below gives a breakdown of Islamic finance segments by region:[458]

Breakdown of Islamic Finance Segments by Region (USD billion, 2015 YTD*)

Region	Banking Assets	*Sukūk* Outstanding	Islamic Funds' Assets	*Takāful* Contributions
Asia	209.3	174.7	23.2	5.2
GCC	598.8	103.7	31.2	10.4
MENA (exc. GCC)	607.5	9.4	0.3	7.1
Sub-Saharan Africa	24.0	0.7	1.4	0.5
Others	56.9	2.1	15.2	-
Total	1496.5	290.6	71.3	23.2

**Data for banking and takāful as of 1H2015, while for sukūk and funds as of 11M15.*
Source: IFSB Secretariat Workings.
Note: Data are mostly taken from primary sources (regulatory authorities' statistical databases, annual reports and financial stability reports, official press releases or speeches, etc.). Where primary data are unavailable, third-party data providers have been used, including Bloomberg, Zawya, EY and World Islamic Insurance Directory 201 In only a few instances where there were still information gaps were data estimated based on historical growth trends and country-specific assumptions. Takāful contributio are used as a basis to reflect the growth in the takāful industry. The breakdown of Islamic funds' assets is by domicile of the funds, while for sukūk outstanding it is by domici of the obligor.

Despite having double-digit growth in 2013, Islamic finance assets represented less than 1% of total global financial assets. They were mainly concentrated in the Gulf Cooperation Council countries, Iran and Malaysia.[459]

Data from the International Monetary Fund suggest that in 2013 Islamic banking surpassed conventional banking and increased its presence in many Muslim countries, accounting for around 15% of the banking system's assets. In 2013, four out of ten courtiers were Gulf Cooperation Council members. In 2015, the number of jurisdictions where the presence of the Islamic financial services industry reached systemic importance increased to

---

[457] Islamic Development Bank: http://www.isdb-pilot.org/; Islamic Financial Service Board, Stability Report, 2016.
[458] *Ibid.*
[459] Islamic Financial Service Board, Stability Report, 2014: http://www.ifsb.org/docs/2014-05-06_IFSI%20Stability%20Report%202014%20(Final).pdf.

11, and the concentration of assets within them remained high. In fact, 88% of the banking assets and 84% of global Islamic bonds outstanding were located within the 11 countries.

The Gulf Cooperation Council comprises the most important region in the Middle East in this regard, accounting for 39.5% of the global Islamic financial services industry.[460] The six GCC countries, by deploying a fixed exchange rate regime, were able to sustain values in US dollar terms.[461]

Besides countries such as Iran and Sudan that operate based on fully Sharia'ah-compliant banking systems (Islamic banking thus has a 100% share of these markets), the market share of Islamic banking in all other Muslim countries improved in 2015. For instance, Islamic banking in both Brunei and Saudi Arabia had approximately 49% of the market, while other important market shares were reported in Kuwait (38.9%), Qatar (26.1%) and the United Arab Emirates (18.4%).[462] Data for 31 countries showed Islamic banking's market share declined very slightly in three of them, while all of the others had stable or increasing market shares.[463]

Iran remained the largest single market for Islamic banking assets, accounting for 37% of the total global Islamic banking industry in 2015. Within the Gulf Cooperation Council countries, Saudi Arabia, the United Arab Emirates and Qatar were the main countries that experienced increases in their share of global Islamic banking assets with respectively 19%, 8.1% and 5.1%.[464] Oman, one of the key partners in the GCC, has a very marginal presence within the overall system although Islamic banking increased rapidly over four years to account for 6.5% of the domestic market.[465]

Of the total Islamic banking assets in all Muslim countries, 92.1% were concentrated in 10 countries in 2015. Although this is down from 94% in 2014, the stability of the Islamic system depends on how these countries function and are governed.[466] Data on Islamic banking assets show steady growth during the seven years to 2015.[467] Analyzing this trend through a sample of 59 banks in 11 countries shows these assets expanded at a compound annual growth rate of 15.4% between 2008 and 2014.[468]

---

460 "Fast Growth, Divergent Paths: GCC Wealth and Asset Management Report," EY, 2015.

461 Bhatty, "The Growing Importance of Takaful Insurance."

462 Islamic Financial Service Board, Stability Report, 2016

463 Ibid

464 Ibid

465 Ajamal Bhatty, The Growing Importance of Takaful Insurance, OECD: http://www.oecd.org/finance/insurance/46116115.pdf

466 Islamic Financial Service Board, Stability Report, 2016

467 Ibid.; Ajamal Bhatty, The Growing Importance of Takaful Insurance, OECD: http://www.oecd.org/finance/insurance/46116115.pdf; Islamic Financial Service Board, Stability Report, 2016.

468 Islamic Financial Service Board, Stability Report, *ibid.*

Islamic Banking Assets Growth Trend (2008–2015F)

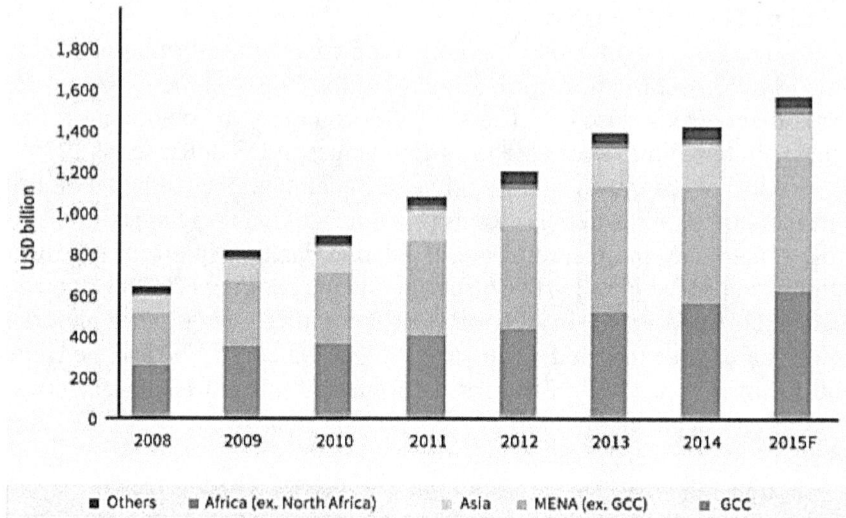

Source: IFSB Secretariat Workings.

An overall breakdown of the system based on 2015 data on a global basis is shown below: [469]

Islamic banks	74.2%
- commercial	71.6%
- investment	0.4%
- specialised	1.7%
- wholesale	0.3%
Takāful	1.8%
Sukūk	16.3%
UIFI	4.6%
- investment firms and funds	2.9%
- financing companies	1.1%
- real estate	0.3%
- others	0.3%
Funds	3.1%
- equity	1.3%
- money market	1.2%
- *sukūk*	0.2%
- others	0.3%
Islamic finance industry	100.0%
Islamic finance industry US$ bn	1,814.1

[469] *Ibid.*

Emerging Issues and Reliability of the System

In addition to historical, philosophical and structural differences, the Islamic system suffers the lack of a robust set of theories which exist for the conventional banking and financial system.[470] The Islamic system is affected by the global business environment and, in general, how the global economy performs. In particular, declines in energy and commodity prices affect the developing countries, and those where the Islamic system operates are not exceptions and face the repercussions.

There is a positive relationship between the oil and gas dependency of a state and the share of Islamic finance within the state's total financial system.[471] As a result, *a priori*, a decline in energy prices would reduce the size of the banking system within the financial system. Reducing the size of Islamic banking is not the only issue that requires the attention of Muslim countries' rulers. Declining oil and gas revenues weaken government expenditures and affect negatively the current account balances of these countries and consequently their populations. Since within the Gulf Cooperation Council countries the relationship between public sector entities and the so-called private sector is positive and intertwined, oil prices affect equity prices and profitability in general.[472]

Islamic countries, especially those that are rich in natural resources such as oil, for many years have spent generous amount of revenues from these resources to guarantee a certain level of standard of living and avoid any social tension that could end in a revolt or uprising. Oil prices will not only affect the size of Islamic banking within these countries, but also other fundamental macroeconomic variables such as investments, consumption and/or imports.[473] Sovereign funds as well as infrastructure and development projects would be affected negatively by declining oil prices. So would Islamic banks that are highly concentrated on consumer finance or commodity investments. However, many scholars and policymakers see opportunities in

---

[470] Nawal Kasim and Zuraidah Mohd Sanusi, "Emerging Issues for Auditing in Islamic Financial Institutions: Empirical Evidence from Malaysia," *Journal of Business and Management*, 8(5), 2013.

[471] Abdul Rafay and Ramla Sadiq, "Problems and Issues in Transformation from Conventional Banking to Islamic Banking: Literature Review for the Need of a Comprehensive Framework for a Smooth Change," *City University Research Journal*, 5, 2015.

[472] *Ibid.*

[473] Chijioke Nwaozuzu, "Dwindling oil revenues: Economic implications for governance, business & development," in *Sweet Crude: A Review of Nigerian Energy Industry, 2016*: http://sweetcrudereports.com/2016/02/29/dwindling-oil-revenues-economic-implications-for-governance-business-development/.

declining oil prices if they force these countries to reform their institutions and diversify their economies.[474]

For the Islamic banking system, long-term resiliency techniques such as diversifying resources are not easily available due to limitations imposed on the system. However, the profitability of the industry has recovered since a dip in 2009. As shown below, the average return on assets (ROA) as well as the return on equities (ROE) have improved, despite remaining lower than they were in 2008, when ROA was 1.3% and ROE was 9.9%.[475]

Selected Islamic Finance Stability Indicators: A Snapshot

Return on Assets		Return on Equity		Net Profit Margin		Cost to Income	
2014	0.95%	2014	8.96%	2014	1.04%	2014	55.88%
2013	0.89%	2013	8.89%	2013	0.96%	2013	55.84%
2014	2.75%	2014	70.50%	2014	16.40%	2014	14.09%
2013	4.12%	2013	81.18%	2013	16.79%	2013	15.23%
Non-Performing Financing		3M Asset Liability Ratio		Total Capital Adequacy		Tier1 Capital Adequacy	

Source: Islamic Banking Sample, IFSB.

Although improvement was registered at an aggregate level, different countries performed differently. Among members of the Gulf Cooperation Council, the United Arab Emirates went back to its pre-2008 record high and reached the threshold of 1.34% in regards to ROA. Saudi Arabia, on the other hand, did not succeed in improving its profitability. Bahrain, after experiencing a negative return on assets, finally had a positive return of 0.7% in 2014. It is worth mentioning that even though Bahrain experienced an

[474] Cyril Widdershowen, "Analysis: Petro-dollar crunch hits GCC sovereign wealth funds, investment and pensions," *Europe*, 2016; Adel Abdel Ghafar, "Will the GCC be able to adjust to lower oil prices?" Brookings Institution, 2016; "Oil and Gas States: After the Party," *Economist*, 2016.

[475] "Oil and Gas States," *ibid.*

improvement, rating agencies such as Standard & Poor's had to downgrade its sovereign rating to BB from BBB-.[476]

Despite some difficulties both internally and at the global level, Islamic banks remain well capitalized; however, they did not improve on indicators such as capital adequacy. Although both the average total capital adequacy ratio and the Tier 1 ratio were above the capitalization standard required by authorities, both have declined since 2008 and stood at 15.79% and 13.89% respectively during 2015. While this reflects changes that have occurred internationally, it can be also be considered as a signal of improved efficiency.

Each Islamic country performed differently in this respect. Overall, the capitalization of the Islamic system is considered as resilient, although the Gulf Cooperation Council countries, though exceeding the high regulatory capital requirement, experienced declines.[477] Nonetheless, due to global economic trends and the lack of diversification in these countries, banks' earnings, and consequently the Islamic system, could be affected.[478]

Besides capital adequacy and other measures such as profitability of the banking system, assessing the stability of the system additionally requires periodic institutionalized reviews of risks and capital management processes.

As noted earlier, the Gulf Cooperation Council countries have a high fiscal dependency on hydrocarbon revenues that is far greater than the total oil and gas exports. The data suggest that during recent years this fiscal dependency has remained high. The effects observed over financial cycles caused by the energy sector's ups and downs are intensified by the sector's importance within the GCC. Both government policies and oil price movements (since the former is influenced by the latter) can augment the financial sector's vulnerabilities, mainly because asset prices and credit can nurture each other. Higher oil prices lead to higher revenues and ultimately create stronger fiscal and external positions. Subsequently, this would produce higher anticipated returns on the equity market due to the impact of higher oil

---

[476] Mamta Badkar, "Bahrain Junked by S&P," *Financial Times*, 2016: https://www.ft.com/content/74f66c57-314a-3f9d-add4-e5e333dfda80.

[477] "Top 50 banks in the GCC," *Gulf Business*: http://gulfbusiness.com/lists/top-50-gcc-banks-2015/#.WE1yh_krLyQ.

[478] "GCC Banking Sector Liquidity Tightens," Bloomberg, 2016: https://www.bloomberg.com/news/videos/2016-08-10/gcc-banking-sector-liquidity-tightens; Padamja Khandelwal, Ken Miyajima and Andre Santos, "The Impact of Oil Prices on the Banking System in the GCC," International Monetary Fund, 2016; "State of GCC Banking System," *International Financial Review*: http://www.ifre.com/state-of-the-gcc-banking-system/610387.fullarticle.

prices on the business sector.[479] The importance of oil revenues relative to the GCC countries' financial systems are shown in the tables here: [480]

GCC: Dependence on Oil Revenues			
	2000-05	2006-10	2011-14
Oil export revenues as percent of total exports of goods and services			
Bahrain	58.7	60.5	65.1
Kuwait	82.7	80.5	87.6
Oman	76.9	69.4	64.3
Qatar	88.5	85.9	88.9
Saudi Arabia	83.4	83.1	83.0
United Arab Emirat	45.0	38.7	32.6
Fiscal oil revenues as percent of total fiscal revenues			
Bahrain	71.7	82.2	87.2
Kuwait	72.7	79.2	83.6
Oman	83.4	83.4	88.7
Qatar	90.5	88.3	90.7
Saudi Arabia	82.8	88.3	90.3
United Arab Emirat	60.2	65.1	69.9

Source: IMF staff calculations.
Note: Fiscal data is of the general government for UAE and central government in other GCC countries

GCC: Size of the Financial System (Percent of GDP)		
	Bank Assets	Market Capitalization
Bahrain	259.7	64.1
Kuwait	165.5	72.8
Oman	121.4	28.1
Qatar	148.7	73.7
Saudi Arabia	92.6	71.0
United Arab Emirates	193.4	59.7

Source: GCC authorities, Bloomberg
Note: United Arab Emirates market capitalization is sum of Abu Dhabi and Dubai stock markets; Market capitalization data is as of Sept. 16, 2015. Banking sector data for Bahrain excludes wholesale banks.

---

[479] Gail Tverberg, "Ten reasons why high oil prices are a problem," Our Finite World, 2013: https://ourfiniteworld.com/2013/01/17/ten-reasons-why-high-oil-prices-are-a-problem/; Roger Showley, "Low oil prices: good or bad for the economy?" *San Diego Union Tribune*, 2015: http://www.sandiegouniontribune.com/business/economy/sdut-econometer-oil-prices-benefit-2015dec18-story.html.
[480] Khandelwal, Miyajima and Santos, "The Impact of Oil Prices on the Banking System in the GCC."

As governments start spending more, non-oil output, liquidity and credit within the banking sector, and real estate prices increase as well.[481] In the GCC countries, the strong banking sector has acted as a buffer in response to lower oil prices since 2014, mainly due to strong capital and liquidity surpluses. Even so, the growth rate of bank deposits and credits decreased, mainly because of withdrawals by governments and related entities.

Since low energy prices can affect the whole system adversely, being dependent on a product with a volatile price, in addition to the vulnerabilities of the financial system, can result in the failure of the real economy.[482] The systemic financial sector risks developed years before the global financial crisis and were mainly due to expansions of the deposit base and liquidity resulting from high oil prices and short-term capital inflows.[483]

The GCC countries that had been experiencing large fiscal surpluses started to deal with the consequences of lower oil prices on both budget balances and the level of expenditures. Saudi Arabia, Qatar and Oman, for example, had to deal with budget deficits. In Saudi Arabia's case, the deficit grew from less than $20 billion in 2014 to nearly $100 billion in 2015 before it was projected to fall back slightly to $87 billion in 2016. Qatar projected a budget deficit in 2016 after 15 years of surpluses. Governments in these and other GCC countries cut their expenditures during 2016.[484]

GCC Nations have Lowered their Spending Levels

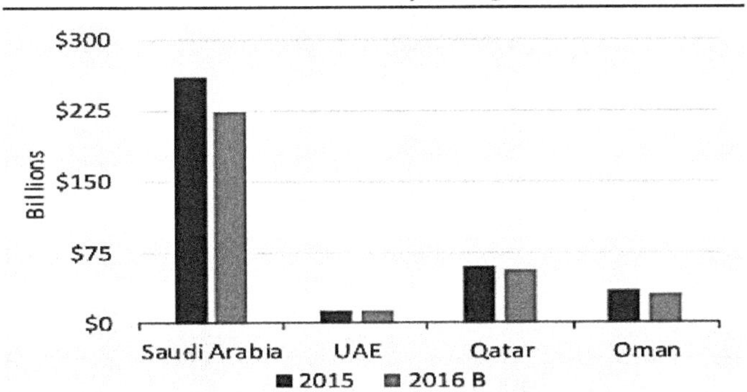

Source: Saudi Ministry of Finance, Alkhabeer Capital

Note: 2015 figures for Saudi Arabia and Oman represent actual expenditures, while 2015 figures for Qatar and UAE represent expenditures forecasted in the previous budget.

[481] *Ibid.*

[482] AlKhabeer Capital, "GCC budgets: Adapting to the new oil reality," 2016: http://www.alkhabeer.com/sites/default/files/GCC%20Budget_Adapting%C2%A0to%C2%A0the%C2%A0New%C2%A0Oil%C2%A0Reality_January%202016%20-%20English.pdf.

[483] *Ibid.*

[484] *Ibid.*

More generally, the previous higher oil prices had been a key driver of stronger macroeconomic and microeconomic variables, both financial and in the real economy.[485] The downturn in these business and financial variables corresponded exactly to the fall in oil prices, as did the real spending of governments.[486]

Conclusion on the Economic Order under Sharia'ah Law

All concepts, principles and institutions that would make an economy function must be regulated through Islamic jurisprudence in order to develop the Islamic economic order. This order needs to be respected for the economy to achieve its objectives. Foremost, people as its main actors are permitted to seek economic well-being but must be capable of differentiating activities that are lawful, Halal, from those that are considered as forbidden, Haram. All economic activities that do not correspond to the system of Islamic jurisprudence would negatively affect everyone and ultimately the society. Nevertheless, wealth and property rights that are legitimately acquired and respect the purposes of God must be utilized prudently while being in accordance with certain limits on accumulation. Although the accumulation of wealth is allowed, margins are controlled for the welfare of the Muslim society as a whole. This system presents itself as a guarantor of social justice, without restraining people from doing business, but it must not go beyond the point of being considered as harmful for both individuals and the society.

The Islamic financial system and Islamic banking are defined through principles such as helping one another, and must be in accordance with concepts such as goodness and piety. The aim of Islam, for many authors, is the elimination of any kind of exploitation. Once achieved, it would ultimately lead to the establishment of a just society. This is supposed to occur through the application of Shari'ah and other Islamic rulings, which must be respected by all banks and financial institutions. This is why, in order to reinforce and monitor the system with the intent of guaranteeing compliance with Islam, banks are provided with religious boards that include Sharia'ah scholars.

---

485 J. Baffes, "The Great Plunge in Oil Prices," World Bank, 2015: http://pubdocs.worldbank.org/en/339801451407117632/PRN01Mar2015OilPrices.pdf.

486 Khandelwal, Miyajima and Santos, "The Impact of Oil Prices on the Banking System in the GCC."

CHAPTER 7

THE GCC'S FINANCIAL SYSTEM AND FINANCIAL FLOWS

For years, most research that had been conducted in regards to evaluating and studying regional integration projects has mainly concentrated on trade flows, with less attention being paid to financial flows and their different aspects. Financial flows are crucial in regional integration initiatives, and international financial aspects are key determinants that must be taken into consideration while evaluating any regional integration project. Based on the importance of a solid, well-functioning financial system for any healthy economy, whether it involves conventional or Islamic financial markets and their institutions, the importance of international financial flows in different stages of the integration process can be identified and observed through three fundamental realities:[487]

1. Common financial markets and institutions in addition to a shared mechanism are essential to first facilitating trade itself and subsequently to the efficient allocation of financial flows created through trade. Given that trade creation and an increase in trade within regional members of a bloc would end in an increase in financial flows, simple issues such as clearing and payment systems must be addressed through the creation of common institutions and mechanisms.
2. Intra-regional investment: More trade stimulates and fosters regional integration initiatives. In the past, foreign direct investment played a determining role in market-driven integration processes.[488] Direct investments also fostered policy-

[487] Steffany Griffinth, Patricia Canto and Monica Ruiz, "Financial Flows for Regional Integration," Institute for Development Studies, University of Sussex, 1995.

[488] Andrew Elek, "Market driven economic integration in the 21st century," East Asia Forum, 2009: http://www.eastasiaforum.org/2009/05/04/market-driven-economic-integration-in-the-21st-century/; Hadi Soesastro, "Regional integration in East Asia: Achievements and Future Prospects," *Asian Economic Policy Review*, 2006; Caren Addis and Mathew Verghis, "Economic Integration in the Western Hemisphere," Kellogg Institute, 1994.

driven processes such as the North American Free Trade Agreement, (NAFTA) or the South American Common Market, Mercosur.

3. The launch of regional integration would generate greater flows of investment from outside the region in addition to the dynamic effects of investment creation. [489] This would have three consequences: (1) a larger market; (2) complementarities in terms of production and resources; and (3) more harmonized policies within the region.

Therefore, the impact of flows from outside the region would not be limited only to an increase of the region's productive capacity. In the larger picture, it would create growth, especially in short term, paving the way for long-term stability. Assessing the feasibility and performance of any regional integration process must also take into consideration the international financial flows into the region as well as intra-regional financial flows. To that end, in this section, we shall examine each Gulf Cooperation Council country in order to evaluate the financial flows side of the integration.

Kingdom of Saudi Arabia

Banking System

The Saudi Arabian banking and financial system is composed of 12 national banks, 12 foreign banks, five credit and lending institutions and the Saudi stock market. All of them are monitored and governed by the Ministry of Finance and two authorities, the Saudi Arabian Monetary Agency (SAMA), the Kingdom's central bank, and the Capital Market Authority (CMA). The banking system is supported through committees such as those that focus on banking disputes and insurance-related disputes, and through internal governing bodies to ensure that regulations are implemented and observed.

With a decline in Saudi reserves since 2014, the money supply increased by 5.7% just in the first quarter of 2015 and at the same time the monetary base increased by 8.1%. Saudi Arabia's share of the Gulf Cooperation Council's money supply in 2014 was 39%, the highest of any

[489] David G. Sirmon and Michael A. Hittm, "Contingencies within dynamic managerial capabilities: Interdependent effects of resource investment and deployment on firm performance," *Strategic Management Journal*, 30, 2009; Csilla Lakatos and Terrie Walmsley, "Investment creation and diversion effects of the ASEAN-China free trade agreement," *Economic Modelling*, 29, 2012, pp. 766-779.

GCC member.[490] This was interpreted as an indication of high bank reserves and a prudent monetary policy with the aim of guaranteeing stability in the economy.[491] One main problem would be the fact that an increase in money supply can lead to higher inflation. However, for instance in the United States, inflation remained stable between 2008 and 2012 despite a tripling of the monetary base.[492] Concerning the Kingdom of Saudi Arabia, studies confirm that the consumer price index is dynamically affected by the money supply.[493]

In fact, the money supply within the economy grew by 60.1% during the period 2010-2014, reaching $466.9 billion in 2014 mainly due to authorities' investments in infrastructure projects and large businesses.[494]

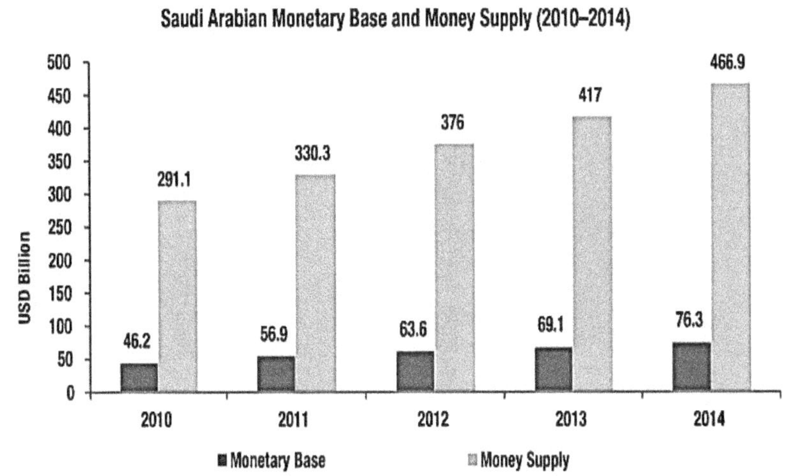

Source: SAMA

In 2015, total banking assets, including those of the central bank, reached $1.1 trillion. That same year, the Saudi stock market's total capitalization accounted for 52% of the Middle East and North Africa region's

---

[490] Saudi Arabian Monetary Authority: http://www.sama.gov.sa/en-us/pages/default.aspx; http://www.jeg.org.sa/data/modules/contents/uploads/infopdf/2792.pdf.
[491] Jeddah Chamber, "Saudi Arabian Banking Sector Report," 2015.
[492] John C. Williams, "Monetary Policy, Money and Inflation," Federal Reserve Bank of San Francisco, 2012: http://www.frbsf.org/economic-research/publications/economic-letter/2012/july/monetary-policy-money-inflation/.
[493] Yousef Nazer, "Causes of Inflation in Saudi Arabia," *Business and Management Review*, 7(3), 2016: http://www.abrmr.com/myfile/conference_proceedings/Con_Pro_65194/conference_71654.pdf.
[494] Saudi Arabian Monetary Authority.

total liquidity. The banking system in KSA is regulated by laws that are put in place to improve the transparency of the system in addition to guaranteeing a more competitive banking system. It is worth mentioning that the system is recognized as one of the safest by the International Monetary Fund. The loan to deposit ratio (LDR), which measures the ability of an institution to cover and guarantee the withdrawals made by its customers, was created to limit the risk within the banking system by discouraging banks from lending loosely. According to the Saudi authorities, aiming to ease tightening liquidity, the loan to deposit ratio increased from 82% to 90% in 2016. Saudi Arabia's LDR, shown prior to that rise, is compared below with those of major developed and developing countries.[495]

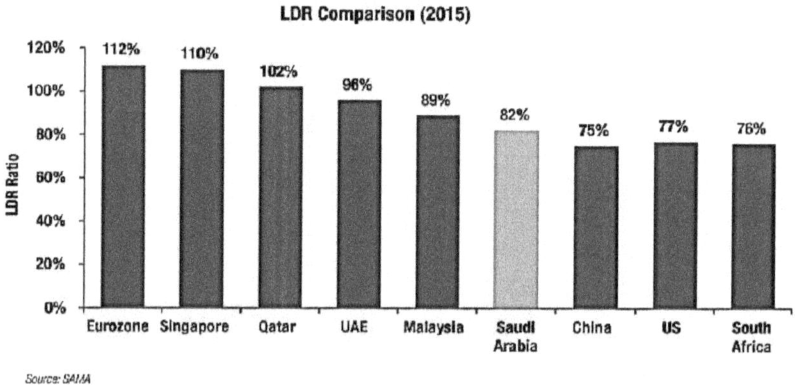

Although a ratio between 80%-90% is considered as an ideal ratio,[496] the increase can be also seen as a solution to the decreasing revenue from the oil business as well as a drop in consumer confidence.[497]

[495] *Ibid.*
[496] "Update 1 –Saudi central bank raises loan to deposit ratio: sources," Reuters, 2016: http://www.reuters.com/article/saudi-cenbank-policy-idUSL8N15T0OK.
[497] Jeddah Chamber, "Saudi Arabian Banking Sector Report."

Saudi Arabian Banking Sector LDR Growth (2009–2017)

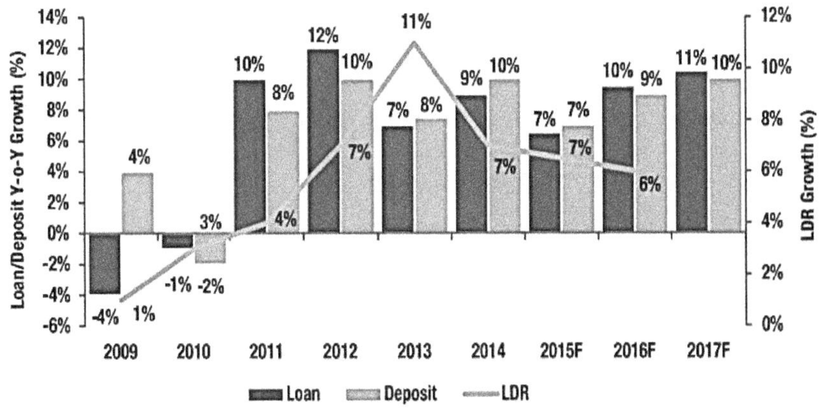

Source: SAMA

The Saudi Arabian banking sector's assets grew by 270%, and by some estimates[498] up to $567.7 billion, between 2005 and 2015. Deposits have grown as much as 284%, reaching $405 billion. This confirms that the Saudi Arabian banking system, under the central bank's monitoring, has evolved into a reliable and attractive destination for both domestic and foreign investors. A set of reforms that further eased restrictions on foreign investment was aimed at making the Kingdom of Saudi Arabia an even better investment destinationn.[499]

Most monetary assets belong to the Saudi central bank.[500] A breakdown of assets held by the Saudi Arabian Commercial Bank shows that the shares of fixed and other assets and of claims on the private sector increased, confirming greater private-sector participation within the economy, which can be ultimately seen as an improvement in the degree of economic development.[501]

A breakdown of bank loans to the private sector confirms that a huge amount of resources was being allocated to sectors such as commerce,

---

[498] "Fitch: New loan to deposit ratio to boost liquidity in Saudi Arabia," Argaam, 2016: http://www.argaam.com/en/article/articledetail/id/410536.

[499] Andrew Critchlow, "Why Saudi Stocks will be your best investment this year," *Telegraph*, 2014: http://www.telegraph.co.uk/finance/markets/10983007/Why-Saudi-stocks-will-be-your-best-investment-this-year.html; Nicolas Parasie, "Saudi Regulator Makes New Moves to Lure Foreign Investors," *Wall Street Journal*, 2016.

[500] "Update 1 –Saudi central bank raises loan to deposit ratio: sources," Reuters; Jeddah Chamber, "Saudi Arabian Banking Sector Report."

[501] Saudi Arabian Monetary Authority.

construction and manufacturing. There was a growth in demand for home and personal loans as well as for corporate loans.[502]

Besides the loan to deposit ratio as a risk-measuring indicator, the safety of the banking system in Saudi Arabia is also confirmed by another indicator, non-performing loans (NPL), as shown below. A loan is considered nonperforming "when payments of interest and principal are past due by 90 days or more, or at least 90 days of interest payments have been capitalized, refinanced or delayed by agreement, or payments are less than 90 days overdue, but there are other good reasons to doubt that payments will be made in full."[503] The Saudi banks are considered as the best within the GCC region by having an NPL ratio of 1.3% in 2015 and remaining in the safe value range.[504] This is mainly because procedures are in place to verify the creditworthiness of borrowers and the feasibility of projects for which funds are borrowed. Overall, the Saudi banking system is considered to have minimum exposure with the global financial market.[505]

[502] "Domestic Credit to Private Sector," World Bank: http://data.worldbank.org/indicator/FS.AST.PRVT.GD.ZS; "Saudi Loan to Private Sector," Trading Economics: http://www.tradingeconomics.com/saudi-arabia/loans-to-private-sector.
[503] Adriaan M. Bloem and Russel Freeman, "The treatment of non-performing loans," 18th Meeting of the IMF Committee on Balance of Payments Statistics, Washington, D.C., 2005.
[504] "Saudi Arabia non preforming loans," The Global Economy.com: http://www.theglobaleconomy.com/Saudi-Arabia/Nonperforming_loans/.
[505] Bank for International Settlements, "Regulatory Consistency Assessment Programme (RCAP) Assessment of Basel III risk-based capital regulations – Saudi Arabia," 2015: http://www.bis.org/bcbs/publ/d335.pdf; Saudi Arabian Monetary Authority.

Based on data from the Saudi central bank, the country's banks have maintained strong positions and levels of profitability despite the fall in oil prices in 2014 and a decrease in consumer confidence, and some banks have even increased their profits. Commercial bank assets grew while overall net profit increased to $11.7 billion in 2014.[506] Underlying this were an increase in efficiency and a rise in non-interest-bearing deposits. However, other data suggest that the downgrading of nine banks by Moody's could dampen banks' profitability for a time.[507]

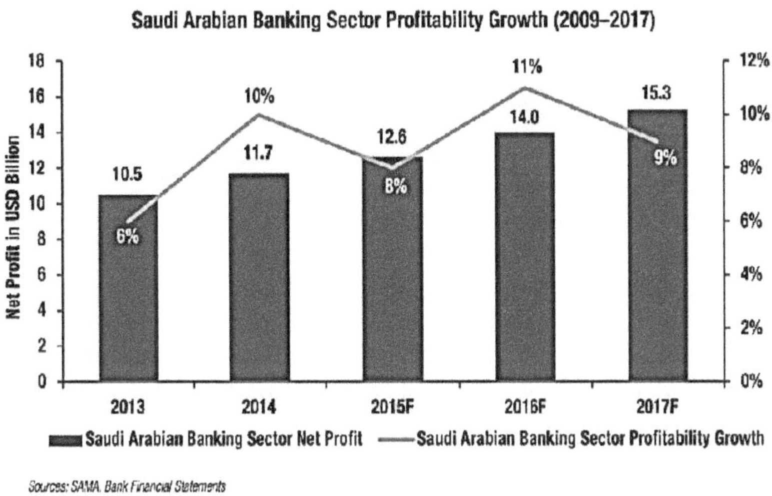

As of 2013, almost 54% of total banking services were Sharia'ah-compliant. Between 2014 and 2015, with an increasing demand for Sharia'ah-complaint instruments such as Takaful and fixed-income funds within the region, Saudi Arabia on a sovereign level issued $4 billion of Sukuk. The Islamic banking system has been growing exponentially and it is estimated to reach the threshold of $683 billion by 2019.[508]

---

[506] Saudi Arabian Monetary Authority.

[507] "Rating Action: Moody's takes rating actions on 11 Saudi banks; concludes review," Global Credit Research, 2016; Saudi Arabian Monetary Authority.

[508] "Fitch: Islamic Banking is dominant in the Saudi Arabia," Reuters, 2016: http://www.reuters.com/article/idUSFit947384; Fayaz Ahmad Lone and Salim Alshehri, "Growth and Potential of Islamic Banking in GCC: The Saudi Arabia Experience," *Journal of Islamic Banking and Finance*, 3(1), 2015, pp. 35-43.

Investment Climate

Saudi Arabia is considered as a relatively attractive and stable market for investment.[509] Despite its economic growth during 2015, lower oil prices created a less transparent economic outlook. With a deficit of $98 billion, Saudi authorities have been trying to diversify the economy. To that end, the government took several steps during 2015 to encourage more investment:[510]

- Opening the Saudi stock market to "qualified" foreign investors
- Moving toward privatizing civil aviation, technology and healthcare
- Removing barriers to full foreign ownership of retail and wholesale businesses
- Designing laws that would facilitate starting new businesses

The General Investment Authority of Saudi Arabia regulates and oversees all foreign investments. Although in theory foreigners are permitted to have access to all sectors of the economy, a "negative list" limits and excludes, for instance, three industrial sectors and 12 service sectors, in addition to prohibiting investments in real estate in Mecca and Medina. The negative list is longer and goes beyond the aforementioned limitations. Overall, the kingdom of Saudi Arabia continues to offer opportunities within a business and investment climate that remains challenging.[511] The table below offers details on key aspects of the investment climate.[512]

Measure	Year	Index/Rank
TI Corruption Perceptions Index	2015	48 of 168
Ease of Doing Business	2016	82/189
Global Innovation Index	2015	43/141
GNI per Capita	2013	$25,140

[509] U.S. Department of Commerce, "Saudi Arabia Country Commercial Guide," 2016.
[510] *Ibid.*
[511] Invest Saudi: https://www.sagia.gov.sa/en/Pages/default.aspx.
[512] "Doing Business," World Bank: http://www.doingbusiness.org/data/exploreeconomies/saudi-arabia; Transparency International – Saudi Arabia: https://www.transparency.org/country/#SAU; The Global Innovation Index: https://www.globalinnovationindex.org/gii-2016-report#; GNI per capita, Atlas Method, World Bank: http://data.worldbank.org/indicator/NY.GNP.PCAP.CD.

Foreign Direct Investment

According to the U.N. Conference on Trade and Development, the Kingdom of Saudi Arabia had $8.012 billion of incoming foreign direct investment in 2014, or 27.4% of the total for all Arab countries. The charts below capture FDI inflows relative to GDP,[513] and show its main sources.[514]

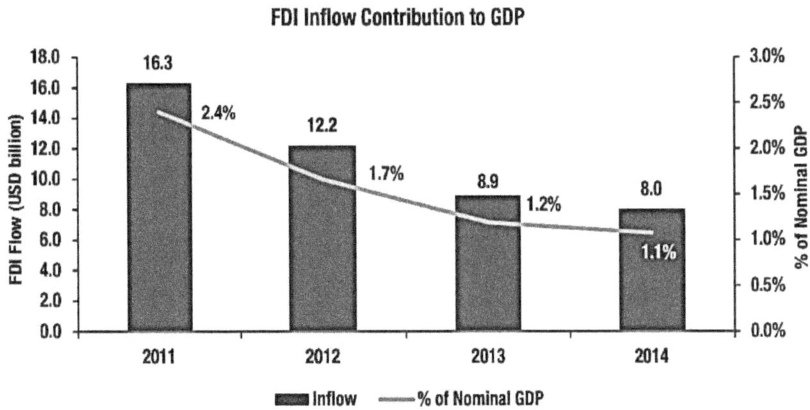

Source: UNCTAD, World Bank

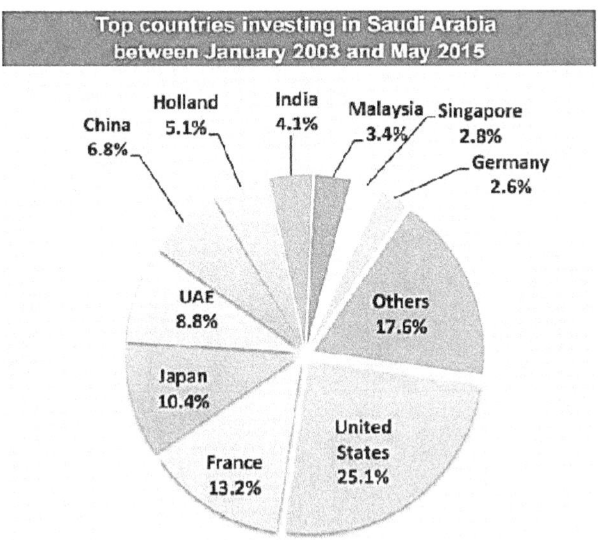

[513] Jeddah Chamber, "Foreign Direct Investment in Saudi Arabia: Jeddah Economic Gateway," 2015.
[514] "FDI Intelligence," *Financial Times*: http://www.fdiintelligence.com/.

The combined share of the top three sources accounted for almost 49% of the total.[515] Of these investments, 31% were made in the chemical industry, followed by 25% in the oil and gas sector.[516]

Inward investment in Saudi Arabia by the sectoral distribution between January 2003 and May 2015						
Rank	Sector	Companies	Projects	Jobs Created	Cost (Million $)	% of Total
1	Chemicals	41	52	17,959	46,769	31
2	Coal, Oil and Natural Gas	28	33	7,154	38,613	25
3	Metals	24	29	15,024	17,151	11
4	Real Estate	44	57	25,581	15,436	10
5	Hotels & Tourism	38	77	10,847	12,176	8
6	Automotive OEM	16	18	7,980	3,412	2
7	Plastics	19	21	3,689	2,606	2
8	Financial Services	79	112	2,059	1,931	1
9	Industrial Machinery, Equipment	81	93	10,196	1,744	1
10	Building & Construction Materials	17	19	2,465	1,492	1
	Others	499	673	66,246	11,730	8
	Total	886	1,184	169,200	153,059	

The Kingdom was successful in exporting FDI as well, and in 2014 its investments amounted to $5.396 billion. A total of 526 projects were implemented by Saudi enterprises abroad,[517] creating a net outflow of 0.72% of GDP.[518] China, Turkey and the United Arab Emirates were among the main destinations of Saudi investments, together accounting for 32% of the total. The chart below captures the FDI outflow trend from 2011 until 2014.[519]

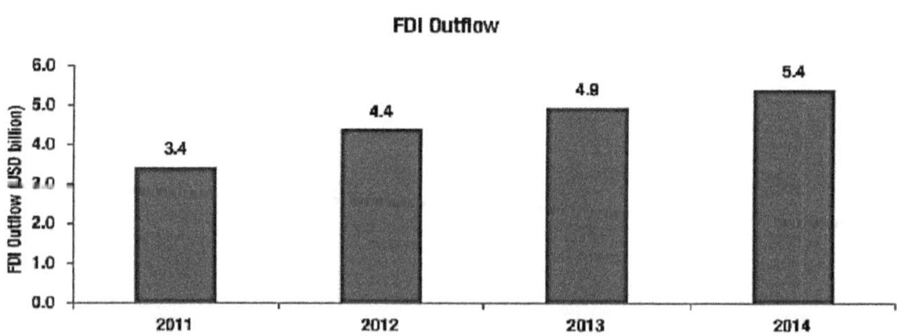

Source: UNCTAD

[515] Arab Investment and Export Guarantee Corporation, Dhaman, 2014: http://dhaman.net/ar/.
[516] "FDI Intelligence," *Financial Times*.
[517] Arab Investment and Export Guarantee Corporation, Dhaman.
[518] "Foreign direct investment net flows, Saudi Arabia," Tradingeconomics: http://www.tradingeconomics.com/saudi-arabia/foreign-direct-investment-net-outflows-percent-of-gdp-wb-data.html.
[519] Jeddah Chamber, "Foreign Direct Investment in Saudi Arabia."

Traditionally, the United States and the European Union were the two main destinations for Saudi investments; however, China has overtaken them as the first destination as it currently offers opportunities to invest in its growing sectors of energy, telecommunications and retail. Although a remarkable decrease of inward FDI flows is observable between 2011 and 2014, during the same period, KSA registered a negative FDI balance as inward stocks exceeded outward stocks.[520]

Foreign Direct Investment (billion USD)

FDI Flow	2011	2012	2013	2014
Inward	16.308	12.182	8.865	8.012
Outward	3.430	4.402	4.943	5.396

FDI Stock	2011	2012	2013	2014
Inward	186.758	199.032	207.897	215.909
Outward	92.958	34.360	39.303	44.699

In regards to portfolio investment flows, Saudi Arabia, through its Capital Market Authority, exercises an effective regulatory system on portfolio investments. Prior to 2015, foreigners were allowed to invest within the stock market through indirect mechanisms such as "swap arrangements." Since then, the market has become accessible to "qualified" foreign investors, but to prevent foreigners from possessing majority stakes in Saudi companies the CMA limited foreign ownership to 49%.[521] Despite the reform-related initiatives in 2015, a decrease in net portfolio investment that year can be observed in the chart on the next page.[522]

520 U.N. Conference on Trade and Development.

521 *Ibid.*; U.S. Department of Commerce, "Saudi Arabia, Efficient Market and Portfolio Investment," 2016.

522 World Bank.

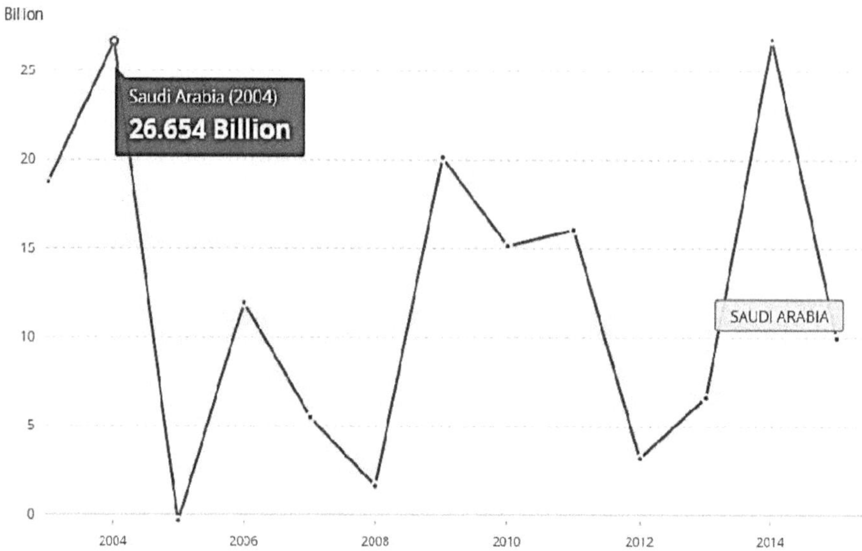

Qatar

Banking System and Investment Climate

The banking system in Qatar is dominated by its oldest and largest bank, which is also a 50% state-owned entity. As of 2013, the Qatar National Bank (QNB) held up to 50.4% of all banking system assets. Beside the QNB, ten other Qatari banks also operate. There are also seven foreign banks that offer their services and operate within the system, among them, HSBC, BNP Paribas and Bank Saderat Iran. In addition to these institutions, since the establishment of the Qatar Financial Center in 2005, over 80 foreign institutions that offer mainly corporate and investment banking services have joined Qatar's financial and banking system. This center, built in order to attract international banks, law firms and insurance companies, offers a modern regulatory framework and is supervised by the center's regulatory authority, QFCRA. Outside the Qatar Financial Center, banks and other financial institutions are supervised by Qatar's Central Bank, QCB. In addition to its functions as a central bank, it requires all banks to meet the IBS standard. In response to volatility during 2013, the QCB succeeded in keeping liquidity and T- bill rates stable.[523]

[523] "Qatar," International Monetary Fund country report, no.15/86; U.S. Department of Commerce, "Qatar – Banking System," 2016.

Bank Sector Liquidity, Nov 2012-Dec 2014

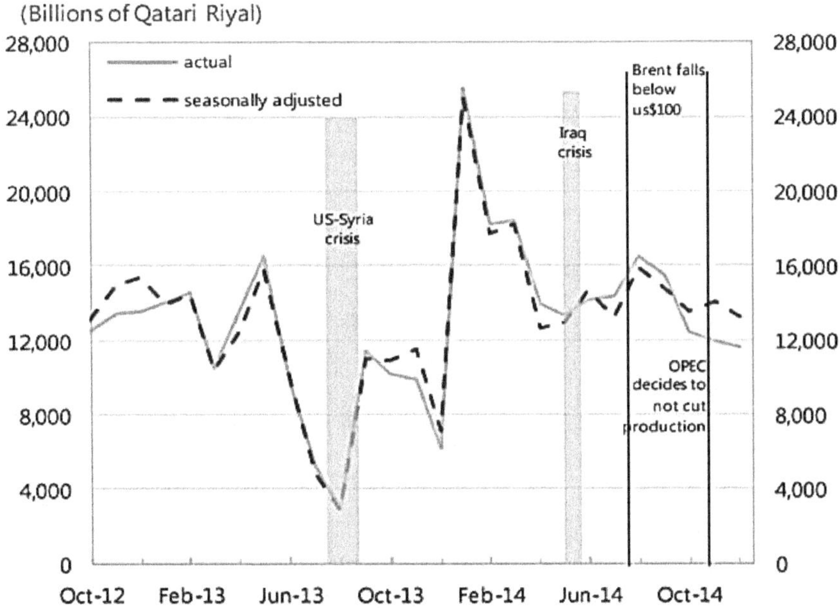

During 2014, domestic credit increased 10%, corresponding to strong demand in the economy as a whole and in particular from sectors such as construction, services and consumers. Domestic credit has been growing, although the pace of growth diminished between 2011 and 2014. During the same period, bank credit to the private sector increased while credit to the public sector decreased.[524]

In 2014, banks in Qatar were well-capitalized and non-performing loans remained below 2%. The other important indicator, the loan to deposit ratio, climbed to 130.4% in 2016. Credit to the government expanded as it had to deal with lower energy prices and a fiscal deficit that has to be nursed.[525] As shown through the table on the next page, banks are sound and the financial sector is reliable; however, despite credit growth, falling oil prices could reduce liquidity.[526]

[524] "Qatar," International Monetary Fund country report, *ibid.*

[525] Arif Sharif, "Qatar Cash Squeeze Seen in Soaring Loan to Deposit Ratio," Bloomberg, 2016.

[526] "Qatar," International Monetary Fund country report.

Financial Soundness Indicators, 2009-14

	2009	2010	2011	2012	2013	2014 1/
Capital adequacy						
Regulatory Tier 1 capital to risk-weighted assets 2/	15.0	15.0	19.9	18.2	15.3	15.4
Regulatory Tier 1 capital to total assets	11.5	11.1	12.6	12.8	9.2	9.9
Regulatory capital to risk weighted assets 2/	16.1	16.1	20.6	18.9	16.0	15.8
Asset quality						
Nonperforming loans	1.7	2.0	1.7	1.7	1.9	1.7
Bank provisions to nonperforming loans 3/	84.5	85.1	87.2	07.5	96.8	100.2
Bank provisions to total loans	1.4	1.7	1.6	1.7	1.0	1.7
Foreign assets to total assets	18.9	16.1	17.2	15.7	17.9	19.6
Earnings and profitability						
Return on assets	2.6	2.6	2.7	2.4	2.1	2.0
Return on equity	19.3	19.9	18.6	17.7	16.5	14.9
Net interest to average total assets	2.7	2.9	2.8	2.6	2.5	2.1
Non-interest expenses to gross income	26.5	24.6	28.2	25.4	26.5	27.2
Wages and salaries to other non-interest expenses	30.8	33.5	31.9	48.5	47.6	48.4
Liquidity						
Liquid assets to total assets	36.3	38.5	36.3	38.1	33.6	32.9
Liquid assets to short-term liabilities	47.0	50.7	47.2	58.5	50.9	50.4
Domestic credit-to-resident deposit ratio (commercial banks)	112.0	106.1	109.6	114.3	103.5	106.1
Other						
Private sector loans (in percent total loans)	72.4	67.0	62.8	56.6	57.8	63.3
Foreign currency assets to liabilities	98.7	97.2	114.6	109.1	76.4	84.0

Sources: Qatar Central Bank; Haver Analytics; and IMF staff calculations and estimates.
1/ Capital adequacy ratios are as of September 2014. Other data are as of November 2014 except for the foreign assets to total assets and the domestic credit to deposits' ratios that correspond to December 2014.
2/ In 2014, Basel III capital adequacy is applied for national banks only. Basel II is applied in earlier years.
3/ In 2014, bank provisions to nonperforming loans include provisions for some performing loans under the special category.

Qatari banks are increasing their presence abroad through acquisitions and loans, although borrowing by foreigners as a share of total liabilities declined between 2011 and 2014.[527]

Overall, Qatar's banking system is a stable one within the region, and the public expenditure guarantees operating conditions that are favorable for banks despite the falling energy prices.[528] However, due to the decline in energy prices, some of Qatar's older banks, such as Commercial Bank of

[527] *Ibid.*
[528] "Moody's maintains stable outlook on Qatar banking system," Moody's, 2016: https://www.moodys.com/research/Moodys-maintains-stable-outlook-on-Qatars-banking-system--PR_351974.

Qatar, have been downgraded by rating agencies while the risk score for the entire banking system has increased.[529]

Foreign Direct Investment

In 2014, Qatar attracted FDI worth of $1.040 billion. FDI balances coming into Qatar represented 3.9% of the Arab total. Between 2003 and 2015, 701 greenfield projects with a total cost of about $110 billion were implemented by 602 enterprises. Among the major countries that invested in Qatar, Bahrain, the United States and Japan together accounted about 40% of the total.[530]

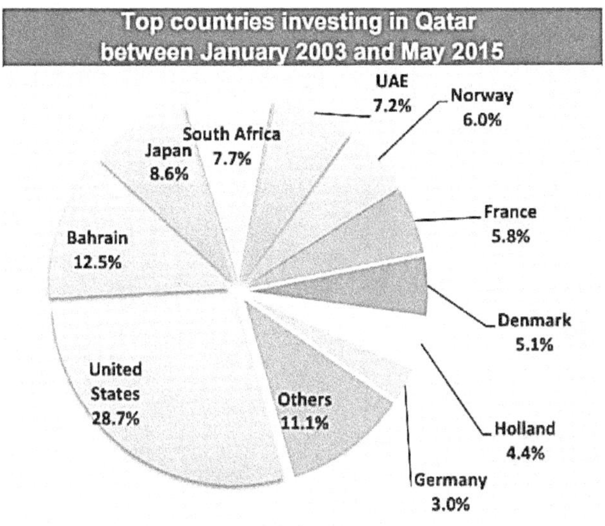

Of these investments, 50% were directed toward the mining and energy sectors. The real estate and chemical sectors, with 15.7% and 6.9% respectively, occupied the second and third positions. Among the enterprises investing in Qatar, Exxon Mobil Oil Company was at the top of the list with five projects.[531] The table on the next page gives more detail on the largest sources of inward investment.[532]

---

[529] Aliya Ram, "Qatari banks' credit outlook cut by S&P," *Financial Times*, 2016.
[530] Arab Investment and Export Guarantee Corporation, Dhaman, "Qatar," 2016.
[531] International Chamber of Commerce, "Qatar: Foreign Investment," Santander Trade Portal, https://en.portal.santandertrade.com/establish-overseas/qatar/investing-3.
[532] Arab Investment and Export Guarantee Corporation, Dhaman, "Qatar," 2016.

Inward investment in Qatar between January 2003 and May 2015					
Rank	Exporting Countries	No. Companies	No. Projects	No. Jobs	Cost (Million $)
1	United States	103	116	11,309	31,439
2	Bahrain	15	17	6,890	13,756
3	Japan	15	15	1,295	9,393
4	South Africa	5	7	3,157	8,417
5	UAE	100	135	21,609	7,897
6	Norway	6	10	4,335	6,575
7	France	35	38	4,529	6,338
8	Denmark	7	8	2,984	5,643
9	Holland	13	15	2,665	4,823
10	Germany	23	26	4,249	3,271

The sectoral distribution of inward investments affirms the areas of concentration, as shown below:[533]

Inward investment in Qatar by the sectoral distribution between January 2003 and May 2015						
Rank	Sector	Companies	Projects	Jobs Created	Cost (Million $)	% of Total
1	Coal, Oil and Natural Gas	24	32	10,491	54,919	50
2	Real Estate	25	30	15,966	17,215	16
3	Chemicals	18	19	7,219	7,560	7
4	Hotels & Tourism	35	45	6,674	7,445	7
5	Metals	8	12	6,847	7,418	7
6	Leisure & Entertainment	8	9	3,720	3,714	3
7	Alternative/Renewable energy	6	6	643	2,613	2
8	Financial Services	81	96	1,811	1,652	2
9	Business Services	148	151	2,994	1,490	1
10	Electronic Components	10	10	4,005	878	1
	Others	239	291	28,807	4,777	4
	الإجمالي	602	701	89,177	109,679	

Source: Tables and Figures in this page: FDI Intelligence from The Financial Times

Concerning outward investments, in 2014, Qatar was able to export FDI valued about $6.748 million, representing 20.2% of the Arab total. The investment costs related to 301 projects implemented by Qatar around the world was about $47.5 billion. The three main destinations for Qatar's projects were Egypt, United Kingdom and Vietnam.[534]

Overall, based on authorities' decisions and policies, and due to the falling of energy prices, restrictions on FDI have been eased in order to promote growth and ultimately make progress toward a more diversified

---

[533] *Ibid.*

[534] Satish Kanady, "Qatar Outward FDI Increases to USD8.2bn," *Zawya*, 2014.

economy.[535] Outward FDI stocks exceeded inward stocks in 2014, registering a positive balance.

Foreign Direct Investment (billion USD)

FDI Flow	2011	2012	2013	2014
Inward	0.939	0.396	-0.840	1.040
Outward	10.109	1.840	8.021	6.748

FDI Stock	2011	2012	2013	2014
Inward	31.502	30.873	29.964	31.004
Outward	22.653	20.413	28.434	35.182

There are no restrictions on capital flows within Qatar, however, it is worth mentioning that according to the Qatar Central Bank, Qatari banks must prioritize Qatari citizens and public projects ahead of private ones in regards to financial operations.[536]

Based on data from the World Bank, portfolio investments (net, balance of payments in current US dollars) in 2015 were calculated at about $16.548 billion. The graph on the next page captures the trend for Qatar between 2011 and 2015.[537]

[535] Oxford Business Group, "Qatar eases restrictions on FDI to boost growth," https://www.oxfordbusinessgroup.com/overview/qatar-eases-restrictions-fdi-boost-growth.
[536] U.S. Department of State, "Executive Summary," https://www.state.gov/documents/organization/231068.pdf.
[537] Portfolio Investment, net, Balance of Payment $US current, World Bank: http://data.worldbank.org/indicator/BN.KLT.PTXL.CD?locations=QA.

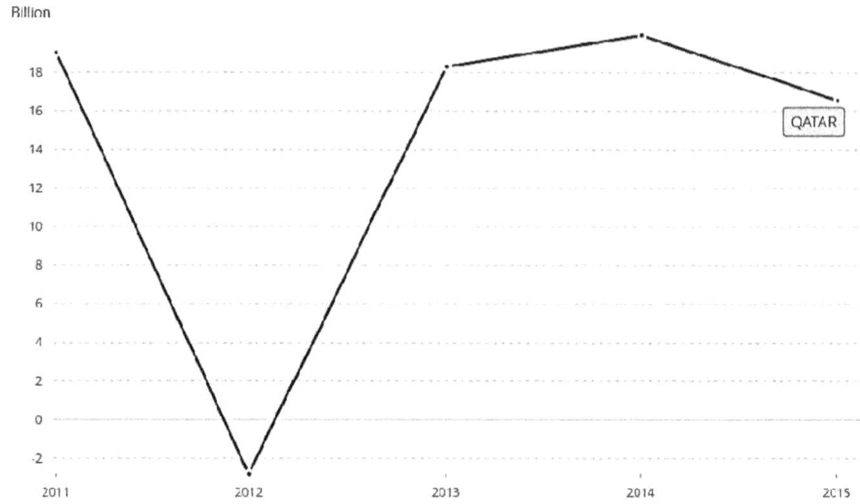

Kuwait

Banking System

The banking System in Kuwait is considered as one of the most fundamentally sound banking sectors within the Middle East and North Africa region. Currently, 23 banks are operating within the country, which are ultimately supervised by Kuwait's central bank. Five are Islamic banks and 12 are foreign banks such as BNP Paribas, Citigroup and HSBC. The banking sector in Kuwait is considered as a well-regulated one. It has confirmed itself as being resilient to the fall in energy prices. With a capital adequacy ratio of 16.9% based on Basel III definitions, it possesses good provisioning buffers. However, the non-performing loan ratio of 2.8% can be considered as a bit high in comparison with some other GCC members.[538] Return on equity increased to 8.9% in 2014, confirming that the sector continues to be profitable.

Concerning the banking sector's exposure to risk, by holding positions directly and indirectly in real estate and the equity market, sufficient

[538] Kuwait Central Bank, "Financial Stability Report," 2015: http://www.cbk.gov.kw/en/images/FSR-2015-En-10-121382-1.pdf; Oxford Business Group, "Kuwait's Banking Industry Looks to the Future." https://www.oxfordbusinessgroup.com/overview/solid-fundamentals-one-country%E2%80%99s-most-stable-industries-looks-future.

capital and implemented buffers guarantee the sector's effective responses to economic shocks.[539]

The stress test conducted by International Monetary Fund also confirms the resilience of the sector and the fact that the combined capital of banks in the sample remained above the minimum required in a moderate scenario. However, in a severe stress scenario, five out of seven banks would not meet the minimum requirement put in place by the Central Bank of Kuwait. In such a case, the sector would see an increase of about 400% in non-performing loans.

Overall, the sector is perfectly capitalized and regulations are complied with and monitored. The central bank continues to strengthen its regulations and the use of macro-prudential approaches to preserve the stability of the system.[540]

Investment Climate

Kuwait's authorities have acted vigorously in regards to easing business constraints within the country and have implemented regulations that are considered as serious intentions toward capturing more investments, in particular from foreigners. The foreign direct investment law of 2013 is an affirmation of how Kuwait has tried to improve its business environment and investment climate. In 2014, for instance, authorities announced that foreign banks could open more than one branch. Regulations also included adopting more standardized measures for business and finance. In 2015, the Financial Action Task Force (FATF) removed Kuwait from its list. Despite these achievements and efforts toward easing the business environment, in 2015, Kuwait ranked lowest within the GCC in terms of the ease of doing business.[541]

---

[539] Kuwait article 4, IMF, 2015: https://www.imf.org/external/pubs/ft/scr/2015/cr15327.pdf; "Kuwaiti banks' risks grow as real estate sales drop," *Saudi Gazette*, 2016: http://saudigazette.com.sa/business/kuwaiti-banks-risks-grow-as-real-estate-sales-drop/; "Kuwait's banks brace for property crash," *Euromoney*, 2016: http://www.euromoney.com/Article/3527346/Kuwaits-banks-brace-for-property-crash.html; "Fitch Affirms Nine Kuwaiti Banks; Upgrades Gulf Bank's VR," Fitch, 2015: https://www.fitchratings.com/site/pr/993657.

[540] Ananthakrishnan Prasad, Heba Abdel Monem and Pilar Garcia Martinez, "Macroprudential Policy and Financial Stability in the Arab Region," International Monetary Fund, 2016; Central Bank of Kuwait, "Macro Prudential Policies and Financial Stability and their Interactions with the Monetary Policy," http://www.cbk.gov.kw/en/index.jsp; Zsofia Arvai Ananthakrishnan and Prasada, "Macroprudential Policy in the GCC Countries," International Monetary Fund, 2014.

[541] World Bank, "Doing Business: Kuwait," http://www.doingbusiness.org/data/exploreeconomies/kuwait/.

Measure	Year	Index/Rank
TI Corruption Perceptions Index	2015	55 of 175
Ease of Doing Business	2016	101/189
Global Innovation Index	2015	77/141
GNI per Capita	2014	$49,300

Tribal and/or family ties as an approach to business in addition to legal and bureaucratic obstacles create difficulties for foreign businesses that seek to have access to the system.[542] Despite these challenges, in 2013, Kuwait attracted $2.3 billion of FDI and surpassed GCC members such as Oman, Bahrain and Qatar.[543]

Foreign Direct Investment

In 2014, Kuwait was able to attract only $486 million of FDI, representing a tiny 1.1% of the Arab nations' total. FDI balances incoming to the country registered $15.4 billion at the end of 2014, a 1.9% share of the Arab total. Between 2003 and 2015, in terms of greenfields, 300 FDI were being implemented through some 258 companies, with total investments of approximately $11 billion. The United Arab Emirates, the United States and France were the main countries in terms of investments in the projects and together accounted for 75% of the total. The following chart shows the major countries investing in Kuwait, with their respective shares, between 2003 and 2015. It is notable that among these countries, only one Gulf Cooperation Council member, the United Arab Emirates, had a significant share – 23.3% of the total – while the others were almost absent in investing in their GCC partner.[544]

---

[542] Institute of Export, "Doing Business in Kuwait," http://www.kuwait.doingbusinessguide.co.uk/the-guide/doing-business/.

[543] U.S. Department of State, "Kuwait Investment Climate Statement,"2015; World Bank, "Doing Business: Kuwait;" Transparency International: https://www.transparency.org/; The Global Innovation Index: https://www.globalinnovationindex.org; GNI per capita, Atlas Method, World Bank: http://data.worldbank.org.

[544] "Foreign investment in GCC drops by 14.6%," *Kuwait Times*, 2014: http://news.kuwaittimes.net/foreign-investments-gcc-drop-14-6/; Kuwait Foreign Investment Data, A European Institutional Investor Company, CEIC:

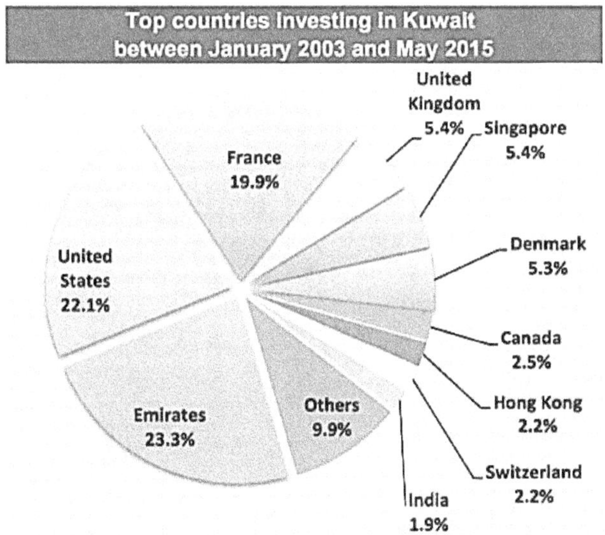

In leading the list, the United Arab Emirates created more than 10,000 jobs in the Kuwaiti economy through its investments of more than $2.5 billion.[545]

Inward investment in Kuwait between January 2003 and May 2015

Rank	Exporting Countries	No. Companies	No. Projects	No. Jobs	Cost (Million $)
1	Emirates	57	79	10,027	2,620
2	United States	41	45	4,325	2,486
3	France	21	21	3,561	2,230
4	United Kingdom	20	20	1,921	602
5	Singapore	1	1	875	601
6	Denmark	1	4	868	590
7	Canada	4	4	361	277
8	Hong Kong	4	4	377	250
9	Switzerland	3	3	648	242
10	India	17	20	1,410	215

https://www.ceicdata.com/en/statistics/Kuwait/Foreign-Direct-Investment-FDI; U.N. Conference on Trade and Development, "World Investment Report," 2016; Arab Investment and Export Guarantee Corporation, Dhaman, "Kuwait," 2016.

[545] Arab Investment and Export Guarantee Corporation, Dhaman, "Kuwait," *ibid.*

While energy and real estate were the main sectors in which FDI occurred, a sectoral distribution shows that Kuwait has had some success in diversifying its economy by attracting investments in other sectors.[546]

Inward investment in Qatar by the sectoral distribution between January 2003 and May 2015						
Rank	Sector	Companies	Projects	Jobs Created	Cost (Million $)	% of Total
1	Coal, Oil and Natural Gas	24	32	10,491	54,919	50
2	Real Estate	25	30	15,966	17,215	16
3	Chemicals	18	19	7,219	7,560	7
4	Hotels & Tourism	35	45	6,674	7,445	7
5	Metals	8	12	6,847	7,418	7
6	Leisure & Entertainment	8	9	3,720	3,714	3
7	Alternative/Renewable energy	6	6	643	2,613	2
8	Financial Services	81	96	1,811	1,652	2
9	Business Services	148	151	2,994	1,490	1
10	Electronic Components	10	10	4,005	878	1
	Others	239	291	28,807	4,777	4
	الإجمالي	602	701	89,177	109,679	

Source: Tables and Figures in this page: FDI Intelligence from The Financial Times

In regards to outward flows, in 2014, Kuwait exported FDI valued at about $13.1 billion, which represented 39.2% of the Arab total. Its outward FDI balances were increasing, and in 2014 they were valued at $36.5 billion. Foreign projects implemented by Kuwaiti enterprises totaled 412 between 2003 and 2015, and their investments in these projects was close to $66.5 billion, creating approximately 130,000 jobs around the world.

The main sector targeted by Kuwaiti investors remained energy. By far the largest investor was Kuwait Petroleum Corporation, which invested $19 billion in 11 projects abroad. Following at some distance were Kuwait Finance House and Gulf Petroleum Investment, whose foreign investments totaled around $5 billion each.[547]

As seen in the next table, the countries receiving these investments included Kuwait's GCC partners, confirming that Kuwait created more financial flows within the GCC than Saudi Arabia or Qatar.[548]

546 *Ibid.*, Kuwait Foreign Investment, Santander, 2016.

547 Mary Ann Tetreault, *The Kuwait Petroleum Corporation and the Economics of the New World Order*, Praeger, 1995; Kuwait, the Business Year, 2016: https://www.thebusinessyear.com/Content/Publication/2c5954f4-3b0e-4012-aea0-67ba8337231f.pdf; Arab Investment and Export Guarantee Corporation, Dhaman, "Kuwait."

548 Kuwait Foreign Investment, Santander, *ibid.*

Kuwait Outwards' Investment between January 2003 and May 2015					
Rank	Hosting Countries	Compa nies	Projects	Jobs Created	Cost (Million $)
1	China	6	6	3,341	9,264
2	Vietnam	3	6	3,342	9,186
3	Bahrain	26	40	17,217	7,176
4	Emirates	44	62	21,138	7,039
5	Egypt	16	22	17,678	5,771
6	Malaysia	8	22	2,802	5,277
7	Syria	8	9	9,210	5,099
8	Lebanon	12	16	5,015	2,026
9	Oman	16	18	7,943	1,585
10	Nigeria	1	2	983	1,408

Overall, Kuwait registered a positive FDI balance, with outward flows considerably higher than inward flows in recent years.[549] For a country that faces lower oil and energy prices, facilitating access to business opportunities abroad can help it face liquidity-related issues and promote economic growth in the long run.[550]

Foreign Direct Investment (billion USD)

FDI Flow	2011	2012	2013	2014
Inward	3.259	2.873	1.434	0.486
Outward	10.773	6.741	16.648	13.108

FDI Stock	2011	2012	2013	2014
Inward	15.176	18.144	16.097	15.362
Outward	32.250	31.023	37.153	36.531

[549] U.N. Conference on Trade and Development, "Kuwait: Country fact Sheet," 2016: http://unctad.org/sections/dite_dir/docs/wir2016/wir16_fs_kw_en.pdf.
[550] "Access to finance 'critical to GCC economies,'" Trade Arabia, 2016: http://www.tradearabia.com/news/REAL_314227.html.

The presence of foreign financial investment companies in Kuwait can also be seen as efforts toward facilitating business investments and project implementation. A very effective regulatory mechanism has been put in place to encourage and facilitate, for instance, issues concerning portfolio investments. Despite all of these efforts, the stock market in Kuwait is not liquid enough and regulations issued in 2015 on portfolio management do not cover foreign investments. However, in the larger picture, we can affirm that the market trend has been positive since 1975. As shown here, net portfolio investments in 2015 were valued at $32.668 billion.[551]

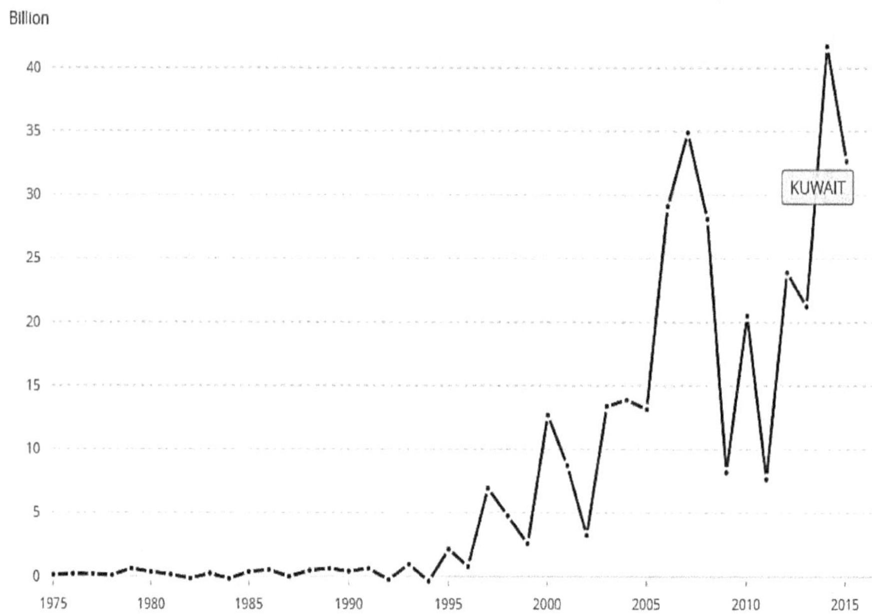

Bahrain

Banking System and Investment Climate

Data from the Central Bank of the Sheikhdom of Bahrain[552] show that as of 31 July 2015 a total of 403 banks and financial institutions were

---

[551] Kuwait, Portfolio Investment, net, PoB current U.S dollar, World Bank, http://data.worldbank.org/indicator/BN.KLT.PTXL.CD?locations=KW.

[552] A Sheikhdom is the land under control of a Sheikh, and a Sheikh in Islamic countries is a chief or patriarch of a tribe or family: Dictionary.com.

registered to operate in the country. This included 79 conventional banks, 24 Islamic banks, 140 insurance companies, 52 investment firms, 82 specialized licensees and 25 capital market operators, as well as insurance representatives and mutual funds. [553]

In 2016, a negative outlook was issued for Bahrain's banking system, mainly due to modest pressure on the quality of loans and profits related to the decline in oil prices. It confirmed that lower oil prices had undermined and would continue to undermine investors' confidence, in addition to causing a decrease in authorities' expenditures. Although the deteriorating conditions would be mitigated by initiatives such as writing off legacy problem loans and a rebound in the tourism sector, the expectations for 2017 remained negative and the system was expected to observe an increase in problem loans from 6.0% to 6.5% of total loans. Financing conditions, though challenging as well, were considered resilient and sustained by high liquidity buffers in addition to loan growth of around 4%. Since the asset-quality issue would result in higher loan-loss provisions, ultimately banks' profitability would be affected as well. In 2016, a decline of 1.2% in tangible assets was registered.[554]

The investment and business climate in Bahrain remains good despite the decline in global oil prices and the presence of state-owned businesses. A liberal approach to investment, as well as reforms such as allowing foreigners to have total ownership of new enterprises, points to a future in which foreign investment would be attracted. However, political instability, violent clashes, favoritism and certain business practices have affected the business environment negatively.[555] Many initiatives have been announced that would facilitate business and the authorities are committed to enhance the circumstances. In that regard, for instance, under a free trade agreement with the United States, Bahrain is committed to strong intellectual property rights. In fact, Bahrain's government currently is focused on attracting and facilitating foreign investment, and to that end, with the aim of diversifying the economy, sectors such as communications and information technology, financial services and tourism are prioritized.[556] The following table gives a clear idea of the business and investment climate in Bahrain.[557]

---

[553] Central Bank of Bahrain: http://www.cbb.gov.bh/page-p-cbb_register.htm.

[554] "Moody's maintains negative outlook on Bahrain's banking system amid weakening operating conditions," Moody's, 2016: https://www.moodys.com/research/Moodys-maintains-negative-outlook-on-Bahrains-banking-system-amid-weakening--PR_350111.

[555] U.S. State Department, Investment Climate 2016: https://www.state.gov/e/eb/rls/othr/ics/2016/nea/254435.htm.

[556] "Committed to enhance Bahrain's investment climate; Industry Minister," 2016: http://www.newsofbahrain.com/viewNews.php?ppId=17357&TYPE=Posts&pid=21&MNU=2&SUB=50; Bahrain Economic Development Board, Key Investment Sectors: http://www.bahrainedb.com/en/investing/sectors/Pages/default.aspx.

[557] Transparency International: http://www.transparency.org/cpi2014/results; The World Bank, Doing Business: http://www.doingbusiness.org/rankings; The Global Innovation Index:

Measure	Year	Index/Rank
TI Corruption Perceptions Index	2014	55 of 175
Ease of Doing Business	2015	65 of 189
Global Innovation Index	2015	59/143
GNI per Capita	2010	$21,060

Foreign Direct Investment

Based on data from 2014, Bahrain was able to attract 2.2% of the total foreign direct investment into Arab countries, valued at about $957 million. At the end of that year, FDI balances incoming to the country were valued at about $18.8 billion, representing 2.4% of the Arab total. Between 2003 and 2015, 567 foreign direct greenfield investment projects with an estimated cost of $31.6 billion were implemented in Bahrain, with the creation of 75,000 jobs. The main investors in Bahrain have been Kuwait, the United Arab Emirates, the United States, France, Germany, India, the United Kingdom and Saudi Arabia. The share of the first three countries accounted for 57% of the total. A privatization program, in addition to other reforms with the aim of offering a business-friendly environment to foreign companies, helped Bahrain to register inward FDI growth during 2015. This allowed it to occupy the tenth position among Middle East and African countries in terms of the number of investment projects.[558]

---

https://www.globalinnovationindex.org/home; The World Bank, Gross National Income per Capita: http://data.worldbank.org/indicator/NY.GNP.PCAP.CD.

[558] fDi Intelligence, the fDi Report 2016: http://forms.fdiintelligence.com/report2016/files/The_fDi_Report_2016.pdf.

FDI INTO MIDDLE EAST AND AFRICA BY PROJECT NUMBERS 2015		
Country	Projects 2015	% change
UAE	298	-2%
South Africa	118	3%
Kenya	84	47%
Saudi Arabia	78	3%
Morocco	71	8%
Egypt	59	14%
Nigeria	51	19%
Ghana	40	21%
Oman	35	9%
Bahrain	34	31%
Other	386	-13%
Total	1254	1%

Source: fDi Markets Note: Percentages rounded up/down

The top 10 sources of foreign investment in Bahrain and their respective shares in terms of total investments are shown below:[559]

Inward investment in Bahrain between January 2003 and May 2015					
Rank	Exporting Countries	No. Companies	No. Projects	No. Jobs	Cost (Million $)
1	Kuwait	26	40	17,217	7,176
2	UAE	71	104	16,353	6,582
3	United States	66	71	7,498	4,336
4	France	20	25	2,470	1,577
5	Japan	10	12	900	1,439
6	UK	62	71	4,860	1,353
7	Germany	23	26	2,103	1,273
8	Saudi Arabia	26	35	3,801	1,099
9	Singapore	6	6	4,120	1,083
10	India	38	43	3,257	963

As is readily seen in the case of Bahrain, the presence of other GCC partners is remarkable. The GCC countries implemented approximately 180 projects between 2003 and 2015.[560] At the top of the list was Kuwait Finance

[559] Arab Investment and Export Guarantee Corporation, Dhaman, "Bahrain," 2016.
[560] *Ibid.*

House, which invested around $4.617 billion between 2003 and 2015.[561] A sectoral distribution of inward foreign direct investment in Bahrain, shown below, reveals that after the real estate sector a priority is being placed on tourism, with the aim of diversifying the economy.

Inward investment in Bahrain by the sectoral distribution between January 2003 and May 2015						
Rank	Sector	Companies	Projects	Jobs Created	Cost (Million $)	% of Total
1	Real Estate	23	27	23,098	8,418	27
2	Hotels & Tourism	25	32	7,095	5,840	18
3	Coal, Oil and Natural Gas	8	8	712	5,013	16
4	Chemicals	12	16	2,661	2,978	9
5	Financial Services	93	123	2,578	2,270	7
6	Communications	22	34	1,945	1,113	4
7	Metals	7	7	2,344	1,014	3
8	Business Services	68	70	8,199	809	3
9	Food & Tobacco	17	25	5,241	645	2
10	Plastics	6	6	1,004	573	2
	Others	191	219	20,043	2,933	9
	Total	472	567	74,920	31,604	

FDI Intelligence from The Financial Times

The outward flow of FDI from Bahrain was negative and valued at about $80 million in 2014. Registering outward FDI balances of $10.7 billion at the end of 2014, Bahrain had a share of 4.3% of the Arab countries' total. Between 2003 and 2015, 206 projects implemented by Bahrain in other countries involved total investments of about $68.4 billion. It is interesting to observe that though Qatar was not among the top ten countries investing in Bahrain, it was among the first three countries that Bahrain invested in.[562] As shown through the table on the next page, 67% of Bahrain's outward investment flows between 2003 and 2015, worth $43.937 billion, were directed toward Libya, Qatar and Kazakhstan.

[561] Kuwait Finance House: https://www.kfh.bh/en/investments/; "KFH-Bahrain wins 'Best Wealth Management Award' in the ME," *Kuwait Times*, 2016: http://news.kuwaittimes.net/website/kfh-bahrain-wins-best-wealth-management-award/.
[562] Arab Investment and Export Guarantee Corporation, Dhaman, "Bahrain."

Bahrain Outwards' Investment between January 2003 and May 2015					
Rank	Hosting Countries	Companies	Projects	Jobs Created	Cost (Million $)
1	Libya	4	4	3,524	20,181
2	Qatar	15	17	6,890	13,756
3	Kazakhstan	1	1	3,000	10,000
4	Tunisia	1	2	6,000	6,000

The main companies that invested outside Bahrain, Gulf Finance House, Khaleej Development House and Arcapita Bank, are committed to Islamic finance and banking, which explains the flow of capital from Bahrain mainly to Muslim countries.[563]

Top important Bahrain companies investing abroad between January 2003 and May 2015				
Rank	Company	Projects	Jobs Created	Cost (Million $)
1	Gulf Finance House (GFH)	19	20,152	32,551
2	Al Khaleej Development (Tameer)	13	7,136	21,634
3	Arcapita Bank	3	3,291	3,692
4	Terra Sola	1	776	3,500
5	Zain (Mobile Telecommunications Company) (MTC)	16	1,929	1,419
6	Investcorp Bank	1	3,000	875
7	Crown Dilmun Development Company	1	3,000	500
8	Bank Alkhair (Unicorn Investment Bank)	16	1,623	458
9	Ithmaar Bank	13	527	339
10	Nader & Ebrahim	1	1,554	300
	Other Companies	122	7,414	3,144
	Total	206	50,402	68,413

563 Tameer, Al Khaleej Development Company: http://www.tameer.com; ARCAPITA: http://www.arcapita.com/; Gulf Finance House: http://gfh.com/.

Overall, Bahrain has registered a negative FDI balance in recent years, as inward FDI stocks have exceeded the outward FDI stocks.[564]

Foreign Direct Investment (billion USD)

FDI Flow	2011	2012	2013	2014
Inward	0.781	0.891	0.989	0.957
Outward	0.894	0.922	1.052	-0.080
FDI Stock	2011	2012	2013	2014
Inward	15.935	16.826	17.815	18.771
Outward	8.776	9.699	10.751	10.672

It should be noted that the country has put in place an effective regulatory system that facilitates and encourages portfolio investments, and that Basel II standards have been implemented and observed. Data from the World Bank confirm that in 2014 net portfolio investments reached $29.609 billion.[565] The following chart gives a clear idea of portfolio investments, in billions of dollars, during the past few decades.

[564] U.N. Conference on Trade and Development.
[565] World Bank, "Portfolio Investment: Bahrain," http://data.worldbank.org/indicator/BN.KLT.PTXL.CD?locations=BH; Central Bank of Bahrain, "Balance of Payment Report," 2011: http://www.cbb.gov.bh/assets/BOPR/2011%20Balance%20of%20Payments%20Report.pdf.

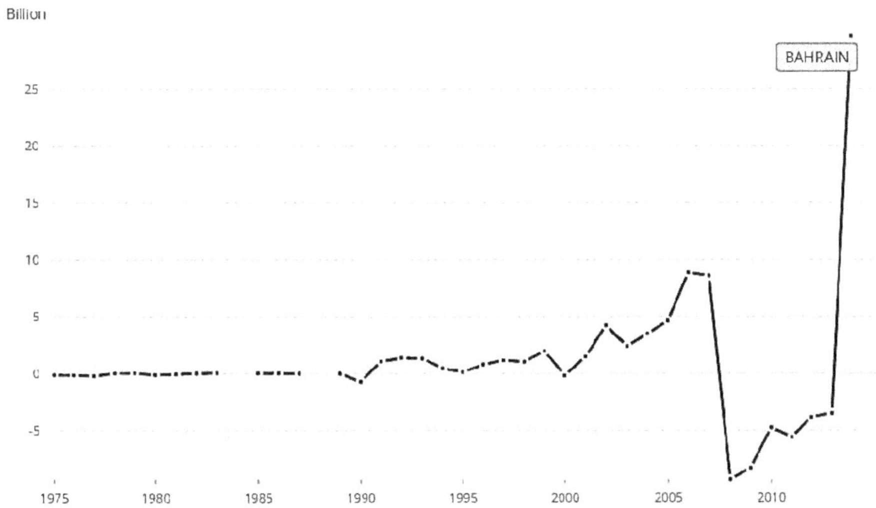

The different sources of portfolio investment assets in 2014 are shown below.[566]

Portfolio Investment Assets (2014)								
Top Five Partners (Millions, US Dollars)								
Total			**Equity Securities**			**Total Debt Securities**		
All Countries	35,416	100%	All Countries	5,835	100%	All Countries	29,581	100%
Turkey	5,947	17%	Cayman Islands	1,113	19%	Turkey	5,905	20%
UAE	3,752	11%	USA	668	11%	UAE	3,423	12%
Qatar	2,797	8%	Luxembourg	519	9%	Qatar	2,603	9%
USA	2,672	8%	KSA	495	8%	USA	2,004	7%
Cayman Islands	1,828	5%	UAE	329	6%	Brazil	1,293	4%

566 U.S. Department of State, "2016 Investment Climate: Bahrain."

United Arab Emirates

Banking System

The banking system in the United Arab Emirates is not very different from the ones of the other GCC partners discussed earlier. A central bank established in 1980 is considered the main authority in regards to deciding regulations, policies and supervision. In regards to foreign banks operating in the UAE, in 2014, 28 banks and their respective branches were on the list of the central bank's licensed banks. Foreign banks' operations and activities are subject to certain limitations put in place by the central bank. In addition to a tax of up to 20% that applies to profits of foreign banks but not domestic ones, foreign banks are affected by other measures related to indicators such as capital adequacy ratios. They are not allowed to calculate loans in connection to their global capital, for example. However, we need to affirm that the number of Islamic banks is growing rapidly and that Islamic banking tools are increasingly used within the conventional banks.[567]

The banking system in the United Arab Emirates, despite lower energy prices that all GCC members have experienced, has reacted well and remained sound in terms of liquidity, profits and asset quality. A high level of liquidity is also required by regulations formulated by the UAE's central bank. However, as is the case for other countries in the GCC club, the lower energy prices can impact the soundness of the system. For instance, the authorities' withdrawals of deposits to finance the deficit caused by lower oil prices can put pressure on liquidity and consequently affect the whole system.[568]

In 2015, the banking system was able to attract new deposits by taking advantage of the wholesale markets, mitigating the decreasing deposit growth. Although credit to the private sector remained within an acceptable range, the government's contribution was negative and thus total deposit growth remained at a low rate of one percent.

As confirmed by authorities and competent institutions, the liquidity of the banking system is not an issue and it remains very good. To help the system, in addition to an increase in government deposits, non-resident deposits and their rise since 2014 are considered as an important factor that has contributed to the system's ability to face the pressure from falling oil

---

[567] U.S. International Trade Administration, "United Arab Emirates – Banking System," 2016, www.export.gov; "Islamic Banks in UAE," Islamic Finance.com, 2016: https://www.islamicfinance.com/islamic-banks-uae/; "Islamic banking gains favor in the UAE," *Khaleej Times*, 2016: http://www.khaleejtimes.com/business/banking-finance/islamic-banking-gains-favour-in-the-uae.
[568] United Arab Emirates, International Monetary Fund, 2016

prices.[569] The recent development of the system's liquidity is captured through the chart below.[570]

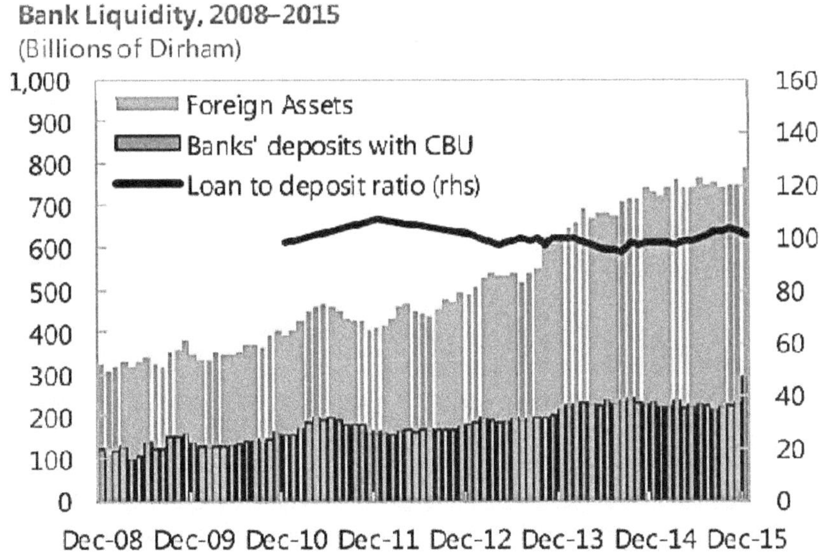

The financial system is considered sound and the asset quality has improved during recent years. In 2015, the nonperforming loan ratio was 4 points lower than the level registered in 2012, and average profitability has improved since 2009.

Other indicators such as the capital adequacy ratio, measuring banks' capital in respect to their risks, was higher than the required regulatory measure of 12, and the important loan to deposit ratio, another risk-measuring indicator, has been stable at around 100% since 2012.[571]

---

[569] *Ibid.*; "UAE central bank chief says liquidity 'very good,'" *Gulf News*, 2016: http://gulfnews.com/business/sectors/banking/uae-central-bank-chief-says-liquidity-very-good-1.1840893; "No pressure on UAE banking sector liquidity, says central bank governor," Reuters, 2016: http://www.arabianbusiness.com/no-pressure-on-uae-banking-sector-liquidity-says-central-bank-governor-634073.html.

[570] United Arab Emirates, International Monetary Fund, 2016.

[571] Central Bank of the U.A.E., "United Arab Emirates Monetary, Financial and Banking Developments," 2016: http://www.centralbank.ae/en/pdf/reports/UAEMonetaryDevelopments-Q1-2016En.pdf; Babu Das Augustin, "Rising liquidity and capital adequacy lifts confidence in UAE banks," *Gulf News*, 2016: http://gulfnews.com/business/sectors/banking/rising-liquidity-and-capital-adequacy-lifts-confidence-in-uae-banks-1.1285218.

Investment Climate

The United Arab Emirates, like its peers, pursues an agenda that focuses on diversifying its economy. To that end, numerous initiatives in the form of laws and regulations have been put in place to facilitate the procedures and promote businesses and startups. Despite all of these efforts, however, bureaucratic as well as underdeveloped mechanisms persist. For instance, each Emirate has its own business registration processes that are different from those of the other Emirates, online mechanisms do not exist, and definitions are not yet standardized among the Emirates for micro, small and medium-sized businesses. In regards to ownership issues, discrimination persists and foreign entities and individuals cannot own more than 49% of a business. In addition, there have been no privatization programs in the UAE as in other GCC countries. However, the UAE has been able to improve on key indicators of its business climate.[572]

Measure	**Year**	**Index/Rank**
TI Corruption Perceptions Index	2015	23 of 168
Ease of Doing Business	2015	31 of 189
Global Innovation Index	2015	47/143
GNI per Capita	2014	$44,600

Overall, the United Arab Emirates is considered as a vibrant free economy that offers a variety of business opportunities to entrepreneurs and entities. Incentives such as tax exemptions and free zones where 100% ownership is allowed are aimed at attracting as much business and foreign investment as possible.[573]

---

[572] World Bank, http://www.doingbusiness.org/data/exploreeconomies/united-arab-emirates; Transparency International, https://www.transparency.org/country/ARE; John Everington, "UAE improves standing in World Bank's Ease of Doing Business Survey," *The National*, 2016: http://www.thenational.ae/business/economy/uae-improves-standing-in-world-banks-ease-of-doing-business-survey; Global Innovation Index, Press release, 2016: https://www.globalinnovationindex.org/media-press-releases.

[573] Global Edge, Michigan State University: http://globaledge.msu.edu/countries/united-arab-emirates/risk; Kothari Auditors and Accountants, http://www.kothariauditors.com/index.html.

Foreign Direct Investment

The United Arab Emirates in 2014 received FDI valued at about $10.066 billion, representing 22.9% of the total FDI into all Arab countries. Foreign direct investment balances coming to the country reached the threshold of $115.6 billion, and in terms of greenfield investments between 2003 and 2015, 3880 projects were implemented in the UAE, with total investments of around $142.3 billion. The key investors, cumulatively representing 40% of the total investments, were India, the United States and the United Kingdom. As in other GCC countries, these inflows mainly went to real estate, tourism and energy-related projects. As shown in the table, the only GCC country among the ten main foreign sources of capital was Kuwait, which implemented 62 projects with a total cost of $ 7.930 billion. Extending the list to the next 10 countries would bring in Saudi Arabia, Bahrain and Qatar, which respectively invested $4.293 billion, $1.179 billion and 983 million.[574]

Inward investment in UAE between January 2003 and May 2015

Rank	Exporting Countries	No. Companies	No. Projects	No. Jobs	Cost (Million $)
1	India	273	339	38,257	25,065
2	United States	724	880	53,007	21,121
3	United Kingdom	551	644	31,998	11,720
4	Germany	193	243	23,172	7,691
5	Japan	95	106	8,222	7,373
6	Kuwait	44	62	21,138	7,039
7	South Korea	30	41	14,137	6,480
8	France	166	215	17,089	6,051
9	Australia	62	68	10,261	4,602
10	Singapore	38	47	10,400	4,545

A sectoral distribution of FDI inflows, shown in the table on the next page, confirms the government's priority of diversifying the economy.[575]

---

[574] Arab Investment and Export Guarantee Corporation, Dhaman, "United Arab Emirates," 2016.
[575] *Ibid.*

Inward investment in UAE by the sectoral distribution between January 2003 and May 2015						
Rank	Sector	Companies	Projects	Jobs Created	Cost (Million $)	% of Total
1	Real Estate	120	150	86,178	32,284	23
2	Hotels & Tourism	114	176	28,751	21,591	15
3	Coal, Oil and Natural Gas	65	71	6,380	18,055	13
4	Financial Services	382	498	12,309	8,925	6
5	Business Services	598	677	19,382	6,378	4
6	Chemicals	65	78	9,909	6,371	4
7	Communications	182	210	11,790	5,309	4
8	Leisure & Entertainment	27	34	12,062	4,570	3
9	Metals	96	105	18,958	3,967	3
10	Consumer Products	144	184	33,814	3,925	3
	Others	1,426	1,697	112,676	30,887	22
	Total	3,219	3,880	352,209	142,262	

Source: Tables and Figures in this page: FDI Intelligence from The Financial Times

Outward investments from the UAE in 2014 represented 9.2% of all such investments from Arab countries and were valued at $3.072 billion. The same year, the outward balances amounted to $66.3 billion. Between 2003 and 2015, Emirati companies implemented 2,456 greenfield projects, mainly in Egypt, India and Iraq. These three countries accounted for 31% of the total in terms of the cost of the projects.

Among the 10 largest recipients of capital from the UAE, Saudi Arabia occupied the seventh position and saw $13.489 billion injected into its economy in terms of FDI from the UAE.[576] Companies investing abroad ranged from energy and property companies to port operators.[577] Overall, in 2014, the UAE registered a negative FDI balance since its inward stocks exceeded the outward ones.[578]

---

[576] *Ibid.*

[577] Al Maabar: http://www.bloomberg.com/research/stocks/private/snapshot.asp?privcapId=47052767; Dubai Holding: http://www.bloomberg.com/research/stocks/private/snapshot.asp?privcapId=12952607; Emaar Property: https://www.emaar.com/en/index.aspx.

[578] Dubai FDI: http://www.dubaifdi.gov.ae/English/DataCenter/Pages/Publications.aspx.

Foreign Direct Investment (billion USD)

FDI Flow	2011	2012	2013	2014
Inward	7.679	9.602	10.488	10.066
Outward	2.178	2.536	2.952	3.072

FDI Stock	2011	2012	2013	2014
Inward	85.406	95.007	105.495	115.561
Outward	57.738	60.274	63.226	66.298

The United Arab Emirates does not report portfolio investment surveys and consequently it publishes no data on the foreign investment portfolio. However, based on information from UAE authorities, the foreign portfolio investment in 2012 was valued at $15.1 billion.[579]

Oman

Banking System and Investment Climate

There are 22 banks operating in Oman. Nine are foreign and two are Sharia'ah-compliant. The leading institution, BankMuscat, accounts for 37.26% of the sector's total assets.[580]

All of the banks in Oman are monitored by the country's central bank, which also manages interest rates and issues regulations. Regulatory amendments and other interventions with the intention of safeguarding the system are common. In recent years, relatively high interest rates on personal loans created a robust flow of revenue to the banking system; however, the authority's conservative response was to intervene through introducing regulatory changes with the aim of depressing the debt levels for both individuals and banks to keep them within desirable ranges. A law put in place in 2012 obliged commercial banks not to deduct more than 50% of borrowers' salaries in regards to their installments. Other measures such as trying to reduce the repayment burdens by imposing a 10-year cap have also been taken. Concerning the overall growth of Oman's economy, authorities decided

---

579 https://www.state.gov/e/eb/rls/othr/ics/2016/nea/254467.htm.

580 Central Bank of Oman, "Financial Stability Report," 2015.

to increase the housing loan limit to 5%. Therefore, as we see, the state's interventions are not limited only to regulations necessary for guaranteeing the soundness of the system, but also to managing the economy as a whole, safeguarding the stability of the Sultanate.[581]

Concerning the resilience of the banking system in Oman, the central bank recently created a financial stability unit with the objective of supervising the system's macro aspects. In addition, the minimum capital requirements were tightened. Authorities, in addition to their own initiatives and measures, also introduced those in accordance with the Basel III framework. Following a long period of low energy prices, an increase in hydrocarbon production as well as public spending through the government's countercyclical policies helped Omani banks to maintain a stable credit profile with a resilient asset quality. Any eventual increase of problem loans would be faced efficiently by the system since available capital buffers would give to the banks a good loan-loss absorbency. Even though the system faces a variety of authorities' interventions, its profitability has been healthy.

The investment climate in Oman is considered favorable since the Sultanate tries to diversify its economy in order to become less vulnerable to global energy prices. To that end, as was the case for other GCC countries, Oman tries to facilitate access to its economy so business opportunities can be exploited. Laws have been put in place, for instance, to provide standardized legal frameworks for investors and businesses. New technologies have helped the registration process to be less time-consuming and more efficient. Although issues such as limiting foreign ownership of companies also exist in Oman, there are exceptions. For instance, based on a free trade agreement with the United States, American firms can open and own businesses in Oman without local partners. In addition to offering privileges to some countries, authorities continue also to privilege and promote industries within the economy that are considered as priorities. The list of privileged and promoted industries begins with manufacturing, mining and shipping, and ends with sectors such as higher education, healthcare and renewable energy.[582] In connection with the aforementioned policies and initiatives, a privatization program has also been introduced.[583] However, the lack of competition laws in concomitance with an unclear legal framework for privatizing has slowed

---

[581] U.S. International Trade Administration, "Oman Executive Summary," www.export.gov; Bank of Oman, "The Business Year," 2015.

[582] U.S. State Department, "Oman: Investment Climate," 2016; Oman Chamber of Commerce and Industry: http://chamberoman.om/En/Content.aspx.

[583] Rejimon K., "100% of ownership for Foreigners in Oman?" *Times of Oman*, 2016: http://timesofoman.com/article/76347/Oman/Government/Expatriates-likely-to-be-allowed-to-start-a-business-in-Oman-without-an-Omani-partner; PWC, "Doing Business in Oman: A Tax and Legal Guide," https://www.pwc.com/m1/en/tax/documents/doing-business-guide-oman.pdf.

the process of attracting investments. The table below describes Oman's business climate by various measures.[584]

Measure	Year	Index/Rank
TI Corruption Perceptions Index	2015	60 of 175
Ease of Doing Business	2015	70 of 189
Global Innovation Index	2015	35 of 141
GNI per Capita	2014	$16,870

Foreign Direct Investment

In 2014, Oman attracted foreign direct investments valued at about $1.180 billion, or 2.7% of the Arab total. At the end of that year, the FDI balances incoming to Oman were $19.7 billion. The Sultanate, between 2003 and 2015, saw 496 greenfield projects implemented with total investments of $39 billion. India, the United Kingdom and China topped the investors' list with combined investments that represented 60% of the total. Again, the presence of GCC partners as investors in Oman was very limited.[585]

Inward investment in Oman between January 2003 and May 2015

Rank	Exporting Countries	No. Companies	No. Projects	No. Jobs	Cost (Million $)
1	India	65	85	17,692	6,313
2	United Kingdom	31	34	6,099	4,575
3	China	3	3	370	3,473
4	United States	38	48	4,915	3,211
5	UAE	81	127	19,013	3,036
6	Qatar	15	21	2,826	2,841
7	Canada	3	4	3,595	2,157
8	Germany	13	13	1,797	1,888
9	South Korea	5	5	1,133	1,746
10	Kuwait	16	18	7,943	1,585

---

[584] Transparency International, https://www.transparency.org/country/; http://www.doingbusiness.org/data/exploreeconomies/oman; Innovation index, http://timesofoman.com/article/90302/Oman/Science-/Oman's-ranking-slips-in-Global-Innovation-Index; GNI per capita, World Bank, Oman: http://data.worldbank.org/indicator/NY.GNP.PCAP.CD?locations=OM.
[585] Arab Investment and Export Guarantee Corporation, Dhaman, "Oman," 2016.

A sectoral distribution of incoming flows between 2003 and 2015 confirms that the real opportunities were in minerals and hydrocarbons. Of the investment projects, 51% were related to the development of natural resources.[586]

Inward investment in Oman by the sectoral distribution between January 2003 and May 2015						
Rank	Sector	Companies	Projects	Jobs Created	Cost (Million $)	% of Total
1	Coal, Oil and Natural Gas	22	23	2,765	12,034	31
2	Metals	17	23	19,108	7,924	20
3	Chemicals	15	15	4,432	4,955	13
4	Real Estate	23	26	15,830	2,864	7
5	Hotels & Tourism	31	38	6,643	2,700	7
6	Financial Services	40	96	1,768	1,648	4
7	Food & Tobacco	17	26	7,536	815	2
8	Business Services	50	50	1,159	785	2
9	Plastics	7	7	533	637	2
10	Building & Construction Materials	5	7	729	569	1
	Others	145	185	22,387	4,198	11
	Total	372	496	82,910	39,128	

Source: Tables and Figures in this page: FDI Intelligence from The Financial Times

In regards to outward investments, Omani FDI totaled $1.164 billion in 2014, and its outward balances amounted to $7.453 billion at the end of that year, which represented 3% of the Arab total. Oman implemented 63 projects between 2003 and 2015 that touched the threshold of $222 million in total investments. Major countries receiving capital from Oman were Saudi Arabia, India and the UAE.[587]

Overall, Oman registered a negative FDI balance as inward stocks exceeded outward stocks.[588] It is worth mentioning that foreign investment is increasing as Oman paves the way for more businesses and foreigners through reforms and incentives such as interest-free loans and exceptions in the areas of customs and corporate taxes.[589]

---

586 "Mining Forum to Highlight Investment Opportunity in Oman," *Times of Oman*, 2016, http://timesofoman.com/article/99116/Business/Mining-forum-to-highlight-investment-opportunities-in-Oman; "Omani, Saudi officials discuss investment opportunities," *Times of Oman*, 2016: http://timesofoman.com/article/98431/Oman/Government/Omani-Saudi-officials-discuss-investment-opportunities; Oman Foreign Investment, Santander, 2016: https://en.portal.santandertrade.com/establish-overseas/oman/investing-3.

587 Arab Investment and Export Guarantee Corporation, Dhaman, "Oman."

588 U.N. Conference on Trade and Development..

589 Gulam Ali Khan, "FDI inflows to Oman touched $822M in 2015, says UNCTAD," *Muscat Daily*, 2016: http://www.muscatdaily.com/Archive/Business/FDI-inflows-to-Oman-touched-822mn-in-2015-says-Unctad-4qt5; U.S. State Department, "Oman: Investment Climate Statements," 2016.

Foreign Direct Investment (billion USD)

FDI Flow	2011	2012	2013	2014
Inward	0.874	1.040	1.626	1.180
Outward	1.233	0.877	1.384	1.164

FDI Stock	2011	2012	2013	2014
Inward	15.861	16.901	18.527	19.707
Outward	4.029	4.905	6.289	7.453

Oman led the GCC countries in portfolio investments by foreigners in 2014. The share of foreigners holding positions within the Muscat Security Market was 29.4% at the end of that year. Despite lower oil prices, the market grew 3% and market capitalization equaled 30% of GDP.[590] Annual portfolio investment inflows averaged $222.56 million between 2003 and 2015, and reached a maximum of $1.939 billion in 2015.[591] However, World Bank data showed net portfolio investments were negative in 2015, as seen below:[592]

[590] A.E. James, "Oman leads in foreign portfolio investment in Gulf region," *Times of Oman*, 2015: http://timesofoman.com/article/65563/Business/Markets/Share-of-foreign-holding-in-listed-companies-of-Muscat-Securities-Market-was-295-per-cent-by-the-end-of-2014-the-highest-among-all-GCC-states-according-to-the-annual-report-published-by-the-Capital-Market-Authority.

[591] "Oman portfolio investment inflows, equity," The Global Economy.com: http://www.theglobaleconomy.com/Oman/Portfolio_investment_inflows/.

[592] http://data.worldbank.org/indicator/BN.KLT.PTXL.CD?end=2015&locations=OM&start=1996.

CHAPTER 8

CONCLUSION

History has taught us that nothing is impossible. In the course of history, human beings have been able to create civilizations, to finish incomplete projects left behind by previous generations and to make progress for the future. They have been able to add value to what nature and life offered them. Despite all of the catastrophes that humanity has witnessed, whether natural or human-made, human beings have been able to reassume standing positions and start rebuilding from scratch. However, history also taught us that what humanity has achieved so far has been based on ideas built upon realistic and scientifically observed assumptions that incorporated precious experiences of others. This work, based on studies done so far with respect to economics and its paradigm, offers a set of conditions that allows us to evaluate the feasibility of the GCC integration project under current circumstances.

As we have seen, the literature on the GCC's integration project gave us an idea about the achievements so far as well as the hurdles ahead. The existing body of economic integration theories, in addition to basic theories of economics discussed during the work, have allowed us to discern the main building blocks of integration projects realized elsewhere, for instance in Europe. Based on what already exists and the experience of other projects, I have identified two determining factors that were present in successful regional integration projects and absent in those that failed to endure. These two factors are part of a larger set of conditions mainly divided into two categories – "demand conditions" and "supply conditions."

The factor coming from the demand condition category is identified as "economic gain," which assesses the potential for economic gain through joining a regional bloc in terms of trade patterns. Here, this potential is analyzed and enforced through financial flows. This gives us an understanding of the rationale behind joining a regional bloc while other alternatives may exist. The potential for economic gain for a whole nation is easily traceable through the way firms operate and perform, since trade is based on what firms within an economy produce and subsequently trade. Integration must provide larger markets to national firms. The European experience has shown this. European firms actively sought deeper integration and lobbied for that.

European countries have well-diversified economies and do not lack complementarities in trade. This is why overlapping trade flows within a region, where everybody produces the same product targeted to the same market, reduces the potential for benefiting from integration.

Concerning the supply category, the conditions that must be met are the presence of an "undisputed leader state" and "commitment institutions." Throughout this work, the presence of commitment institutions is identified and developed in connection with the Gulf Cooperation Council's integration project. The absence of an undisputed leader state was easy to detect under current circumstances, considering politically motivated conflicts of interest among the GCC countries. The definition of "institution" as "a custom, practice, relationship or behavioral pattern of importance in the life of a community" is inclusive. Moreover, in the context of regional integration, it has enabled us to offer a presentation of the Islamic banking and financial system and to compare the structural differences it has with the conventional system. European countries function based on a set of assumptions, concepts and practices that enabled them to develop their economies through trade and later by seeking deeper integration, guaranteeing prosperity for the community. This took place through the tenet of natural and civil rights, where, for instance, property rights belong to individuals.

GCC and Demand Conditions

The main rationale behind entering into any trade agreement or regional bloc must be justified *a priori* through a verifiable potential for economic gain or benefit. The assumption that countries that are involved in bilateral trade and trade in general would gain may not be valid for regional blocs and regional integration projects. Adhering to a regional integration project can deprive participating countries from certain autonomies in terms of economic and trade policies. Clearly, furthering integration would demand giving up more. Within a monetary union, for instance, a country's central bank would forgo its autonomy in terms of monetary policies essential for managing the overall economy, as presented and elucidated through the section dedicated to the Federal Reserve banking system in the United States. The Europeans had to prepare themselves years ahead of launching the euro by having the European exchange rate mechanism. The GCC currencies are mainly pegged to the U.S. dollar or a basket of developed-country currencies. As a reminder, The Gulf Cooperation Council was formed mainly with the intent of countering external threats and facing security related issues.

For the GCC, however, the potential gain from trade as a key determinant for countries to join a regional bloc is not satisfied. The phenomenon called "overlapping production and trade flows" has undermined the prospect for intra-regional trade, despite the increase that has been registered since the launch of GCC customs union. Trade among the six countries represented only 7% of their total foreign trade conducted in 2013. The overlapping production and trade flows are foremost confirmed by how the main sectors of their economies are formed. Hydrocarbons are the primary motor of their economies, although these natural resources are not equally distributed among the six of them. Efforts toward diversifying their economies have not succeeded despite some achievements. The primary and secondary sectors are dominant, and consequently industries are formed accordingly. Those related to minerals, chemicals and plastics together produce the same categories of products, such as petroleum, refined petroleum, fertilizer, propylene, etc., to name a few.

The weight of such an industrial skeletal support for the economy is visibly marked through analyzing trade patterns. The GCC countries import machinery, transportation equipment, chemical and mineral products, textiles, vegetable products and foodstuffs because they are not producers themselves. They export crude oil, refined petroleum, natural gas and minerals as their main sources of revenue. The East Asian countries, India, China, Europe and the United States are the main export destinations as well as sources of imports for the six partners of the Gulf Cooperation Council. Their trade patterns confirm the lack of complementarity in production. As a result, they compete for the same markets, not having diversified economies, in addition to living in the globalization era, and they are vulnerable to the performance of their trading partners' economies. The GCC countries for years remained justly focused on their comparative advantage and tried to develop and specialize on that. Efforts to diversify their economies did not translate into the creation of new markets that would ultimately augment intra-regional trade.

The GCC countries have tried to diversify their economies through developing sectors such as tourism, finance and/or transportation. Interestingly, they compete in these regards as well, although the problem is not competition *per se*. The problem is that markets developed through these sectors are mainly targeted to attract, augment and facilitate extra-regional trade. The absorptive capacity of increased intra-regional trade is not present and the complementarity in production and trade flows are absent. This is why the potential for economic gain is not realized.

Financial flows foster regional integration projects. Because intra-regional trade is limited, the financial flows created through trade are not considerable. However, analyzing the financial flows created through foreign direct investments has helped us to evaluate the potential for economic gain that can be realized through investments. Data confirmed the same tendency that had been registered concerning the trade flows. The GCC countries are hosts to foreign enterprises based in countries outside of the region, and these invest mainly in the real estate sector or in the exploitation of natural resources. China, the United States, France, Germany, the United Kingdom, India and Japan are among the main foreign direct investors within the GCC.

These investments might develop sectors such as tourism, real estate or mining within the GCC members' economies, but they would not cause the economies to diversify to the point of producing a larger and broader market that would ultimately guarantee substantial and durable intra-regional trade. The outflows of foreign direct investment confirm the same conclusion. The GCC countries, overall, invest outside of the region rather than in their GCC partners. In connection with financial flows, data retrieved for portfolio investments within the region confirm the same attitude.

Therefore, the potential economic gain that is crucial for a successful economic integration is sought elsewhere, rather than within the region. Firms are therefore not able to achieve economies of scale through the larger market that is supposed to be created once countries are joined together. Specialization which is important to develop sectors where comparative advantages are identified does not happen through a larger market. In addition, all of the GCC members have more and less the same comparative advantage, with different degrees of intensity.

Moreover, economic prosperity due to overall trade creation is not observed, and there are doubts about whether its effects would outweigh those of trade diversion. For instance, Saudi Arabia exports refined petroleum and at the same time imports the same product from India, Turkey and Oman. Therefore, Turkey and India are subject to tariffs where Oman is not. As a result, the more efficient producers lose out to the less efficient ones and trade diversion occurs. The GCC countries compete for the same markets located outside of the region. They receive huge investments from outside of the region to develop sectors where their comparative advantages are identified to be. In connection with this, finances go to diversify sectors that ultimately do not offer larger markets to businesses and consumers within the region. All of this is affirmed by the fact that the GCC countries also heavily invest outside of the region because they can obtain higher returns on investments made externally compared to those made regionally.

Thus, under current circumstances, the GCC countries are better off unilaterally rather than being part of a regional bloc since the demand condition of potential economic gain is not realized.

GCC and Supply Conditions

For a successful integration project, in order to assess its feasibility, in addition to the potential for economic gain, certain institutional conditions are required. Adjusting the definition of "institution" to regional integration projects, it is defined as a "set of formal and informal rules, regulations, and compliance procedures designed to constrain and shape human interaction and structure the incentives of actors involved in an exchange relationship in order to maximize the wealth or unity of these actors." The latter is actualized through established organizations that are dedicated to particular tasks.

Regarding the GCC charter, the six countries confirm that they are fully aware of the ties of special relations, common characteristics and similar systems founded on the creed of Islam which bind them; and that by signing the charter the Arab and Islamic causes would be served and reinforced through the integration project. Islamic civilization is a source of human culture and it shares many aspects with other cultures. Therefore, scrutiny of its economic and financial system was deemed necessary. As it was examined in the sections of this work it, became evident that Sharia'ah can be considered as an institution *per se* that affects the entire system. Important conceptual functionalities built upon the theoretical frameworks of both the Islamic and conventional systems were also introduced.

Economic integration and related theories and concepts, such as customs union, monetary union, trade, investment, etc., are based on a consolidated paradigm of modern economics. In conventional economics, wage is defined as the marginal product of labor, rent as the marginal product of land and interest as the marginal product of money. Within conventional banking, the system of fractional reserve money guarantees the efficient functioning of the relationship between central banks and commercial ones. The whole system operates based on interbank interest rates, reserve/deposit ratios and interventions by the central bank. In regards to finance, concepts such as the time value of money, the cost of capital and techniques such as the present value of money, as well as cash flow analysis in general, together are considered as *modus operandi* of the financial system and its institutions. It is obvious that the macroeconomic factors of a nation, such as growth and employment, are influenced by the way the banking and financial system and their institutions function.

The Islamic system offers a banking and financial system based on Islamic jurisprudence, which has its salient features. For instance, interest is identified as usury and as such is firmly prohibited, even if the two are different concepts. Within the conventional system, modern interest is the price of capital, which is considered as a resource in the economy. However, the way interest is treated as an added value reveals fundamental contradictions. Thus, as is clear, altering the conventional system without offering an alternative that is based on strong theoretical and conceptual grounds cannot guarantee the main objective of allocating resources efficiently within the economy.

The Islamic system, loyal to its principles, coexists with the conventional system in these countries. The share of Islamic banking and finance is increasing as it is considered safer and in accordance with Sharia'ah. On the other hand, the economic integration theory and other regional integration initiatives are built upon modern economics and its consolidated paradigm, which offer a robust theoretical and conceptual basis for their implementation.

This is how, in the European Union, institutions such as the ECB, the ESCB, the Economic and Financial Committee and ECOFIN are created and currently operate. Therefore, the idea of regional integration being simply a process that provides common rules, regulations and policies for a region cannot be built upon theories, concepts and institutions that do not reflect the reality of that particular region. Ignoring the demand for institutional change that comes from the population of a country through political parties, interest groups, associations, etc., would only guarantee the failure of the regional integration project.

Political divisions are sources of conflicts, and political leaders in order to further the integration process must sacrifice national sovereignty in terms of economic policies and politics. In connection with the GCC project, the emergence of an undisputed leader has not taken place so far. Political actors within the region have not yet decided firmly to shift their powers and authorities to supranational institutions, and as such, the whole project lacks liveliness. Therefore, the supply conditions are not met. Commitment institutions do not exist and an undisputed leader must still emerge.

Thus, it is to conclude that, overall, under the current circumstances, the feasibility of the GCC integration project, evaluated through both the potential for economic gain for participating countries and the presence of committed institutions, does not exist.

BIBLIOGRAPHY

Aaron and Boskin, *The Economics of Taxation*, Brookings Institution Press, 2011.

Abdulaal and Hakimian, *GCC Economic Integration: Fiction or Reality?* Khamsoon, 2015.

Abdullah, *Gulf Cooperation Council's Challenges and Prospects*, Aljazeera Center for Studies, 2014.

Abramovitz, *The Allocation of Economic Resources*, Stanford University Press, 1959.

Academy for International Modern Studies, Islamic Finance Training & Research Division, "Takaful Models," https://uaelaws.files.wordpress.com/2012/02/takaful-models.pdf.

"Accounting and Auditing Organization for Islamic Financial Institutions, Securitizations and Permissible Categories," http://aaoifi.com/?lang=en.

Acemoglu and Robinson, *Why Nations Fail: The Origins of Power, Prosperity, and Poverty*, Crown Business, 2012.

Acemoglu, Johnson and Robinson, "Institutions as a Fundamental Cause of Long Run Growth," *Handbook of Economic Growth*, Elsevier, 2005.

ADB Institute, *Financial System Stability, Regulation, and Financial Inclusion*, Springer, 2015.

Addis and Verghis, *Economic Integration in the Western Hemisphere*, Kellogg Institute, 1994.

Afxentiou, "Convergence, the Maastricht Criteria, and Their Benefits," *Brown Journal of World Affairs*, 7(1).

Ahmad, "Riba, Its Economic Rationale and Implications," Institute of Islamic University, Pakistan.

Ahmad, *Theory and Practice of Modern Islamic Finance: The Case Analysis from Australia*, Universal Publishers, 2010.

Ahmad and Hassan, "The Time Value of Money Concept in Islamic Finance," Islamic Economics and Finance Pedia, http://iefpedia.com/english/wp-content/uploads/2009/11/The-Time-Value-of-Money-Concept-in-Islamic-Finance.pdf.

Ahsanuddin, "Lights," Middle Eastern Studies Students' Association's Subcommittee of Publications, University of Chicago, Spring 2013, https://lucian.uchicago.edu/blogs/messa/files/2013/08/Lights-Spring-2013-FINAL.pdf.

Akram Khan, *An Introduction to Islamic Economics: Islamization of Knowledge*, International Institute of Islamic Thought and Institute of Policy Studies, 1994.

Akram Khan, *Islamic Economics and Finance: A Glossary*, Routledge, 2004.

Al Alekri, Janahi and Hafith, "Civil Society in the Gulf Cooperation Council (GCC) Region: A Literature Review," National Center for Studies, Manama.

Al-Islam.org, "Khums in the Qur'an and History," https://www.al-islam.org/khums-islamic-tax-sayyid-muhammad-rizvi/khums-quran-history.

Al Maneh, "Joint declaration at GCC summit raises hopes and Expectations," *The National*, 2016, http://www.thenational.ae/opinion/comment/joint-declaration-at-gcc-summit-raises-hopes-and-expectations.

Al Tamimi & Co., http://www.tamimi.com/en/magazine/law-update/section-11/february-7/business-conditions-in-the-arabian-gulf.html.

Ali, "Introduction to Ijarah Sukuk: Current Structures and Future Prospects," Monetary and Banking Research Institute, http://new.mbri.ac.ir/userfiles/file/Islamic%20Banking/%D8%A8%D8%A7%D9%86%DA%A9%20%D9%85%D9%82%D8%A7%D9%84%D8%A7%D8%AA/sukuk/introduction%20to%20ijarah%20sukuk%20current%20structures%20and%20future%20prospects.PDF.

Ali and Ahmad, "Islamic Banking and Finance: Fundamental and Contemporary Issues," Islamic Research and Training Institute, 2004.

AlKhabeer Capital, "GCC budgets: Adapting to the new oil reality," 2016, http://www.alkhabeer.com/sites/default/files/GCC%20Budget_Adapting%C2%A0to%C2%A0the%C2%A0New%C2%A0Oil%C2%A0Reality_January%202016%20-%20English.pdf.

Alkholifey and Alreshan, "GCC Monetary Union," Bank of International Settlements, IFC Bulletin no. 32.

Allen, Gasiorek and Smith, "Trade Creation and Trade Diversion," Single Market Review Series, European Commission, 1996.

Alm, Vazquez and Rider, *The Challenges of Tax Reform in a Global Economy*, Springer Science & Business Media, 2005.

Al-Sabah, *Gender and Politics in Kuwait: Woman and Political Participation in the Gulf*, I.B. Tauris, 2013.

Anderson, *Regional Integration and Global Trading System*, Prentice-Hall, 1993.

Andriamananjara, "Customs Unions," World Bank, https://siteresources.worldbank.org/INTRANETTRADE/Resources/C5.pdf.

Ansary, "A Brief Overview of the Saudi Arabian Legal System," Hauser Global Law School, 2008.
Aravi, Prasad and Katayama, "Macro Prudential Policy in the GCC Countries," International Monetary Fund, 2014.
Ariff, Iqbal and Mohamad, *The Islamic Debt Market for Sukuk Securities: The Theory and Practice of Profit Sharing Investment*, Edward Elgar, 2012.
Auty, *Resource Abundance and Economic Development*, Oxford University Press, 2001.
Aziz, *Introduction to Islam*, Ahmadiyya Anjuman Ishaat Islam Lahore USA, 2011.
Badinger and Nitsch, *Routledge Handbook of the Economics of the European Integration*, Routledge, 2015.
Badkar, "Bahrain Junked by S&P," *Financial Times*, 2016, https://www.ft.com/content/74f66c57-314a-3f9d-add4-e5e333dfda80.
Baffes, "The Great Plunge in Oil Prices," World Bank, 2015: www.worldbank.org/content/dam/Worldbank/.../PRN01_Mar2015_Oil_Prices.pdf.
Bahrain Business Law Handbook, International Business Publications, 2007.
Bahrain Economic Development Board, "Key Investment Sectors," http://www.bahrainedb.com/en/investing/sectors/Pages/default.aspx.
Balamir-Coskun and Demirtaş-Coşkun, *Neighborhood Challenge: European Union and Its Neighbors*, Universal Publishers, 2009.
Balassa, *The Theory of Economic Integration*, Routledge, 2011.
Balassa, "Towards the Theory of Economic Integration," *Kyklos*, 1.
Balassa, "Trade Creation and Trade Diversion in the European Common Market: An Appraisal of the Evidence," *The Manchester School*, 42(2), 1974.
Baldwin, "In or Out: Does It Matter? An Evidence-Based Analysis of the Euro's Trade Effects" Centre for Economic Policy Research, 2006.
Baldwin, *The Development and Testing of Heckscher-Ohlin Trade Models, A Review of Ohlin Lectures*, MIT Press, 2008.
Baldwin and Venables, *Handbook of International Economics*, Elsevier, 2014.
Baldwin-Edwards, *Labor Immigration and labor Markets in the GCC Countries: National Patterns and Trends*, LSI, 2011.
Bank for International Settlements, "Regulatory Consistency Assessment Program (RCAP) Assessment of Basel III Risk-based Capital Regulations – Saudi Arabia," 2015, http://www.bis.org/bcbs/publ/d335.pdf.
Basu, "Economics of Scale and Imperfect Competition," *International Economics, Finance and Trade*, Vol.1, Encyclopedia of Life Support.

Basu, Prasad, and Rodriguez, "Monetary Operations and Islamic Banking in the GCC: Challenges and Options," International Monetary Fund, 2015.
"Beginning of Revelation, Mission Islam," https://www.missionislam.com/quran/beginrevelation.htm.
Bekaert and Harvey, "Capital Market: An Engine for Economic Growth," Duke University, https://faculty.fuqua.duke.edu/~charvey/Research/Published_Papers/P58_An_engine_for.pdf.
Bergeijk and Brakman, *The Gravity Model in International Trade: Advances and Applications*, Cambridge University Press, 2010.
Berger and Bouwman, *Bank Liquidity Creation and Financial Crises*, Academic Press, 2015.
Bhatty, "The Growing Importance of Takaful Insurance," OECD, http://www.oecd.org/finance/insurance/46116115.pdf.
Bloomberg Markets: Americas, Bloomberg, 2016, https://www.bloomberg.com/markets/stocks.
Bloomberg Markets: Asia Pacific, Bloomberg, 2016, https://www.bloomberg.com/markets/stocks.
Bloomberg Markets: Europe, Middle East and Africa, Bloomberg, 2016, https://www.bloomberg.com/markets/stocks.
Bogdanov, "Liberalized Capital Accounts and Volatility of Capital Flows and Foreign Exchange Rates," European Commission, *Economic Papers* 521, 2014.
Bojarczyk, "The Gulf Cooperation Council, Regional Integration Mechanism," University Marie Curie, Poland, 2013.
Borensztein, De Gregorio and Lee, "How does foreign direct investment affect economic growth?" *Journal of International Economics*, 1998, http://www.olemiss.edu/courses/inst310/BorenszteinDeGLee98.pdf.
Bosworth and Collins, "Capital Flow to Developing Economies: Implication for Investment and Savings," Brookings Paper on Economic Activities, Brookings Institution, 1999.
Bowles and Pagano, "Economic integration, cultural standardization, and the politics of social insurance," Universita degli Studi di Siena.
Brada and Mendez, "An Estimate of the Dynamic Effects of Economic Integration," *The Review of Economics and Statistics*, 70(1), 1988.
Braithwaite and Drahos, *Global Business Regulation*, Cambridge University Press, 2000.
British Broadcasting Corporation, "Sharia," http://www.bbc.co.uk/religion/religions/islam/beliefs/sharia_1.shtml.

Brulhart, "Scale Economies, Intra-Industry Trade and Industry Location in a 'New Trade Theory,'" *Trinity Economic Papers*, Technical Paper no. 95/4.
Brulhart, "Trading Places: Industrial Specialization in the European Union," Journal of Common Market Studies, 36(3), 1998.
Buch, *Globalization of Financial Markets: Causes of Incomplete Integration and Consequences for Economic Policy*, Springer, 2004.
Buigut, "Feasibility of Proposed Monetary Unions in the Eastern and Southern Africa Region," Georgia State University, 2007.
Buiter, "Economic, Political, and Institutional Prerequisites for Monetary Union among the Members of the Gulf Cooperation Council," *Open Economic Review*, 19(5), 2008.
Cakir and Raei, "Sukuk Vs. Eurobonds: Is There a Difference in Value-at-Risk?" International Monetary Fund, 2007.
Carnery, *Lessons from Asian Financial Crisis*, Routledge, 2009.
Carpenter and Dunung, "Challenges and Opportunities in International Business," v.1.0.
Central Bank of Kuwait, "Macro Prudential Policies and Financial Stability and their Interactions with the Monetary Policy," http://www.cbk.gov.kw/en/index.jsp
Central Bank of Oman, "Government development bond auction results," http://www.cbo-oman.org/circulars/2016/BM1144.pdf.
Centre d'information sur les institutions européennes, "Detailed Explanations about the Institutions of the European Union," http://en.strasbourg-europe.eu/detailed-explanations-about-the-institutions-of-the-european-union,3214,en.html.
Chadha and Tsiddon, "Inflation, Nominal Interest Rate and Variability of Output," International Monetary Fund, 1996.
Chang and Katayama, "Imperfect Competition in International Trade," 1995.
Chik, "Sukuk: Shari'ah Guidelines for Islamic Bonds, Islamic Banking Operations and Regulatory Framework," Centre for Banking Studies, Central Bank of Sri Lanka, 2012.
Choudhury, *The Islamic World-System: A Study in Polity-Market Interaction*, Routledge, 2005.
Clark, *Islam Charity and Activism*, Indiana University Press, 2004.
Cohen, *Multinational Corporations and Foreign Direct Investment: Avoiding Simplicity, Embracing Complexity*, Oxford University Press, 2007.
"Committed to enhance Bahrain's investment Climate; Industry Minister," 2016, http://www.newsofbahrain.com/viewNews.php?ppId=17357&TYPE=Posts&pid=21&MNU=2&SUB=50.
Cordesman and Obaid, *National Security in Saudi Arabia: Threats, Responses, and Challenges*, Greenwood Publishing Group, 2005

Crane, *Gravediggers of the Gulf*, Jacobin, 2015.
Crescent Petroleum, http://www.crescentpetroleum.com/html/oil_gas_overview.html.
Crystal, *Kuwait: The Transformation of an Oil State*, Routledge, 2016.
Czinkota and Zeneli, "Why the Transatlantic Trade and Investment Partnership Is More Important Than TPP," *The Diplomat*, 2016, http://thediplomat.com/2016/01/why-the-transatlantic-trade-and-investment-partnership-is-more-important-than-tpp/.
Davidson, *Abu Dhabi: Oil and Beyond*, Hurst Publishers, 2011.
De Bel-Air, "Demography, Migration, and Labor Market in Qatar," Gulf Research Center, no 8, 2014.
Dedman, *The Origins and Development of the European Union 1945-2008: A History of European Integration*, Taylor and Francis, 2010.
Denisia, "FDI theories: An overview of the main theories of FDI," *European Journal of Interdisciplinary Studies*, 2, 2010.
Dew, *Doing Business with Bahrain*, Kogan Page, 2002.
Diaw, Bacha and Lahsasna, *Incentive-Compatible Sukuk Musharakah for Private Sector Funding*, ISRA I*nternational Journal of Islamic Finance*, 4(1) 2012.
Dieter, "Report on East Asian Economic Integration, Opportunities and Obstacles to Enhance Economic Cooperation," *Notre Europe* 47.
U.S. Federal Reserve System, "Directors of Federal Reserve Banks and Branches," https://www.federalreserve.gov/aboutthefed/directors/about.htm.
"Disadvantages of Foreign Direct Investment," Economy Watch, 2010, http://www.economywatch.com/foreign-direct-investment/disadvantages.html.
Dorgan, "Purchasing Power Parity, Swiss Franc Overvalued?" 2016, SNBCHF.com.
Draper, "Rethinking the foundation of sub-Saharan African regions' economic integration," VOX CEPR's policy portal, 2011.
Ebert, *Intra Industry Trade and Shock Asymmetry in a Monetary Union: A Study of Trade Evolution in the Eurozone*, GRIN Verlag, 2013.
Economist Intelligence Unit, "Economies of scale: How the oil and gas industry cuts costs through replication," 2011.
Economist Intelligence Unit, "Kuwait," http://country.eiu.com/kuwait.
Elek, "Market driven economic integration in the 21st century," East Asia Forum, 2009, http://www.eastasiaforum.org/2009/05/04/market-driven-economic-integration-in-the-21st-century/.
El-Gamal, *Islamic Finance: Law, Economics and Practice*, Cambridge University Press, 2006.
Embassy of the State of Kuwait, Ottawa, Canada, "Natural Resources," http://kuwaitembassy.ca/pages/GeneralInfo/Natural-Resources.htm.

European Central Bank, "Financial Integration in Europe: Eurosystem," 2014.
European Central Bank, Occasional Paper Series, no. 92, 2008.
European Central Bank, https://www.ecb.europa.eu/ecb/orga/escb/html/mission_eurosys.en.html.
European Commission, "Benefits of Trade for Developing Countries," http://trade.ec.europa.eu/doclib/docs/2012/january/tradoc_148991.pdf.
European Commission, "EU-GCC Cooperation Agreement," http://trade.ec.europa.eu/doclib/docs/2008/september/tradoc_140300.pdf.
European Commission, "Foreign Direct Investment," 2014.
European Commission, "Trade Creation and Trade Diversion," 1997.
European Commission, "Treaty on European Union, https://europa.eu/european-union/sites/europaeu/files/docs/body/treaty_on_european_union_en.pdf.
European Parliament, "Adjustment to asymmetric shocks," 1998, http://www.europarl.europa.eu/workingpapers/econ/104/chap1_en.htm.
European Parliament Think Tank, "One Belt One Road (OBOR): China's Regional Integration Initiative," http://www.europarl.europa.eu/thinktank/en/document.html?reference=EPRS_BRI(2016)586608.
European Union, "Import and Export," http://europa.eu/european-union/business/import-export_en#trading-in-and-with-the-eu.
Eurostat, "External and Intra-European Union Trade," 2010, http://ec.europa.eu/eurostat/documents/3930297/5966458/KS-CV-10-001-EN.PDF/c43ee937-2072-4d35-b46f-c73ae20c41bf.
Eurostat, "Intra EU Trade in Goods: Recent Trends," http://ec.europa.eu/eurostat/statistics-explained/index.php/Intra-EU_trade_in_goods_-_recent_trends.
Fabozzi, Modigliani, Jones and Ferri, *Foundations of Financial Markets and Institutions*, Prentice Hall, 2002.
Fama, "Efficient Capital Markets: A Review of Theory and Empirical Work," *Journal of Finance*, 25(2), 1969.
Farah, *Islam*, 7th ed., Barron's Educational Series, 2003.
Fasano and Schaechter, "Monetary Union Among Member Countries of the Gulf Cooperation Council," International Monetary Fund, 2003.
Fasano, Filho and Schaechter, "Monetary Union Among Member Countries of the Gulf Cooperation Council," International Monetary Fund, 2003.

"Fast Growth, Divergent Path: The EY GCC Wealth and Asset Management Report," 2015, http://www.ey.com/Publication/vwLUAssets/EY-gcc-wealth-asset-management-report-2015/$FILE/EY-gcc-wealth-asset-management-report-2015.pdf.

Fatemi, "International Finance and Banking," lecture notes, European Center for Advanced International Studies, Baruch College, International Finance Program, 2009.

"FDI in Green Buildings in China, A solution for its affordable housing problems," *China Business Review*, 2016, http://www.chinabusinessreview.com/fdi-in-green-buildings-in-china-a-solution-for-its-affordable-housing-problems/.

"FDI Intelligence," *Financial Times*, http://www.fdiintelligence.com/.

Federal Reserve Bank of Dallas, "Becoming a Member Bank of the Federal Reserve System," http://www.dallasfed.org/banking/apps/faq.cfm.

Federal Reserve Bank of Philadelphia, https://www.phil.frb.org/-/media/publications/economic-education/first-100-years.pdf?la=en.

Feenstra, "Product Variety and the Gains from International Trade," 2010.

Feldstein, "The case against EMU," *Economist*, June 13, 1992.

"Fitch Affirms Nine Kuwaiti Banks, Upgrades Gulf Bank's VR," Fitch, 2015, https://www.fitchratings.com/site/pr/993657.

"Fitch: New loan to deposit ratio to boost liquidity in Saudi Arabia," *Argaam*, 2016, http://www.argaam.com/en/article/articledetail/id/410536.

"Forex Glossary," http://www.cmsfx.com/en/forex-education/Forex-Glossary/counterparty/.

Forex Trading Charts.com, http://forex.tradingcharts.com/glossary/Forex%2BTrading/Counterparty.html.

Frankel and Rose, "The Endogeneity of the Optimum Currency Area Criteria," Berkeley University, 1997.

Fromherz, *Qatar: A Modern History*, Georgetown University Press; 2012.

Fuchs, Bahrain: *The Exception in the Gulf*, GRIN Verlag, 2013.

Furman, Porter and Stern, "The Determinant of National Innovative Capacity," *Research Policy*, 31(6), 2002.

Galal and Hoekman, *Between Hope and Reality: An Overview of Arab Integration*, Brookings Institution Press, 2003.

Galati and Melvin, "Why has FX trading surged? Explaining the 2004 triennial survey," Bank for International Settlements, 2004, http://www.bis.org/publ/qtrpdf/r_qt0412f.pdf.

Gandolfo, *International Trade Theory and Policy*, Springer Science and Business Media, 1998.

"GCC Banking Sector Liquidity Tightens," Bloomberg, 2016, https://www.bloomberg.com/news/videos/2016-08-10/gcc-banking-sector-liquidity-tightens.

Geithner, "Liquidity and Financial Markets," Federal Reserve Bank of New York, 2007, https://www.newyorkfed.org/newsevents/speeches/2007/gei070228.
Ghabra, "Kuwait: At the Crossroads of Change or Political Stagnation," Middle East Institute, 2014, http://www.mei.edu/content/article/kuwait-crossroads-change-or-political-stagnation.
Ghafar, "Will the GCC be able to adjust to lower oil prices?" Brookings Institution, 2016.
Ghazaleh, *Held in Trust: Waqf in the Islamic World*, Oxford University Press, 2011.
Ghazali, *The Socio-Political Thought Of Shah WaliAllah*, Adam Publishers, 2004.
Giles, Alexeeva and Buxton, *Managing Collective Investment Funds*, John Wiley & Sons, 2005.
Gonzalez, Karoly, Constant, Salem and Goldman, "Facing Human Capital Challenges of the 21st Century: Education and Labor Market Initiatives in Lebanon, Oman, Qatar, and the United Arab Emirates: Executive Summary," Rand Corporation, 2009.
Gregoriou, *Stock Market Volatility*, CRC Press, 2009.
Griffinth, Canto and Ruiz, "Financial Flows for Regional Integration," Institute for Development Studies, University of Sussex, 1995.
Grossman, *Imperfect Competition and International Trade*, MIT Press, 1992.
Gulf Research Center, http://gulfmigration.eu/total-population-and-percentage-of-nationals-and-non-nationals-in-gcc-countries-latest-national-statistics-2010-2015/.
GulfBase, http://www.gulfbase.com/GCC/Index/6.
Haas, *The Unity of Europe: Political, Social and Economic Forces*, rev. ed., University of Notre Dame Press, 2004.
Hafer and Hein, *The Stock Market*, Greenwood Publishing Group, 2007.
Hakkio, "Is purchasing power parity a useful guide to the dollar?" *Federal Reserve Bank of Kansas Economic Review*, 1992.
Hall, *Varieties of Capitalism: The Institutional Foundations of Comparative Advantage*, Oxford University Press, 2001.
Hamed, "Seeing the Environment through Islamic Eyes: Application of Shari'ah to Natural Resources Planning and Management," Texas Tech College, www.arch.ttu.edu/scienceandspirituality/hamed_sands_colloquium_paper.pdf.
Hammond, "Qatar Leadership Transition: Like Father, Like Son," European Council on Foreign Relations, 2014.

Haneef, "Retail Sukuk and SRI Sukuk: The Malaysian Experience," 1st Annual Islamic Finance Conference, Jakarta, Islamic Research and Training Institute, 2016.

Hannan, "Islamic Jurisprudence: Analogical Deduction, Qiyas, Muslim Tent," http://www.muslimtents.com/aminahsworld/Islamic_jurisprudence_qiyas.html.

Harmsen, *Islam, Civil Society and Social Work*, Amsterdam University Press, 2008.

Hassan and Mervyn Lewis, *Handbook of Islamic Banking*, Edward Elgar, 2009.

Helpman, "Monopolistic competition in trade theory," Special Papers in International Finance, Princeton, Library of Congress, 16, 1990.

Hennigan, *The Birth of a Legal Institution*, Brill, 2004

Herb, *All in the Family: Absolutism, Revolution and Democracy in Middle Eastern Monarchies*, SUNY Press, 1997.

Herb, *The Wages of Oil: Parliaments and Economic Development in Kuwait and the UAE*, Cornell University Press, 2014.

Heritage Foundation, "Index of Economic Freedom," 2016, http://www.heritage.org/index/.

Hertog, "The Private Sector and the Reform in GCC," LSE, 2013.

Hoekman, "Intra- Regional Trade: Potential Catalyst for Growth in the Middle East," Middle East Institute, 2016.

Hopwood, *The Arabian Peninsula: Society and Politics*, Routledge, 2015.

Human Rights Watch, "Qatar: Migrant Construction Workers Face Abuse," https://www.hrw.org/news/2012/06/12/qatar-migrant-construction-workers-face-abuse.

http://www.uaeinteract.com/government/political_system.asp.

https://snbchf.com/fx-theory/real-effective-exchange-rate/.

Hummel, *The Euro Financial Crisis: Impacts on banking, capital markets, and regulation: Report of the international workshop in Potsdam*, Potsdam University Press, 2013.

Hussain, Shahmoradi and Turk, "An Overview of Islamic Finance," International Monetary Fund, 2015.

Hvidt, "Economic diversification in GCC: Past records and future trends," Kuwait Program on Development, Governance and Globalization in the Gulf States.

Imam and Kpodar, "Is Islamic Banking Good for Growth?" International Monetary Fund, 2015.

Index Mundi, "Oman GDP: Composition by sector," http://www.indexmundi.com/oman/gdp_composition_by_sector.html.

Institute for Capacity Development and International Monetary Fund, "Economic Diversification in GCC: Past, Present and Future," 2014.

International Monetary Fund, "Economic Diversification in Oil Exporting Arab Countries," 2016.
International Monetary Fund, "Kuwait: Selected Issues Paper," 2014.
Iqbal and Lewis, *An Islamic Perspective on Governance*, Edward Elgar, 2009.
Ismael and Perry, *Government and Politics of the Contemporary Middle East: Continuity and Change*, Routledge, 2015.
ISN, ETH Zurich, "Charter of the Gulf Cooperation Council (GCC)."
"Issues in Islamic Liquidity," *International Financing Review*, 2007, http://www.ifre.com/issues-in-islamic-liquidity/552713.fullarticle
Jackson, "Is government regulation really so bad for business?" *Business Journal*, 2016, http://www.bizjournals.com/bizjournals/how-to/growth-strategies/2016/03/is-government-regulation-really-bad-for-business.html.
Jaffer, "Infrastructure Sukuk," World Bank, 2015, http://pubdocs.worldbank.org/en/109671448479782899/pdf/islamic-finance-2015-11-18-Sohail-Jaffer-Infrastrcture-Sukuk.pdf.
Jamaluddin, *Islamic Finance for Dummies*, John Wiley & Sons, 2012.
Janin and Kahlmeyer, *Islamic Law: The Sharia from Muhammad's Time to the Present*, McFarland & Company, 2007.
Jevčák, Setzer and Suardi, "Determinants of Capital Flows to the New EU Member States Before and During the Financial Crisis," European Commission, *Economic Papers*, 425, 2010.
John, "GCC to stick to Dollar peg," *Khaleej Times*, 2016, http://www.khaleejtimes.com/business/banking-finance/gcc-to-stick-to-dollar-peg.
John, "Qatar, GCC Countries with Dollar peg to face challenges when Fed hikes rate," *Gulf Times*, 2015, http://www.gulf-times.com/story/463341/Qatar-GCC-countries-with-dollar-peg-to-face-challe.
Kamar and Bakardzhieva, "The Appropriate Monetary Policy Coordination for the GCC Monetary Union: Proposal for the Twenty-sixth Annual Meeting of The Middle East Economic Association (MEEA)," 2006.
Kamilil, "Factors affecting economic integration in East African Community in ARUSHA," 2015.
Kammer, Norat, Piñón, Prasad, Towe and Zeidane and IMF Staff, "Islamic Finance: Opportunities, Challenges, and Policy Options," International Monetary Fund, 2015.
Kanady, "Qatar Outward FDI Increases to USD8.2bn," *Zawya*, 2014.
Karim and Archer, *Islamic Finance: The Regulatory Challenge*, Wiley Finance, 2007.
Kasim and Sanusi, "Emerging Issues for Auditing in Islamic Financial Institutions: Empirical Evidence from Malaysia Nawal," *IOSR Journal of Business and Management*, 8(5), 2013.

Kastrati, "The Effects of Foreign Direct Investments for Host Country's Economy," American University of the Middle East, Kuwait, 2013.
Kerr and Gaisford, *Handbook on International Trade Policy*, 2007.
Khadduri and Liebesny, *Origin and Development of Islamic Law*, Lawbook Exchange, 2010.
Khan , *Woman in Islamic Shariah*, Goodword Books, 1995.
Khan, "Takaful versus Conventional Insurance," Monetary and Banking Research Institute, http://new.mbri.ac.ir/userfiles/file/Islamic%20Banking/%D8%A8%D8%A7%D9%86%DA%A9%20%D9%85%D9%82%D8%A7%D9%84%D8%A7%D8%AA/Takaful/Takaful%20vs%20Conventional%20Insurance.PDF.
Khan, "Takaful: Concepts and Models," https://zulkiflihasan.files.wordpress.com/2009/11/takaful-dlc.pdf.
Khandelwal, Miyajima and Santos, "The Impact of Oil Prices on the Banking System in the GCC," International Monetary Fund, 2016.
Khandelwal, COMESA and SADC: "Prospects and challenges for Regional Trade Integration," International Monetary Fund, 2004.
Kheder, "Kuwait's Legal System and Legal Research," Hauser Global Law School, 2010.
Kim, Shin and Yun, "Monetary Aggregates and the Central Bank Financial Stability," The Federal Reserve Board, 2012.
King and Kurmann, "Expectations and the Term Structure of Interest Rates: Evidence and Implications," *Federal Reserve Bank of Richmond Economic Quarterly*, 88(4), 2002.
Klug, *Theories of International Trade*, Routledge, 2006.
Knaul, "Rapport of Special Rapporteur on the Independence of Judges and Lawyers," U.N. Human Rights Council, 2015.
Komai, "A Brief History of Regulations Regarding Financial Markets in the United States," National Bureau of Economics, 2011, http://www.nber.org/papers/w17443.pdf.
Kondakov, *How to View and Forecast the Market: Forex Fundamental Indicators*, Bookbaby, 2013.
Kotilaine, "GCC Agriculture," NCB Capital, 2010.
Kritzer, *Forex for Beginners: A comprehensive guide to profiting from the global currency market*, Apress, 2013.
Krugman, *Rethinking International Trade*, MIT Press, 1994.
Kubursi, *Oil, Industrialization and Development in the Arab Gulf States*, Routledge, 2015.
"Kuwait's banks brace for property crash," *Euromoney*, 2016, http://www.euromoney.com/Article/3527346/Kuwaits-banks-brace-for-property-crash.html.

"Kuwaiti banks' risks grow as real estate sales drop," *Saudi Gazette*, 2016, http://saudigazette.com.sa/business/kuwaiti-banks-risks-grow-as-real-estate-sales-drop/.
Laabas and Limam, "Are GCC Countries Ready for Currency Union?" Arab Planning Institute, 2002.
Laffan, Donnell and Smith, *Europe's Experimental Union: Rethinking Integration*, Routledge, 2013.
Lai, *Financial Crisis and Institutional Change in East Asia*, Springer, 2012.
Lambert, "Political Reform in Qatar: Participation, Legitimacy and Security," Middle East Policy Council Journal, 18(1), 2011.
Latham and Watkins, "The Sukuk Handbook: A Guide to Structuring Sukuk," https://www.lw.com/thoughtLeadership/guide-to-structurings-sukuk-2015.
Laursen, "Theory and Practice of Regional Integration," Jean Monnet and Robert Schuman Paper Series, 8(3), University of Pittsburgh, 2008.
Lee, "The European Union: A Failed Experiment," *Harvard Business Review*, 2013.
Lengyel, "Socio-economic Indicators, Theories and Applications," *International Social Science Journal*, 27(1), 1975.
Lindberg, *The Political Dynamics of European Economic Integration*, Stanford University Press, 1963.
Lipsey, "The Theory of Custom Unions: Trade Diversion and Welfare," *Economica*, 24(93), 1957.
Lipsey and Lancaster, "The General Theory of Second Best," *Review of Economic Studies*, 24(1), 1956.
Lipsey and Mucchielli, *Multinational Firms and Impacts on Employment, Trade and Technology: New Perspectives for a New Century*, Routledge, 2003.
Lone and Alshehri, "Growth and Potential of Islamic Banking in GCC: The Saudi Arabia Experience," *Journal of Islamic Banking and Finance*, 2015.
Lopes, "Inching toward Integration," *Finance and Development*, 53(2), 2016.
Loungani and Razin, "How beneficial is foreign direct investment for developing countries?" International Monetary Fund, *Finance and Development*, 38(2), 2001.
Mackay, "The effects of economic integration on lesser developed countries," University of Edinburg, 1984.
Madura, *Financial Markets and Institutions*, 3rd ed., West Publishing Company.
Madura, *International Financial Management*, Cengage Learning, 2008.
Magee, "New Measures of Trade Creation and Trade Diversion," *Journal of International Economics*, 75(2), 2008.

Maghyereh and Awartani, "The effect of market structure, regulation, and risk on banks' efficiency," *Journal of Economic Studies*, 41(3).
Mangus, "China's currency policies need an overhaul," Bloomberg.
Manhal, "The Attractiveness of Qatar to Foreign Direct Investment, 1980-2002," Applied Econometrics and International Development, AEID, 5(3), 2005.
Mankiw and Taylor, *Economics*, Thomson.
Mankiw, *Macroeconomics*, 5th ed.
Mansfield and Milne, *The Political Economy of Regionalism*, Columbia Univesrity Press, 1997.
Mansoor, "Modern Finance and the Phenomenon of the 'Islamic Banking,'" Diplomatic Academy of London, 2001.
Maqsood, *Teach Yourself Islam*, Teach Yourself Books, 2003.
MarketWatch, "These are the most heavily traded stocks on Wall Street," http://www.marketwatch.com/story/these-are-the-most-heavily-traded-stocks-on-wall-street-2015-05-29.
Martin, "Growth, Specialization and Economic integration in Europe," University of London, 2013.
Mattli, *The Logic of Regional Integration: Europe and Beyond*, Cambridge University Press, 1999.
McEvoy, "Brexit: Uncertain times ahead, but let's focus of what we can manage," *Drogheda Independent*, 2017.
McGee, *The Ethics of Tax Evasion: Perspectives in Theory and Practice*, Springer, 2011.
McHugh, "Irish job creation and employment: Growth set to continue in 2017," *Business World*, 2017.
Mechantaf, "The Constitutional Law and the Legal System of the Kingdom of Bahrain," Hauser Global Law School Program, 2010.
Media Committee of the Supreme Preparatory Committee of the Thirtieth Session of the Summit Conference of Gulf Cooperation Council, "The Thirtieth Gulf Summit: Accomplishments and Aspirations," 2009.
Melendez, "Wall Street Reporter," Huffington Post, Feb 2013, http://www.huffingtonpost.com/2013/02/14/financial-crisis-cost-gao_n_2687553.html.
Michigan State University, "GlobalEDGE," https://globaledge.msu.edu/.
Milenkovic, Vukmirovic, Bulajic and Radojicic, "A multivariate approach in measuring socio-economic development of MENA countries," *Modelling Economy*, 38, 2014.
Ministry of Economy, Trade and Industry of Japan, "Regional Integration," http://www.meti.go.jp/english/index.html.

Minor, “Zakat and Development Finance: Filling the Gaps,” AidData, Open data for International Development, 2014, http://aiddata.org/blog/zakat-and-development-finance-filling-in-the-gaps.

Mitrany, *A Working Peace System*, Quadrangle Books, 1966.

Molyneux and Iqbal, *Banking and Financial Systems in the Arab World*, Springer, 2016.

Money, Capital Mobility and Trade, Essays in Honor of Robert A. Mundell, MIT Press, 2001.

Moody’s Investor Service, “Malaysia's Sukuk volumes will be stable, driven by corporate and sovereign refinancing,” 2015, https://www.moodys.com/research/Moodys-Malaysias-sukuk-volumes-will-be-stable-driven-by-corporate--PR_325842.

Moody’s Investor Service, “Moody’s maintains negative outlook on Bahrain's banking system amid weakening operating conditions, 2016, https://www.moodys.com/research/Moodys-maintains-negative-outlook-on-Bahrains-banking-system-amid-weakening--PR_350111.

Moody’s Investor Service, “Moody’s maintains stable outlook on Qatar banking System,” 2016, https://www.moodys.com/research/Moodys-maintains-stable-outlook-on-Qatars-banking-system--PR_351974.

Moran, “Foreign Direct Investment,” Wiley Online Library, 2012.

Moss, *Monetary Union in Crisis: The European Union as a Neo-Liberal Construction*, Springer, 2004.

Moya, “Case Study of 1997 Asian Financial Crisis,” GreenMango Research and Trading, 2015, https://greenmangotrading.wordpress.com/category/case-studies/.

Muhammad, “Sukuk and the problem of short term liquidity,” Global Home of the Sukuk Industry, 2014: https://www.sukuk.com/article/sukuk-problem-short-term-liquidity-3508/.

Mundell, “A Theory of Optimum Currency Area,” *American Economic Review*, 51(4), 1961.

Mundell, *Flexible Exchange Rate and Employment Policy*, University of Toronto Press, 1961.

Mundell, “The International Monetary Dilemma,” Interamerican Institute of Capital Markets, 1979.

Nagraj, “Stalled EU-GCC Free Trade Agreement Should be Passed – UK’s Mandelson,” *Gulf News*, 2015, http://gulfbusiness.com/stalled-eu-gcc-free-trade-agreement-passed-uks-mandelson/

NASDAQ, “Glossary,” http://www.nasdaq.com/investing/glossary/s/securities.

Nazar, "Regulatory and Financial Implications of Sukuk's Legal Challenges for Sustainable Sukuk development in Islamic Capital Markets," 8th International Conference on Islamic Economics and Finance, Hamed Bin Khalifa University, http://www.hbku.edu.qa/en/cis, http://webcache.googleusercontent.com/search?q=cache:v0XE0hIq9pcJ:conference.qfis.edu.qa/app/media/298+&cd=2&hl=en&ct=clnk&gl=fr#1.

Nazer, "Causes of Inflation in Saudi Arabia," *Business and Management Review*, 7, 2016.

Nee, "Key Facts on Kuwait," *Internationalist*, 2014.

Nkombo, McCoy and Harrison, "Impediments to economic integration in Africa: The case of COMESA," *Journal of Business in Developing Nations*, 2, 1998.

Nofal, "Al-Ghazali's Theory of Education," Muslim Heritage, http://muslimheritage.com/article/al-ghazalis-theory-education.

Nomani and Rahnema, *Islamic Economic Systems*, Zed Books, 1994.

North and Tripp, *Culture Shock! Saudi Arabia: A Survival Guide to Customs and Etiquette*, Cavendish Square Publishing, 2007.

North, *Structure and Change in Economic History*, Norton, 1981.

Nwaozuzu, "Dwindling oil revenues: Economic implications for governance, business & development," *Sweet Crude*, 2016, http://sweetcrudereports.com/2016/02/29/dwindling-oil-revenues-economic-implications-for-governance-business-development/.

Nyrop, *Area Handbook for the Persian Gulf States*, WildSide Press, 2014.

Ohlin and Sandelin, *Interregional and International Trade*, Routledge, 1998.

"Oman to issue first sovereign Sukuk by mid-2015," Reuters, 2015, http://www.reuters.com/article/oman-sukuk-idUSL5N0W30G420150301.

Organisation for Economic Co-Operation and Development, "Assessing investment policies of member countries of the Gulf Cooperation Council," 2011, http://www.oecd.org/mena/competitiveness/Preliminary%20assessment%20GCC%20invt%20policies.pdf.

Organisation for Economic Co-operation and Development, "The Economic Significance of Natural Resources: Key points for reformers in Eastern Europe, Caucasus and Central Asia," 2011.

Osberg and Sharp, "Comparisons in trends of GDP and economic well-being: The impact of social capital," OECD, https://www.oecd.org/innovation/research/1824740.pdf.

Oseni and Hassan, "Regulating the governing law clauses in Sukuk transactions," *Journal of Banking Regulations*, 2014.

"Over the Counter Markets," http://press.princeton.edu/chapters/s9623.pdf.

Oxford Business Group, "A broader scope: Qatari developers continue to invest in major International Projects," https://www.oxfordbusinessgroup.com/analysis/broader-scope-qatari-developers-continue-invest-major-international-projects.
Palan, *The Efficient Market Hypothesis and its Validity in Today's Market*, GRIN Verlag, 2007.
Peterson, Shackleton, *The Institutions of the European Union*, Oxford University Press, 2012.
Pfaffermayr and Egger, "The Pure Effects of European Integration on Intra-EU Core and Periphery Trade," *The World Economy*, 36(6), 2013.
Porter, *The Competitive Advantage of Nations*, Free Press, 1998.
Porter, "The Role of Location in Competition," *Journal of the Economics of Business*, 1994.
Poser, *The Asian Financial Crisis*, GRIN Verlag, 2008.
Prasad, Monem and Martinez, "Macro Prudential Policy and Financial Stability in the Arab Region," International Monetary Fund, 2016.
U.S. Federal Reserve System, "Procedures for Elections of Class A and Class B Directors," https://www.federalreserve.gov/aboutthefed/directors/PDF/procedure-for-elections-classes-a-b.pdf.
Qatar Investment Authority, http://www.qia.qa/.
"Qatar: Foreign Investment," Santander Trade Portal, International Chamber of Commerce, https://en.portal.santandertrade.com/establish-overseas/qatar/investing-3.
Rafay and Sadiq, "Problems and Issues in Transformation from Conventional Banking to Islamic Banking: Literature Review for the Need of a Comprehensive Framework for a Smooth Change," *City University Research Journal*, 5, 2015.
Rahman, "Exploring Sharia'ah Views on the Practice of Takaful Company Reinsuring with Reinsurance Company," Department of Sharia'ah and Economics, Academy of Islamic Studies, University of Malaya.
Ram, "Qatari banks' credit outlook cut by S&P," *Financial Times*, 2016.
Ramady, *Political, Economic and financial Country Risk: Analysis of the Gulf Cooperation Council*, Springer Science and Business Media, 2013.
Ramazani and Kechichian, *The Gulf Cooperation Council: Record and Analysis*, University of Virginia Press, 1988.
"Rating Action: Moody's takes rating actions on 11 Saudi banks, concludes review," Global Credit Research, 2016.
Rauf, *Islam: A Sacred Law: What Every Muslim Should Know About the Shariah*, Threshold Books 1999.

Razak, "Overview of Zakat Collection in Malaysia: Regional Analysis," *American International Journal of Contemporary Research*, 3(8), 2013, http://www.aijcrnet.com/journals/Vol_3_No_8_August_2013/17.pdf

Razin and Sadka, *Foreign Direct Investment: Analysis of Aggregate Flows*, Princeton University Press, 2007.

Razin, "The contribution of FDI flows to domestic investment in capacity and vice versa," University of Chicago, 2004, http://www.nber.org/chapters/c10747.pdf.

Read, *The Efficient Market Hypothesists: Bachelier, Samuelson, Fama, Ross, Tobin and Shiller*, Springer, 2012.

"Regional Economic Integration in Global Framework," European Central Bank, G20 Workshop, 2004.

Reuters, "Financial Glossary," http://glossary.reuters.com/index.php?title=Reporting_Dealer.

Rieley, "Understanding the Circular Flow of Income and Spending," Tutor2u, http://www.tutor2u.net/economics/reference/circular-flow-of-income-and-spending.

Roberts, "The case for regulation: The failure of free market economics," Center for Research on Globalization, 2011.

Rutledge, *Monetary Union in the Gulf*, Routledge, 2015.

Sachedina, "Al-Khums: The Fifth in the Imami Shi I Legal System," *Journal of Near Eastern Studies*, 39(4), 1980.

Sahib and Kari, "Analysis of Intensity of Intra-regional Trade in GCC Countries, 1998-2008," *International Journal of Trade, Economics and Finance*, 3(3), 2011.

Sait and Lim, *Land, Law and Islam*, Zed Books, 2006.

Salacalin, "Oil and Gas Reserves: How long Will They Last," BQ, 2015, http://www.bq-magazine.com/energy/2015/02/oil-and-gas-reserves-in-the-gcc.

Salvatore, *Schaum's Outline of International Economics*, McGraw-Hill, 1995.

Salvini, "The Kuwaiti labor market and foreign workers," International Labour Organization.

Sami, "Three Essays on Financial Markets and Monetary Behavior in GCC Countries," ProQuest, 2008.

Samuelson, *Economics*, McGraw-Hill, 2010.

Sapwarabol, "Essays on regional economic integration in East Asia," Claremont Graduate University, 2012.

Saripudin, Mohamad, Razif, Abdullah and Rahman, "Case Study on Sukuk Musharakah Issued in Malaysia," *Middle-East Journal of Scientific Research* 12, 2012.

U.S. International Trade Administration, "Saudi Arabia: Efficient Market and Portfolio Investment," 2016.

Saudi Arabian Monetary Authority, http://www.sama.gov.sa/en-us/pages/default.aspx.
Sayigh, *The Economies of the Arab World*, Routledge, 2014.
Schiel, *Monarchy: A Primary Source Analysis*, Rosen Publishing Group, 2005.
Schreyer and Koechlin, "Purchasing power parities – measurement and uses," OECD, 2002.
Schumacher, "Adam Smith's theory of absolute advantage and the use of doxography in the history of economics," *Erasmus Journal for Philosophy and Economics*, 5(2), 2012.
Schutter, Swinnen and Wouters, *Foreign Direct Investment and Human Development: The Law and Economics of International Investment Agreements*, Routledge, 2013.
Kalemli-Ozcan, Sørensen and Yosha, "Asymmetric shocks and risk-sharing in a monetary union: Updated evidence and policy implications for Europe," European Commission, http://ec.europa.eu/dgs/policy_advisers/docs/3_kalemli_may05.pdf.
Sexton, *Exploring Economics*, Cengage Learning, 2015.
Shafi, "The Qur'an: How it was revealed and compiled," Daralislam, http://www.daralislam.org/.
Sharif, "Qatar cash squeeze seen in soaring loan to deposit ratio," Bloomberg, 2016.
Sheikh, "The Moral Economy of Classical Islam: A FiqhiConomic Model," Hartford Seminary, Blackwell Publishing, 2008, http://ierc.sbu.ac.ir/File/Article/The%20Moral%20Economy%20of%20Classical%20Islam%20A%20FiqhiConomic%20Model_94660.pdf.
Sheng, "A strong US dollar, Global Trade and Crisis," *The Straits Times*, 2015, http://www.straitstimes.com/opinion/a-strong-us-dollar-global-trade-and-crises.
Sherif and Shaairi, "Determinants of Demand on Family Takaful in Malaysia," *Journal of Islamic Accounting and Business Research*, 2010.
Shihata, "Some Observations on the Question of Riba and the Challenges Facing 'Islamic Banking,'" *Internet Journal of the Centre of Energy, Petroleum and Mineral Law and Policy*, 1998.
Shourie and Saxena, "World of Fatwas: Shariah in Action," ASA, 1995.
Showley, "Low oil prices: good or bad for the economy?" *San Diego Union Tribune*, 2015, http://www.sandiegouniontribune.com/business/economy/sdut-econometer-oil-prices-benefit-2015dec18-story.html.
Siddiqui, *Islamic Sharia and the Muslims*, Kazi Publications, 1972.
Silva and Tenreyro, "Currency Unions in Prospect and Retrospect," *Annual Review of Economics*, 2, 2010.

Simoes, Observatory of Economic Complexity, 2014, http://atlas.media.mit.edu.
Singer, *Charity in Islamic Societies*, Cambridge University Press, 2008.
Sirmon and Hittm, "Contingencies within dynamic managerial capabilities: Interdependent effects of resource investment and deployment on firm performance," *Strategic Management Journal*, 30, 2009.
Smith, *An Inquiry into the Nature and Causes of the Wealth of Nations*, W. Strahan and T. Cadell, 1776.
Smits, *The European Central Bank: Institutional Aspects*, Kluwer Law International, 1997.
Soesastro, "Regional Integration in East Asia: Achievements and Future Prospects," *Asian Economic Policy Review*, 2006.
Sokoloff and Engerman, "Institutions, Factor Endowments, and Paths of Development in the New World," *Journal of Economic Perspectives*, 14(3), 2000.
Spangler, *The Law of Private Investment Funds*, Oxford University Press, 2012.
Stabb, *The European Union Explained: Institutions, Actors and Global Impact*, Indiana University Press, 2008.
Staff of the International Monetary Fund, "Economic Prospects and Policy Challenges for the GCC Countries' Annual Meeting of Ministers of Finance and Central Bank Governors," Riyadh, Saudi Arabia, 2016.
"State of the GCC Banking System," *International Financial Review*, http://www.ifre.com/state-of-the-gcc-banking-system/610387.fullarticle.
Stevens, "The Asian Crisis: A Retrospective," Reserve Bank of Australia, 2007: http://www.rba.gov.au/speeches/2007/sp-gov-180707.html.
Stratfor, "The Gulf Cooperation Council: Finding safety in numbers," 2016, https://www.stratfor.com/analysis/gulf-cooperation-council-finding-safety-numbers.
Sulaiman and Galadanci, "Islamic Banking and Finance: General Framework and Case Studies," International Institute of Islamic Thoughts, Nigeria Office, 2003.
Swartz and Coetzer, "Takaful: An Islamic insurance instrument," *Journal of Development and Agricultural Economics*, 2(10), 2010.
Swoboda, "Mundell and Theoretical Foundation for the European Monetary Union," International Monetary Fund, 1999.
Szczepański, "Adopting the euro convergence criteria and state of play," European Parliamentary Research Service, 2015.
Tahir, Ataullah and Mahmood, "Right to Basic Necessities of Life in Islam: Meaning and Concept," Qurtuba University, http://www.qurtuba.edu.pk/thedialogue/The%20Dialogue/11_2/Dialogue_April_June2016_202-212.pdf.

Takagi, "Establishing Monetary Union in the Gulf Cooperation Council: What Lessons for Regional Cooperation?" Asian Development Bank Institute, no. 390, 2012.
Talha and Rahama, "Zakat, Waqf and Sadaqa and their roles against fighting poverty," UNESCO, 2016.
Tas, "Money-Price Relationship in GCC Countries," *Journal of Economic Cooperation and Development*, 33(2), 2012.
Taylor, "Snapshots of Foreign Direct Investment," Conversable Economist, 2014, http://conversableeconomist.blogspot.fr/2014/06/snapshots-of-foreign-direct-investment.html.
Thakor, "International Financial Markets: A Diverse System Is the Key to Commerce," Center for Capital Markets, 2015.
The Banking Association, South Africa, http://www.banking.org.za/consumer-information/conventional-banking/what-are-interest-rates.
The Economist, "Big Mac Index," http://www.economist.com/node/21542840/print.
Trading Economics, http://www.tradingeconomics.com/kuwait/unemployment-rate.
Trandafir, http://mirceatrandafir.com/teaching/econ435/Chapter_12.pdf..
Trebilcock , Howse and Eliason, *The Regulation of International Trade*, Routledge, 2012.
Turak, "U.S Secretary of Commerce Lauds TPP and Free Trade," FDI Intelligence, 2016, http://www.fdiintelligence.com/Locations/Americas/USA/US-secretary-of-commerce-lauds-TPP-and-free-trade.
Tverberg, "Ten reasons why high oil prices are a problem," Our Finite World, 2013, https://ourfiniteworld.com/2013/01/17/ten-reasons-why-high-oil-prices-are-a-problem/.
U.K. House of Commons Education and Employment Committee, "Employment Consequences of European Economic and Monetary Union," House of Commons Paper Series, 1999.
Ulrichsen, *The Gulf States in International Political Economy*, Springer, 2016.
Ulrichsen, *The United Arab Emirates: Power, Politics and Policy-making*, Taylor & Francis, 2016.
University of Toronto, Department of Economics, https://www.economics.utoronto.ca/jfloyd/modules/ppar.html.
"Update 1: Saudi central bank raises loan to deposit ratio: sources," Reuters, 2016, http://www.reuters.com/article/saudi-cenbank-policy-idUSL8N15T0OK.
U.N. Conference on Trade and Development, "World Investment Report 2015," http://unctad.org/en/PublicationsLibrary/wir2015_en.pdf.

U.N. Development Programme, "Human Development Index," http://hdr.undp.org/en/content/human-development-index-hdi.
U.N. Food and Agriculture Organization, "Regional Integration and Food Security in Developing Countries: Regional Integration in Africa," http://www.fao.org/docrep/004/y4793e/y4793e0a.htm.
U.N. High Commissioner for Refugees, http://www.refworld.org/pdfid/48eca8132.pdf.
U.N. International Children's Emergency Fund, http://www.unicef.org/gender/files/Qatar-Gender-Eqaulity-Profile-2011.pdf.
United Nations, "Report on international definition and measurement of standards and levels of living," 1961.
U.S. Bureau of Labor Statistics, Economic News Release, http://www.bls.gov/news.release/mslo.t02.htm.
U.S. Department of Energy, http://www.eia.gov/beta/international/analysis_includes/countries_long/Qatar/qatar.pdf.
U.S. Department of State, "Investment Climate 2016," https://www.state.gov/e/eb/rls/othr/ics/2016/nea/254435.htm.
U.S. Department of State, "Organization," http://www.state.gov/documents/organization/160079.pdf.
U.S. Department of the Treasury, https://www.treasury.gov/resource-center/data-chart-center/interest-rates/Pages/TextView.aspx?data=yieldYear&year=1991.
U.S. Federal Reserve Board, "Board of Governors of the Federal Reserve System," https://www.federalreserve.gov/aboutthefed/bios/board/default.htm.
U.S. Federal Reserve Board, "Federal Reserve Districts," https://www.federalreserve.gov/otherfrb.htm.
U.S. Federal Reserve Board, "Structure of the Federal Reserve System: Board of Governors," https://www.federalreserve.gov/aboutthefed/structure-federal-reserve-system.htm.
U.S. Federal Reserve Board, "What are Fed objectives in conducting monetary policy?" https://www.federalreserve.gov/faqs/money_12848.htm.
U.S. Government Accountability Office, http://www.gao.gov/products/GAO-16-175.
U.S. Securities and Exchange Comission, https://www.sec.gov.
Valeri, *Oman: Politics and Society in the Qaboos State*, Hurst Publishers, 2009.
Vamvakidis, "Regional Integration and Economic Growth," *The World Bank Economic Review*, 2(2).
Viner, *The Customs Union Issue*, Oxford University Press, 1950.

Wagenaar, *Government Institutions: Effects, Changes and Normative Foundations*, Springer Science & Business Media, 2012.

Wahab, Lewis and Hassan, *Islamic Takaful: Business Models, Shariah Concerns, and Proposed Solutions*, Wiley, 2007.

Wall, "Failure of integration projects in South Caucasus," *Europe-Asia Studies*, Carnegie Europe, 64(9).

Wall, "The Role of Liquidity in the Financial Markets," Federal Reserve Bank of Atlanta, 2015, https://www.frbatlanta.org/cenfis/publications/notesfromthevault/1511.aspx.

Walz, "Dynamic Effects of Economic Integration," *Open Economies Review*, 8(3), 1997.

Weaver and Rockman, *Do Institutions Matter? Government Capabilities in the United States and Abroad*, Brookings Institution Press, 2010.

Welfens, *European Monetary Integration: EMS Developments and International Post-Maastricht Perspectives*, Springer Science & Business Media, 2012.

Wells Fargo, "Small Businesses Enter 2016 with More Optimism," https://www.wellsfargo.com/about/press/2016/small-business-optimism_0216/.

Whittaker, "The Gulf Currency: Lessons from the Euro," Lancaster University, 2010, http://www.lancaster.ac.uk/staff/whittaj1/Gulf%20Currency%20Report%20Final.pdf.

Widdershowen, "Analysis: Petro-dollar crunch hits GCC sovereign wealth funds, investment and pensions," *Europe*, 2016.

Wigglesworth, "UAE quits Gulf Monetary Union," *Financial Times*, 2009.

Williams, "Monetary Policy, Money and Inflation," Federal Reserve Bank of San Francisco, 2012, http://www.frbsf.org/economic-research/publications/economic-letter/2012/july/monetary-policy-money-inflation/.

Wippel, *Regionalizing Oman: Political, Economic and Social Dynamics*, Springer, 2013.

World Bank, "The Economic Integration in the GCC," 2010, http://siteresources.worldbank.org/INTMENA/Resources/GCCStudyweb.pdf.

World Intellectual Property Organization, http://www.wipo.int/edocs/lexdocs/laws/ar/ae/ae017ar.pdf.

Wynbrandt, *A Brief History of Saudi Arabia*, InfoBase, 2014.

Yarbrough and Yarbrough, *Cooperation and Governance in International Trade: The Strategic Organizational Approach*, Princeton University Press, 1992.

Yeats, *Trade and Development Policies: Leading Issues for 1980*, Palgrave Macmillan, 1981.

Zahlan, *The Origins of the United Arab Emirates: A Political and Social History of the Trucial States*, Routledge, 2016.

Zaidan and Al-Aqily, "The legislation guarding five necessities," Islam House, 2009, https://islamhouse.com/en/articles/228515/.

Zenker, *Currency Speculation in Fixed Exchange Rate Regimes: Theory and Empirical Evidences*, Springer Business and Science Media, 2014.

Zuriah, "Takaful: Potential Demand and Growth," *Islamic Economic Journal*, Islamic Economic Institute, 2010, http://www.kau.edu.sa/Show_Res.aspx?Site_ID=121&LNG=EN&RN=57694.

Structures éditoriales du groupe L'Harmattan

L'Harmattan Italie
Via degli Artisti, 15
10124 Torino
harmattan.italia@gmail.com

L'Harmattan Hongrie
Kossuth l. u. 14-16.
1053 Budapest
harmattan@harmattan.hu

L'Harmattan Sénégal
10 VDN en face Mermoz
BP 45034 Dakar-Fann
senharmattan@gmail.com

L'Harmattan Cameroun
TSINGA/FECAFOOT
BP 11486 Yaoundé
inkoukam@gmail.com

L'Harmattan Burkina Faso
Achille Somé – tengnule@hotmail.fr

L'Harmattan Guinée
Almamya, rue KA 028 OKB Agency
BP 3470 Conakry
harmattanguinee@yahoo.fr

L'Harmattan RDC
185, avenue Nyangwe
Commune de Lingwala – Kinshasa
matangilamusadila@yahoo.fr

L'Harmattan Congo
67, boulevard Denis-Sassou-N'Guesso
BP 2874 Brazzaville
harmattan.congo@yahoo.fr

L'Harmattan Mali
Sirakoro-Meguetana V31
Bamako
syllaka@yahoo.fr

L'Harmattan Togo
Djidjole – Lomé
Maison Amela
face EPP BATOME
ddamela@aol.com

L'Harmattan Côte d'Ivoire
Résidence Karl – Cité des Arts
Abidjan-Cocody
03 BP 1588 Abidjan
espace_harmattan.ci@hotmail.fr

L'Harmattan Algérie
22, rue Moulay-Mohamed
31000 Oran
info2@harmattan-algerie.com

L'Harmattan Maroc
5, rue Ferrane-Kouicha, Talaâ-Elkbira
Chrableyine, Fès-Médine
30000 Fès
harmattan.maroc@gmail.com

Nos librairies en France

Librairie internationale
16, rue des Écoles – 75005 Paris
librairie.internationale@harmattan.fr
01 40 46 79 11
www.librairieharmattan.com

Lib. sciences humaines & histoire
21, rue des Écoles – 75005 Paris
librairie.sh@harmattan.fr
01 46 34 13 71
www.librairieharmattansh.com

Librairie l'Espace Harmattan
21 bis, rue des Écoles – 75005 Paris
librairie.espace@harmattan.fr
01 43 29 49 42

Lib. Méditerranée & Moyen-Orient
7, rue des Carmes – 75005 Paris
librairie.mediterranee@harmattan.fr
01 43 29 71 15

Librairie Le Lucernaire
53, rue Notre-Dame-des-Champs – 75006 Paris
librairie@lucernaire.fr
01 42 22 67 13

www.ingramcontent.com/pod-product-compliance
Lightning Source LLC
Chambersburg PA
CBHW071436230926
51846CB00001B/248
* 9 7 8 2 3 4 3 1 6 4 4 8 9 *